S0-BRZ-761

A History of the English Monarchy

from Boadicea to Elizabeth I

by

Gareth Russell

A History of the English Monarchy

from Boadicea to Elizabeth I

Copyright © 2015
MadeGlobal Publishing &
Gareth Russell

ISBN-13: 978-84-943721-2-4

All rights reserved. No part of this publication may be reproduced, stored in a retrieval system, or transmitted, in any form or by any means, electronic, mechanical, photocopying, recording or otherwise, except as permitted by the UK Copyright, Designs and Patents Act 1988, without the prior permission of the publisher.

M

MadeGlobal Publishing

For more information on
MadeGlobal Publishing, visit our website:
www.madeglobal.com

This book is dedicated to my grandparents
Richard and Iris Mahaffy
With love and gratitude

CONTENTS

Cover image © 2015 MadeGlobal - Artist Aleksandra Klepacka.
From top, clockwise: Boadicea, Henry V, Elizabeth I, Alfred the Great.

AUTHOR'S NOTE

TRYING TO strike a balance between what is familiar against what is accurate is a constant difficulty for any medievalist, not least because words and titles evolved so much over the course of that era. For instance, the use of prince or princess to denote the son or daughter of a king did not seem to develop until the fourteenth century and it was not assumed as automatic in England until the sixteenth. Prior to that, a monarch's children were often referred to as lord, lady, dame, etc. Hence why Edward II's future bride, Isabella of France, would have regarded it as an honour to be referred to as the Lady Isabella in the thirteenth century, but Henry VIII's eldest daughter considered it a humiliation to be the Lady Mary in the sixteenth. For clarity's sake, I have used the former throughout, on the understanding that my readers will appreciate how fluid the period's attitude towards titles was. In modern scholarship, we do not usually capitalise royal or aristocratic titles, in contrast to the syntax of etiquette, where it is still required. Since no one ever erred in choosing the side of politesse, for the most part the titles remain in their capitalised form, particularly when referring to a specific individual. When referring to the title in passing and plural, I have stuck with modern sensibilities and used lower case.

Where possible, I have tried to give the modern equivalent of the prices mentioned, but this is an inexact science – as even economic predictions for the next few months, let alone the past millennium, show us every day in our newspapers.

All quotes from the Bible are taken from the Douay-Rheims translation. On the issue of Irish and Welsh names, today there are numerous spellings for these vis-á-vis their English equivalents, and even someone fluent in modern Irish might struggle with medieval Ireland's spelling of certain Christian names. Dermot/Diarmait and Rory/Ruaidhri, the two kings central to part of this story, have their anglicised names given alongside their Hibernian equivalents. Where there is no direct English equivalent, as with King Muircheartach, I left the names untranslated.[1]

Finally, the title of this book proved a challenge, and a thought-provoking one. While the English monarchy became the British in the centuries after Elizabeth I's death, it is technically incorrect to refer to it as that prior to 1603 – according to some, before 1707 and for an even smaller group of academics, before 1801. This book is anglocentric, it is a history of the kings and queens of England, yet it does also try to explain how and why that monarchy interacted with Ireland, Wales and Scotland in more detail than is usually given in anglocentric histories of the Crown. I hope, therefore, that the title selected is an acceptable compromise and I take comfort from the fact that if neat labels and neat translations were possible, it would no longer be possible for us to grapple with History's magnificent inconsistencies.

Gareth Russell

PROLOGUE

THE SWORD GLEAMED

O N THE Tuesday after Easter in 1278 an extraordinary ceremony took place at the Benedictine abbey at Glastonbury. Torches flickered in the springtime twilight, knights in their armour stood alongside monks holding tapers, gorgeously dressed ladies-in-waiting attended to help their mistress if she called on them as Eleanor of Castile, England's Spanish-born Queen, tenderly wrapped a centuries-old set of bones in the finest of silks. Next to her, her towering and terrifying husband, King Edward I, did the same to another set of remains. The chroniclers claimed that Edward was binding the remains of King Arthur 'of wondrous size', as Queen Eleanor cared for the skeleton of Camelot's long-dead Queen, 'Guinevere, of marvellous beauty'.[1]

King Arthur is one of fiction's great heroes. He was either based on no man or a hundred. Folk tales, Nordic deities, Christian aspirations and the fragmented and, perhaps, distorted biographical details of chieftains and warriors separated by centuries were the interweaving threads of his legend. That spark was fanned into a flame by medieval writers like Geoffrey of Monmouth, whose history of the early British Isles was the era's equivalent of a bestseller, and who insisted that Arthur had been a human king who ruled a vast and noble empire from his court at Camelot in the mist-shrouded centuries of antiquity.[2]

The English believed him, so did the Welsh, who claimed Arthur for their own and clung to the variation of the legend that spoke of Arthur carried, wounded and comatose, to the mysterious island of Avalon, from whence he would return to drive-out his people's enemies. The English did not much care for this twist on the tale and as the English Crown's relations with the Welsh princes deteriorated, they were keen to show that the centre of Arthur's kingdom had been in England where, like all mortal men, he had died. There was no 'once and future king'. Edward I, his ancestors and his descendants, were Arthur's successors, not his replacements.

Belief in the myth of Camelot as historical fact was thus widespread by the thirteenth century. Indeed, to the upper classes it constituted a communal obsession. Edward I's uncle, the Earl of Cornwall, had built a hugely expensive castle at Tintagel, which had absolutely no strategic value, because it was the alleged site of great Arthur's conception.[3] There were numerous aristocratic jousting tournaments at which the competitors could adopt the persona of one of Arthur's knights. Queen Eleanor, like most of her literate contemporaries, devoured Arthurian romances. En route to Glastonbury she had hosted parties at her manor near South Cadbury, a ruined Iron Age fort that English scholars at the time believed to be a likely locale for the original Camelot.

At the end of the ceremony, Edward I and his Queen, described by her modern biographer as 'a fine-looking Spanish lady, whose eyes and hair were probably her greatest beauty, with a determined chin and a winning smile', set the skeletons – and whose they actually were is still a mystery – aside until the King financed the construction of a lavish new tomb for the iconic couple upon whom rested so much of his kingdom's sense of destiny.[4]

King Arthur had been brave, a great warrior who ruled his people in their best interests rather than his own. He was surrounded by a glittering court that advertised his kingdom's splendour and provided a venue in which the most noble men could pledge their service to the Crown. Camelot's famous Round Table implicitly preached participation alongside obedience and a monarchy whose power was checked by honour and responsibility.

In the legends Arthur's vanished sword, Excalibur, had been plucked and held aloft as the initial proof of his right to the throne. It does not take a literary scholar to decipher the place that this metaphor gave to battlefield prowess in medieval ideals of a successful ruler. Edward I and Eleanor of Castile processed and paid homage to the shrine of the English monarchy. Excalibur's promises shone throughout the Middle Ages, but so too did the believed-in court that had never existed – a world where consensual government, idealism and monarchical resplendence competed and interacted with one another. If Camelot had never existed, its devotees did and they produced one of the world's most controversial, awe-inspiring and important institutions.

CONQUEST

THE VIOLENT BIRTH OF THE MONARCHY

'The sword gleamed and the flames crackled round them on every side.'

Gildas, *On the Ruin and Conquest of Britain* (6th century AD)

THE SUICIDE of Cleopatra VII of Egypt on 12 August 30 BC was a rare moment in history that truly constituted a *fin-de-siècle*. Not only was it the last act of a brilliant and ambitious individual, but it also brought to a close the longest-running monarchy in human history. So ancient was the Egyptian royal system that Cleopatra is still closer to Elizabeth II than she was to the first pharaoh, who had unified Egypt nearly three millennia before her.[1]

The kingdom of the pharaohs was the ancient Mediterranean's monarchy par excellence, in which the power of royalty was underpinned by the belief that kings and queens stood far closer to the gods than they did to the rest of humanity. Testaments to this belief system dotted the Egyptian landscape, in the impressive monuments of previous dynasties and in temple shrines where prayers and offerings were still made to royals who had been dead for centuries. Yet for all its splendour and supreme self-confidence, Egypt was no longer the dominant power in the region by the time Cleopatra VII came to the throne. That honour was held by the upstart Roman republic, which had spread inexorably from its homeland in the Italian peninsula. On some level it must have seemed laughable that this xenophobic, oligarchic republic could challenge a country as ancient as Egypt. Cleopatra's kingdom possessed two of the seven wonders of the ancient world and its capital city, Alexandria, was a glittering jewel of multiculturalism and royal power. It was built from marble, while Rome was still built predominantly from brick. The visual contrast between the rivals was deceptive, however. As one historian elegantly put it, the differences between Alexandria and Rome were 'akin to sailing from the court of Versailles to eighteenth-century Philadelphia. In Alexandria, the glorious past was very much in evidence. Rome's glorious future was from Cleopatra's quarters nowhere visible. It was just still possible to mistake which was the Old World and which was the New.'[2]

One person who was not fooled was Cleopatra herself and she knew that for one empire to prosper, the other must perish. Or, at the very least, submit. A ruler with less self-belief, like her late and incompetent father, might have quailed at such a task, but Cleopatra was clever, capable, glamorous, beautiful and utterly determined – a foe to be reckoned with.[3] She set herself the task of charming, seducing and exploiting the power of Rome, with the ultimate intention of establishing her own empire at Rome's expense. It is a testimony to Cleopatra's capabilities that she very nearly succeeded. She did not, of course, and in 30 BC she took her own life rather than face the ignominy of being paraded through the streets of Rome as a captive. A few loyal slave girls accompanied her in death, since a Queen could not be expected to go anywhere on her own. Cleopatra's eldest son and heir was quietly murdered, Rome occupied Egypt and the throne that claimed descent from the gods Amun-Ra, Horus and Osiris passed out of existence. Cleopatra's dour-faced opponent, thirty-two-year-old Octavian, returned to Rome to be fêted and honoured as the great hero who had secured republicanism's victory over the last independent absolute monarchy of the Mediterranean basin.

Yet, in much the same way as Cleopatra's stage-managed suicide had turned her defeat into a kind of emotional victory, Rome's conquest of Egypt did not mark the end of imperial monarchy, as the more zealous of Roman republicans had so fervently hoped. Monarchism was to have the last laugh. Two-and-a-half-years after Cleopatra's death, Octavian renamed himself Augustus and was installed as the first Roman Emperor, complete with de facto absolute power and the requisite divine lineage. The 'known world' was under the authority of a monarchy, just as Cleopatra had hoped; sadly for her, it was Augustus who took the prize.

Roman rule first came to Britannia (their name for most of modern-day England and Wales) thanks to the military endeavours of Julius Cæsar, Cleopatra's second husband and Rome's first dictator.[†] Britannia was still technically subject to Rome twenty-eight years later when Cæsar's great-nephew Augustus took things a step farther than Uncle Julius had Britannia

There had been no real discernible sense of unity in pre-Roman Britain and those internal divisions went a long way in explaining why it had been unable to repulse the armies of either Julius Cæsar or those of the Emperor Claudius, who came to extend and solidify the conquest later. When it colonized a new piece of earth, the Roman Empire sought homogeny in law, finance, politics and architecture. Like other parts of the empire, the Britons did occasionally object to this cultural autocracy. The most famous of several outright rebellions occurred during the reign of the Emperor Nero, who was so badly shaken by the strength of British opposition that he apparently considered withdrawing Roman troops from the region altogether. The uprising took place either in AD 60 or AD 61 and it was led by the woman commonly known as Boudica or Boadicea, Queen regent of a British tribe called the Iceni. Boadicea had been publicly flogged by the Romans after her husband died without bequeathing his kingdom directly to the Emperor, as had been expected of him. As she was beaten, the Romans raped both of her daughters.

It was this kind of tact and compassion that provoked the British insurrection. If a Queen and her daughters could be treated so abominably, it was not only an insult to all Britons but also a chilling

---

[†] Her first had been her younger brother, Ptolemy XIII. It was an arranged marriage, designed to mirror the incestuous unions that the Greek-descended royal family had embarked upon to prove themselves closer to Egyptian gods like Osiris and Isis, who were mythological sibling-spouses. Unlike the marriage between Osiris and Isis, the match between Cleopatra VII and Ptolemy XIII was one of mutual loathing that resulted in Ptolemy ending his life face-down in a small lake just outside Alexandria after unsuccessfully attempting to oust his sister from power.

reminder of what less-exalted personages could expect if they got in Rome's way. What happened in AD 60-61 was not a minor uprising led by a grieving widow, but rather a war of attrition. Boadicea's first major victory, and first major slaughter, came when her army captured the Roman town of Camulodunum (modern-day Colchester), which they systematically destroyed, including a temple dedicated to the late Emperor Claudius. (Like the pharaohs they had replaced in Egypt, the Roman emperors had acquired a fondness for being posthumously worshipped.) After that, the warrior-Queen's armies captured and destroyed Londinium and Verulamium (London and St Albans, respectively). In a revealing insight into the era's gender expectations, the historian Dio Cassius later wrote, 'Moreover, all this ruin was brought upon the Romans by a woman, a fact which in itself caused them the greatest shame.'[4]

Boadicea, who had ridden into battle with her abused daughters in her chariot as a visible reminder of the brutality of Rome, finally lost her war at the Battle of Watling Street. As with Cleopatra before her, it is likely that the defeated Boadicea chose suicide over the indignity of capture.[5] It has also plausibly been suggested that her two daughters followed her in hastening their own ends.[6] Given what had already happened to them at Roman hands before the rebellion, it is unlikely that they had any illusions about the horrors awaiting them if they were captured afterwards. The theory that Boadicea was given a splendid Celtic funeral at Stonehenge is a pretty legend that dates from the seventeenth century, but it has no basis in fact.[7]

In the aftermath of Boadicea and the Iceni's rebellion, Roman rule became harsher and more direct. There was less reliance on, and interaction with, client regional monarchies, as there was in other parts of the Roman Empire, like Judea, where readers of the Bible will be familiar with this political set-up thanks to the gospel interactions between Herod, the client King, and Pontius Pilate, the Roman governor.[8] The Emperor who made the most visible impact on Britannia's landscape was Hadrian, who ruled from 117 until his death in 138. Hadrian was an intellectual who understood the importance of travel when ruling such a vast empire. Although he was married to his second cousin, the Empress Vibia Sabinia, the great love of Hadrian's life was a spectacularly good-looking man called Antinous, from the Greek-speaking city of Bithynia.[9] It was Antinous who accompanied Hadrian on his lengthy travels throughout the Roman Empire and it was on a visit to Egypt that tragedy struck, when Antinous accidentally drowned in the Nile. Hadrian was understandably devastated by his lover's death, but an Emperor's grief is not quite the same as a mere mortal's. Following in the footsteps of Alexander the Great's insistence that his dead lover-cum-general Hephaestion should be deified, Hadrian had Antinous posthumously declared a god.[10] (Apparently, since the days of Cleopatra and Augustus, the divinity club had become a lot easier to get into.) Hadrian's construction of a new city called Antinopolis was a similarly-understated expression of the imperial grief.

Hadrian is most famous in Britain for building the wall that bears his name, rather than for building the city that bore Antinous'. Today, Hadrian's Wall is little more than an incomplete yet sombrely beautiful set of disjointed ruins across the landscape of northern England, but in the second century AD, it was a paradoxical tribute to both Roman power and Roman nerves. The fact that the empire could construct such an enormous wall separating Britannia from the unconquered lands of Caledonia to the north was an indicator of how complete Roman domination over parts of the British Isles had become. Equally, the fact that they felt the need to build it in the first place reflected lingering unease about the loyalty of Britannia and concerns over Rome's inability to subdue its barbarian neighbours. Two years after Hadrian's accession and three years before his visit to Britain, there had been yet another rebellion and Hadrian's Wall thus stands as a tribute to his monarchy's strength that it could build the wall, and weakness that it had to.

The next monarch to make an enormous impact on Britannia left his mark on its soul, rather than its geography. The monarch known to history as Constantine the Great inherited the imperial throne in his mid-thirties in the year 306. Seven years later, he issued the Edict of Milan, which ended the persecution of Christians. Under previous emperors, the Christian community had been treated with 'the utmost refinements of cruelty' and eyewitnesses described how 'their death was made a matter of sport: they were covered in wild beasts' skins and torn to pieces by dogs; or were fastened to crosses and set on fire in order to serve as torches by night when daylight failed'.[11] It was Constantine's mother, the Empress Helena, who undertook the first major step in this specific part of the story and thereby started a curious trend in British history whereby the country's major changes in religion all seem to have come through the bodies and brains of royal women. (There is an unverifiable legend, repeated by G. K. Chesterton, that the Empress Helena actually started her life in Britannia by being born in the city of Colchester, but cities in Palestine and Turkey have also claimed the honour. Like so much in this period, it is sadly impossible to say either way with any degree of surety.) What is certain is that at some point in his reign, Constantine the Great, to all intents and purposes, converted from the paganism of his ancestors to embrace the relatively new religion of Christianity and that his mother's faith played a role in that decision.[12]

Both Constantine and Helena had led particularly torturous private lives prior to this, with allegations that they had ordered the murder of Constantine's possibly-treacherous wife, the Empress Fausta, by drowning her in her bath after she falsely accused Crispus, Constantine's son from his first marriage, of attempting to seduce her. Crispus had been executed on his father's orders. Months later, the Emperor discovered that Fausta had lied and in a fit of grief and rage, he and his mother had her killed.[†] Later pagan writers like Zosimus rather spitefully suggested that the Empress Helena's mania for Christianity was due primarily to her guilt over her grandson and daughter-in-law's deaths.[13]

Whatever the vagaries of her earlier private life, Helena's devotion to Christianity was passionate and sincere. With her son's blessing, and his money, she went on pilgrimage to the Holy Land to track down relics associated with Christ, the Holy Family and the Apostles. Ambrose of Milan wrote later that the Empress 'burned with an earnest desire' at beholding remnants of the True Cross.[14] A shrine to the Graeco-Roman goddess Aphrodite, built by the late Emperor Hadrian on the alleged site of the Crucifixion, was demolished and replaced with the church of the Holy Sepulchre, which is today one of Christianity's most cherished shrines.[15]

The impact of Roman imperialism on Christianity's subsequent journey is difficult to understate. It gave it automatic entry into

---

† It has also been suggested that Crispus and Fausta were, in fact, lovers and that Fausta's life was only spared for longer so that she could give birth to the child she had illegitimately conceived with her stepson. Once that child was born, Constantine then felt morally justified in punishing the mother for her adultery. The deaths of Crispus and his stepmother were certainly linked, but in what way is frustratingly unknowable. Both versions of events – that Crispus had been complicit with Fausta or that she had unfairly framed him for a crime he did not commit – were current at the time, with the latter being the most popular.

places like Britannia and Gaul which, otherwise, it might have taken centuries to reach. However, the empire did not just shape Christianity's geographical access, but also its character for future generations. Like his predecessors, Constantine the Great was keen on uniformity and, to that end, he involved himself in ironing-out Christianity's numerous internal disputes. All well and good to debate the two natures of Christ or the nitty-gritty of eschatology when one was only a persecuted minority sect, but when after being elevated to the state religion, unity of purpose and creed were required. In pursuit of this, Constantine the Great summoned the Council of Nicea, an ecclesiastical conference held in modern-day Turkey, to define in detail what Christians should believe and why. Far from being the diktat depicted by modern conspiracy theorists, the Council of Nicea was an energetic and spirited set of theological debates. Nonetheless, they did have the Emperor breathing down their necks to make sure they reached a final decision. Constantine's monarchy had appropriated some of the culture, theories and rituals of earlier Hellenistic and Persian monarchies, which stressed the importance of a sovereign holding power in secular and spiritual matters.[16] That theory developed into something that scholars subsequently dubbed caesaropapism, a concept that would later have enormous significance in England when it was used to justify splitting the Church, rather than uniting it, as it had at Nicea.[17] It was at Nicea that the Church finally decided which books should go into the Bible and which should be left out – it is wholly untrue that they wrote any of the books themselves – formally defined the theological interpretation of the nature of Christ and produced the famous Nicene Creed under Constantine's aegis that defined the core tenets of the Christian faith. A few important spiritual upgrades and qualifications were added by later gatherings, particularly at the Council of Constantinople in 381 and the Council of Ephesus in 431, where particular attention was paid to formally emphasising Christ's Divine Nature, in part by defining the role of the Virgin Mary as Theotokos or 'god-bearer' (more often transliterated today as 'Mother of God'). The credo defined at Nicea in 325 and expanded upon later remains Christianity's equivalent of the Bill of Rights – the codification and refinement of its original constitution.[18]

I believe in one God the Father Almighty,
Maker of heaven and earth, And of all things
visible and invisible:

And in one Lord Jesus Christ, the only-
begotten Son of God, Begotten of His Father
before all worlds, God of God, Light of Light,
Very God of Very God, Begotten, not made,
Being of one substance with the Father, By
whom all things were made: Who for us men,
and for our salvation, came down from heaven,
And was incarnate by the Holy Ghost of the
Virgin Mary, And was made man, And was
crucified also for us under Pontius Pilate. He
suffered and was buried, And the third day
He rose again according to the Scriptures,
And ascended into heaven, And sitteth on the
right hand of the Father. And He shall come
again with glory to judge both the quick and
the dead: Whose Kingdom shall have no end.

And I believe in the Holy Ghost, The Lord and
Giver of Life, Who proceedeth from the Father
and the Son, Who with the Father and the Son
together is worshipped and glorified, Who spake
by the Prophets.

And I believe in one Holy Catholic and
Apostolic Church. I acknowledge one Baptism
for the remission of sins. And I look for the
Resurrection of the dead, And the Life of the
world to come.

Amen.[19]

Constantine was pleased. The faith was propagated. For good
or for ill, the alliance between monarchy and Christianity, between
throne and altar, had been forged and, with it, the full force of
Christianity came sweeping over Britannia. One of Constantine's
sons and successors, the Emperor Constantius II, began the attack
on paganism by closing down its temples and in 391 the Emperor

Theodosius, an intolerant ascetic with an obsession for controlling other people's morality, launched an all-out, iconoclastic attack on the remaining polytheist cults. For the first time, the Christian faith also began to turn on its Jewish cousins, with a set of homilies and increasingly anti-Semitic invectives thundering forth from the clergy. Despite his undoubted unpleasantness, Theodosius, who had spent time as a young man in Britannia, did manage to resist cries from his bishops that he should attack Judaism as violently as paganism.

More and more people converted to Christianity as it became not just the easiest religion to follow but also the surest path to career promotion in imperial service. By 417, Spanish subjects of the Emperor, like the historian Orosius, could start their sentences with the words 'As a Christian and as a Roman ...', the two adjectives having become nearly axiomatic.[20] Wealth poured from the hands of the Roman aristocracy as they rushed to fund churches, reliquaries, monasteries and shrines. Some, particularly female aristocrats, did so in a burst of pious devotion, others undoubtedly did it to impress the Emperor, impress their friends or advertise their wealth. As he laboured in his monastery to translate the Bible into the beautiful Latin text that would become known as his Vulgate, Saint Jerome was horrified at the money being flung at the Christian faith – sure and certain in the knowledge that Mammon could only bring corruption and the dilution of Christ's gospel. 'Parchments are dyed purple,' wept Jerome, 'gold is melted in lettering, manuscripts are dressed up in jewels, while Christ lies at the door naked and dying.'[21] Perhaps he should not have been so harsh, for this wealth was to help keep Christianity's pulse beating when it faced the lean years ahead. Churches sprang up the length and breadth of the Roman world, even as the empire nurturing them slipped inexorably into its twilight.

THE BARBARIAN CONSPIRACY

IN 367, Britannia was attacked on all sides by the peoples beyond its borders. The empire provoked both resentment and envy in the barbarian countries around it and as Rome weakened they seized their opportunity to strike. Hadrian's famous wall failed and the Picts, who populated what is now Scotland, invaded Britannia from the north. This sweeping-south trauma was supplemented by incursions from the west and the south. The invasion in the west came from the Scots in Ireland – or Hibernia, as the Romans had called it.[†] The invasion on the southern coastline was led by the Saxons, a seafaring tribe of Germanic pagans, who the Briton-Christian chronicler Gildas described as 'a race hateful to God and men'.[22] At the time of these attacks, the Roman Empire's power may have been declining, but it was not yet broken and Britannia was exceptionally lucky that the imperial throne had recently been taken by the Emperor Valentinian, who had undertaken the promethean task of trying to hold the decaying empire together, through which he earned his future sobriquet of 'the Great'. Livid at the 'barbarian conspiracy' to end Roman rule in the British Isles, Valentinian set off for Britannia himself. When he was delayed in Gaul, he dispatched one of his most competent generals, Flavius Theodosius, to expel the invaders. He was successful in completing the task the Emperor set for him, but the three-pronged invasion of Roman Britannia, defeated though it was, confirmed how seriously the empire's power was deteriorating.

In 409, the barbarians struck again. This time, the throne was not held by a man like Valentinian, but by the weak and unlucky Honorius. Honorius was an erratic monarch who scandalised his Christian subjects by developing an incestuous passion for his younger sister, Galla Placidia, who fled to the eastern city of Constantinople to escape his attentions. The entirety of the Roman Empire was weakened by incursions and attacks; Rome itself was threatened and the imperial capital was relocated to the city of Ravenna, since Rome could no longer be adequately defended. Britannia, as an island on the farthest reaches of the empire with hostile neighbours on every side,

---

† Confusingly, 'Scots' was a catch-all term in the fourth and fifth centuries that eventually came to refer to all the Gaels. The links between Scotland and Ireland at the time were sufficiently close that the Scotch-Irish kingdom of Dál Riata was actually located in both countries – with land in western Scotland and on the coastline of County Antrim, in what is now Northern Ireland.

was particularly vulnerable. The soldiers stationed there made clear their dissatisfaction with the Emperor by backing several rebellions against him. In 409, this instability was added to when Britannia was once again attacked by Rome's enemies. Confronted by the erosion of imperial rule and overstretched resources, Honorius could or would do nothing for the Britons. In 410, he declared the province must look after itself for the time being and recalled the Roman legions to Italy to defend the empire's heartlands.

As with so many regime changes in history, the price of this freedom was a devastating loss of security. Initially, the Britons coped badly and the archaeological evidence left to us suggests that the implosion of Roman Britain was a bloody affair. Eventually, however, the Britons grew up, as all children must, and acquired something of the independent collective thought process the empire had so long discouraged them from possessing. Some of the lessons of imperial rule were remembered and, in order to face the invaders, the Britons knew that they must unite behind a strong leader. That leader's name is given by tradition as Vortigern, but that may be a later fiction. Whatever his name, it seems that the dominant warlord in Britain decided that the main threat lay with the Celtic invaders from the north. Operating under the mentality of 'my enemy's enemy is my friend', the man known as Vortigern decided to ally with the other invading force, the Saxons, and the former were allowed to flood into the country to aid Vortigern's attack on the northern Celts. It turned out to be Britain's equivalent of the Trojan horse.

The Saxons originated from today's Germany, hence the province of Saxony. In the fifth century they were still unrepentantly pagan and at the end of each season of pirating, raiding, enslaving and raping, they drowned one out of every ten of their prisoners as human sacrifices to the Saxon gods. Given that this religion was essentially the living, breathing reality of Christianity's worst nightmare of paganism, it is unsurprising to find that British Christians generally regarded the Saxons with horror. The short-lived alliance between the two was born from necessity not sentiment. However, by inviting the war-like Saxons into their country in the first place, the Britons had advertised their own weakness. When or why Vortigern's pact with the Devil broke down into an orgy of ethnic cleansing is impossible to pinpoint, but it may have been that the Britons lacked the money to pay the Saxons what had been promised or that the Saxons had been planning to break their word from the beginning. The Saxons turned on the Britons and the results were unspeakable. The Briton priest Gildas, who wrote a vivid account of post-Roman Britain called *De Excidio et Conquestu Britanniæ* ('On the Ruin and Conquest of Britain'), spoke of the mass rape of British women, frequent massacres, of villages, towns and cities burned to the ground, constant fighting and thousands forced into slavery. The Saxons were soon joined by two other tribes – the Jutes from modern-day Denmark and the Angles from the northern shores of Germany. Nearly two hundred thousand Saxons, Jutes and Angles landed in Britannia over the course of the invasion. Their coming resembled not so much mass immigration as the four horsemen of the Apocalypse. Two million Britons are believed to have died as a direct or indirect result of the Saxon invasion, with the overall population dropping by nearly fifty percent in the course of a generation. In the south of the country, where the invasion had been at its most sustained and most vicious, evidence indicates that ninety percent of the native male population was sold into slavery, driven into exile or butchered. The result was a complete re-alignment of Britain – racially, religiously and politically. The native Britons coalesced in the north and the west; the south and the east were lost to them. So complete was the Saxon invasion that Britannia ceased to exist. The dominance of the Saxons, the Jutes and the Angles gave the land a new name – 'Ængla Land', in time, 'England'.

SEVEN KINGDOMS

THE THREE centuries that followed the establishment of the Anglo-Saxon kingdoms in the south-east of Britain saw a slow but steady progression towards the unification of England under a single monarchy. If the story of that era was to be reduced to two dominant narrative themes then they would be the march towards unification and the second coming of Christianity. It was a period known as the Heptarchy, an age of seven kingdoms. Less flatteringly, it has also been dubbed 'the Dark Ages', a dismissive and derogatory term that is likely to produce tiny aneurysms in modern-day specialists. Even the concept of the heptarchy or the seven kingdoms has been queried, since power and borders were in a constant state of flux, producing short-lived or small sub-kingdoms that do not quite fit neatly into the narrative of seven kingdoms ultimately merging into one. However, for simplicity's sake it is just about possible to tell the story as that of the seven kingdoms of Wessex, Essex, Sussex, Kent, East Anglia, Mercia and Northumbria.

All were technically ruled by the Angles, the Saxons, the Jutes or, as they inter-married and reproduced, the Anglo-Saxons. Northumbria, the northern-most and largest of the seven, occupied land in what is now central and northern England, and southern parts of Scotland. It had the most pronounced native Briton influence. Mercia sat in the Midlands, around the River Trent. Neighbouring East Anglia, the kingdom of the eastern Angles, covered most of modern-day Norfolk and Suffolk. Essex was relatively fragile, despite possessing the former Roman strongholds of London and Colchester. Sussex lay along the southern coast. Kent, an area so beautiful that it was later nicknamed 'the garden of England', was in the south-east, and Wessex, which lasted the longest to become the most powerful of the seven, was in the south-west. For centuries, these kingdoms co-existed and competed. As generations passed, one would emerge as overlord, only to slip into decline to yield its dominance to another.

Initially, the Briton communities in the north clung to Christianity, while the majority of Anglo-Saxons remained pagan for a century or so after the invasion. For a time, Christianity's zeal for proselytising was stayed by the Britons' fear and loathing for the newcomers. When Christianity did come to the Anglo-Saxons, it was through Bertha, a fourth-generation Christian princess whose father, Charibert, was the ruler of Paris. In the 560s, Charibert negotiated a marriage for Bertha with Æthelbert, pagan King of the southernmost kingdom of Kent. There was no question of Bertha endangering her immortal soul by turning apostate and so part of the marriage contract allowed for the princess and her household to be granted access to Christian worship once they arrived in Kent. The little church provided, Saint Martin's at Canterbury, had apparently been built during the days of Roman rule but then fallen into disuse after the Saxon invasion. Queen Bertha and her private chaplain, Liudhard, restored it and it survives to this day as the oldest parish church in continual use in the Anglican communion.[23]

Kent under Bertha's husband, King Æthelbert, was the most powerful of the English kingdoms. Like most of the Anglo-Saxon territories, it remained officially non-Christian and, like most princesses before and after her, Bertha was under considerable pressure to bring her husband, and thus his subjects, to the light. The long-dead Empress Helena had established a precedent for royal women to be living aqueducts of the Christian creed – Bertha must live up to it. But like most royal women whose religion was at odds with their adopted homeland's, Queen Bertha found herself having to juggle the spiritual duty she owed her faith with the obedience she was supposed to owe her husband. It was a difficult and often thankless position, with a queen criticised for doing either too much or too little. Many in Rome, including the Pope, felt that neither Bertha nor Liudhard were working hard enough to bring the gospel beyond the restored walls of Saint Martin's. The non-Christians surrounding the King tried to limit the pair's opportunity to evangelise by defining Liudhard's role as adiutor fidei, that is, solely and specifically as Bertha's 'faith helper' or spiritual adviser. Letters from Pope Gregory the Great, one of the most brilliant pontiffs in history, exhorted Bertha to do more. Luckily, he understood that the Queen could not convert a nation on her own. Even the best generals needed foot soldiers. To that end, in 595, the Holy Father dispatched a team of missionaries to help. The group was led by a man called Augustine, a prior held in high regard by Pope Gregory and with a great working knowledge of the scriptures. He would go down in history as 'the Apostle to the English'.

As with all good saints' lives, Augustine suffered a pang of human weakness en route to Kent, when someone unhelpfully informed him of the full extent of Anglo-Saxon savagery. A horrified Augustine rushed back to Rome and tried to wriggle out of his mission. The Pope, who had put the re-Christianisation of southern England high on his list of Papal priorities, was unmoved and commanded Augustine to get back on the road. The forty-or-so-person-mission, led by a reluctant missionary, reached Kent in 597. Thanks no doubt to the influence of Queen Bertha, they were given a fairly warm reception by King Æthelbert at Canterbury, Kent's capital. The King granted Augustine permission to preach freely in his kingdom, but avoided committing to a conversion himself.

For someone who had shown great reluctance in going there in the first place, Augustine of Canterbury quickly showed why the Pope had such faith in him. He began by using the Queen's chapel at Saint Martin's as a base, but his mission soon outgrew the little church. By Christmas, he had secured the conversion of ten thousand people. At some point before 601, King Æthelbert became a Christian as well.[24] The Pope's joy can be imagined and Bertha finally received those longed-for letters comparing her to Helena. Equally effusive pontifical letters were dispatched to Æthelbert, assuring him that his conversion would 'make your glorious name still more glorious even to posterity'.[25] The fact that pure Roman Catholicism arrived on the shores of England through Kent and that the subsequent royal conversion took place at Canterbury was to have a lasting impact on British Christianity. Even today, the archbishopric of Canterbury, created for Augustine in 597, remains the highest-ranking episcopal see in Anglicanism. In recognition of their efforts in bringing Christianity back to southern Britain, both Queen Bertha and Archbishop Augustine were posthumously declared saints.

From Kent, Roman Christianity made rapid progress. The model established by Bertha and her priests was followed by her daughter, Æthelberg, when she married the pagan Angle King of Northumbria. A few generations later, Christianity made in-roads in another of the seven kingdoms, Mercia, when a Northumbrian princess called Osthryth married the future King, Æthelred. As with Bertha, these royal women could not have succeeded had the main body of work not been done by dedicated priests, monks, theologians and preachers working beyond the walls of the court – in Northumbria, an Irish monk, Saint Aidan, was dubbed 'the Apostle to the Northumbrians' in much the same way as Augustine of Canterbury's efforts in the south had earned him the epithet of 'Apostle to the English'.[26] Christianity had also come to Wales, where a local king, Cadfan of Gwynedd, was buried as a Christian in Anglesey and eulogised by his subjects as the 'wisest and most renowned of all kings'.[27]

With so much missionary activity garnering so many conversions, there was inevitably renewed tension with the remnants of Anglo-Saxon paganism, especially in Mercia, but, as always with Christianity, some of its greatest disputes were internal. The queens and princesses who sprang from the tradition and lineage of Bertha of Kent were Roman Catholics, in that their faith followed the order and structure established by the Papacy in Rome. They belonged to a European religion that owed much of its character to what had been established by Constantine the Great and the Council of Nicea three centuries earlier. However, Constantine had intended for this version of the Christian faith to sit alongside the power of Roman imperialism. With the subsequent disintegration of that power and Britain's estrangement from the continent thanks to the Saxon invasions, British Christianity had moved closer and closer to the Gaelic Christianity of Ireland and Scotland which, having developed separately from Rome's, was far more Celtic than Catholic.

Links between the northern British Christians had been fostered in the sixth and seventh centuries by their shared sense of faith, with Ireland, as a centre of missionary activity, often leading the way. King Oswig of Northumbria, who reigned in the north-east from 642 to 670, spent part of his childhood in Ireland, he was fluent in the Irish language and both his culture and his Christianity owed a lot more to Hibernia than it did to Rome. The chronicler Bede, a scholar later dubbed the 'father of English history', wrote that Oswig thought that 'nothing could be better than the Irish teaching'.[28] His first wife, Fín, was an Irish princess from modern-day County Tyrone in Northern Ireland, who shared Oswig's religious views.

However, after Fín's death, Oswig married a princess of Kent, Eanflæd, who had been raised in the Catholic tradition. It was a mixed marriage with the result that the King's household stuck to the Gaelic traditions while the Queen's entourage emulated her by adhering to continental Catholicism. The differences were particularly obvious during the faith's great penitential season of Lent, which requires forty days of self-denial and intermittent fasting, followed by what was (and is supposed to be) Christianity's major festival, Easter. Trivial as it may seem to us today, the Gaelic Church calculated Easter by a different calendar to Rome's, meaning that Queen Eanflæd and her servants were still starving themselves in the sombre spirit of Lent, while King Oswig's half of the court were busy celebrating Easter. In 664, Oswig decided to resolve the issue and paid tribute to the tactics of Constantine by summoning a Church council, or synod, at the seaside town of Whitby. It was the Synod of Whitby's job to decide between Gaelic or Roman Christianity. Momentously, it sided with the Queen's Catholicism, on the basis that the Roman Church could trace its foundation back to the career of Saint Peter, chief of Christ's Apostles, but the Gaelic Church could only trace its historical precedent to the missionary activity of Saint Columba, a sixth-century Irish monk, sometimes known as Saint Columcille, who had established famous monasteries in Derry (north-western Ireland), Durrow (central Ireland) and Iona (off the coast of western Scotland) and who, according to his biographer Adomnán, abbot of Iona, had brought the Irish version of Christianity to mainland Britain: 'In the forty-second year of his age Columba sailed from Ireland to Britain, wishing to be a pilgrim of Christ.'[29] For the rest of his life, Columba had travelled back and forth between northern Britain and Ireland, solidifying the cultural ties between them and founding a monastic network that ensured the region's commonality of faith survived Columba's own death in 597. At Whitby, that legacy was overturned. Peter trumped Columba and Rome therefore trumped the Gaels. From 664, Roman Catholicism enjoyed ascendancy in the British Isles and the links between Irish, Scottish and northern English Christianities gradually weakened – although neither as quickly nor as thoroughly as Rome would have liked.

PRAYING MEN, FIGHTING MEN AND WORKING MEN

THE SYNOD of Whitby took place during a century-and-a-half when Northumbria had emerged as the dominant power in England. The southern kingdoms of Kent and East Anglia had gone into decline to be superseded by the rising north-east. Northumbria was a vibrant and wealthy kingdom, not just in terms of its political influence but also in its culture. Wealthily endowed monasteries and churches simultaneously expressed the region's temporal economy as well as its spiritual fervour. As with Ireland in previous generations, Northumbria became a hotspot for missionary zeal, dispatching many expeditions across the North Sea to convert the Germanic tribes. Part of what made Northumbria so exciting was its cosmopolitan interpretation of Christianity, which borrowed from the Celtic, Anglo-Saxon and Catholic traditions. Even after Catholicism's victory at Whitby in 664, the Northumbrian monasteries continued to preserve vestiges of the area's numerous cultures. Perhaps the greatest surviving expression of this was a book produced by Northumbria's most famous monastery, the island abbey of Lindisfarne, founded by Saint Aidan. The stunningly beautiful Lindisfarne gospels still have the power to dazzle and move, much like the equally inspiring Book of Kells, now kept at Trinity College, Dublin. The two books spring from the same artistic heritage and the rich, impossibly detailed scrollwork of the gospel narratives, as transcribed by the monks of Lindisfarne, is a testament to the artistic vibrancy of Northumbria at its zenith. Its gradual decline coincided with the strengthening of another of the seven kingdoms, Mercia. It was under its eighth-century King, Offa, that Mercia's rise accelerated at the expense of its neighbours. Shortly after becoming King, Offa conquered Kent and then East Anglia, where he had the former King beheaded. A bloody and ruthless conqueror with something of a Cæsar-complex, Offa also constructed his own slightly less impressive version of Hadrian's Wall, Offa's Dyke, a large ditch to separate Mercia from the allegedly troublesome Welsh, in much the same way as Hadrian had once sought to limit contact between the Romans and the Picts.

At the turn of the century, shortly after Offa's death, Prince Egbert, who had been driven into European exile by Offa's armies, returned to England to claim the throne of the south-western kingdom of Wessex. Egbert's vengeance against Mercia was as thorough as it was brilliant. He repeatedly defeated their armies, encouraged rebellions in East Anglia, had his son occupy Mercian territory in Essex, Kent and Sussex and finally, in 829, after a long campaign, Egbert conquered Mercia itself. Wessex had not just become the dominant English kingdom, but also the crown that would play the crucial final role in unifying the country under a single government.

Wessex's contribution to the unification of England went far beyond the territorial ambitions of its monarchs. Unlike Mercia, Wessex had a relatively participatory political system, which gave its kings not just a bedrock of popular support, but also created a population with a vested interest in seeing the monarchical system work. It was Wessex that gave us shires, a word that still possesses a nostalgic cachet for English traditionalists. Shires were administrative districts that devolved a significant amount of day-to-day government to the localities. These shires could, for instance, levy taxes and raise troops in the King's name, but also administer justice by resolving legal disputes. Despite what one might have read during the misleading 'Ricardian' zeal of 2013, Richard III no more invented trial by jury than he did time travel. It was the shire courts of Anglo-Saxon Wessex that gave birth to trial by jury in England. They also allowed the kings of Wessex to sub-divide their territories into manageable districts, as did that other great Wessex innovation – the burhs. The ancestor of modern boroughs, the burhs of Wessex were a crucial part in the evolution of British towns and cities; by allowing towns to heavily fortify themselves against the threat of invasion, they helped the evolution of city- or town-specific urban civic culture in England, which would later become such a fundamental part of medieval political life.

Above the shires and the burhs but, just, below the King was the body of men later referred to as the Witanagemot, a sort of proto-parliament. Despite the fact that it never met regularly or on anything like what we would now recognise as a democratic or constitutional basis, historians worried that referring to this council as the Witanagemot endows it with a sense of parliamentary permanence are perhaps underestimating the intelligence of their readers. A truly remarkable institution to co-exist so productively alongside a monarchy at that stage in history, the Witanagemot, whose members were known as the Witan, was an advisory body that met inconsistently and only when called to by necessity. It consisted of representatives drawn from both the laity and the clergy and it possessed tangible political power, in that it was the Witans' job not simply to advise their kings, but also, from time to time, to confer the crown upon the rightful heir. The Witanagemot was to grow, evolve and change alongside Wessex, surviving until the Norman conquest of 1066.

Wessex's role in uniting the country was helped greatly by the Vikings, whose rapacious raids on the English coast gave the English a common enemy to unite against. Enticed by the great wealth of Anglo-Saxon England, the initial spate of Viking raids from their native Scandinavia were mostly along the north-eastern coastline. Despite recent attempts to rehabilitate the reputation of the Vikings, who have traditionally been seen in Britain as nothing more than a gang of plundering rapists and murderers, there can be little doubt that their raids were fearsome events. In 793, they laid waste to one of the jewels of Anglo-Saxon Britain, the abbey at Lindisfarne. It was solely down to the grace of God or the vagaries of luck that a copy of the monastery's beautiful gospels managed to survive the rampage, thanks to the actions of a few quick-thinking monks, who also saved the bones of Saint Cuthbert, which had been buried and revered on 'the holy island'.

Intermittent and isolated raids, such as those that had destroyed Lindisfarne, continued on-and-off for nearly half-a-century, before the Vikings realised that the disunited but wealthy land was ripe for a more thorough kind of pillaging. Three decades of deeper raids into enemy territory followed, culminating in an all-out invasion of England, which conquered Northumbria in 867 and East Anglia in 869. Their vanquished kings were allegedly submitted to the gruesome ritual of human sacrifice to Odin, the Viking deity believed to rule over Valhalla. A second invading force arrived in 871 and by the end of the decade most of Mercia had also fallen. Representing the only major Anglo-Saxon kingdom left, the Witan of Wessex, met to advise their King, Æthelred, on how to respond. The path chosen was a war in which King Æthelred and his younger brother Alfred both fought valiantly. Their courage may have been enough to win them the applause of the chroniclers and balladeers, but it was not enough to expel the Vikings. Halfway through the campaign, Æthelred died and the Witanagemot convened to award the crown to Alfred, who was destined to be remembered by History as Alfred the Great.

A large painting by Colin Gill, showing Alfred the Great and his men smiting the Viking invaders, still hangs in the Palace of Westminster, the seat of British parliamentary government. Alfred's victory from the jaws of defeat, coupled with his personal chivalry, helped make him a hero in his own lifetime. Much later, the Victorians were particularly fond of invoking him at a time when the success of the British Empire made it seem as if the expansion first experienced under Alfred was part of Britain's manifest destiny and that a direct line could be drawn from the resurgence of Wessex to the vast nineteenth-century empire on which, it was boasted, the sun never set. They did, however, downplay Alfred's devotion to the Papacy as unbefitting in the hero of a resolutely Protestant empire like Victoria's.

Alfred the Great was born the youngest of the five sons of King Æthelwulf of Wessex and his first wife, Osburga of Coventry, 'a most religious woman [and] noble in character'.[30] As a young boy, he had accompanied his father on a pilgrimage to Rome, where he had been formally blessed by Pope Leo IV. It was a ceremony and a journey that left a deep mark on Alfred. His exposure to the ruins of ancient Rome gave him a sense of culture far beyond most of his contemporaries' and his meeting with the Pope nurtured a lifelong commitment to the Roman Catholic faith. For Alfred there was none of the muddied theological waters of his ancestors, but rather total trust in the one, true, holy and indivisible Church of Rome. Nor was Alfred simply a wide-eyed youth so overawed by the rituals of the Holy See that he blindly followed what he had been taught in Rome for the rest of his life. Rather, here was a King who could articulate with precision why he was a Christian. For instance, his writings reveal a conscious rejection of pagan ideas like Fate, or what we might now call karma: 'I hold, as do all Christian men, that it is Divine Providence that rules, and not fate.'[31]

He was heir to a monarchy that was gradually and consciously aggrandising itself, appropriating the imagery of Imperial Rome and Christian kingship by turns. His stepmother, Judith, was the first recorded Queen in British history to have her own consecration or coronation.[32] Such were Alfred's capabilities that four hundred years later chroniclers were still remembering him as 'the famous, the warlike, the victorious; the careful provider for the widow, the helpless, the orphan and the poor, the most skilled of all Saxon poets, most dear to his own nation, courteous to all, most liberal, endowed with prudence, fortitude, justice and temperance [...] the most discerning investigator in executing justice, most watchful and devout in the service of God'.[33] Even allowing for the hyperbole of medieval chroniclers (and it is not true, as we shall see, that they always praised their kings), Alfred emerges both from his own writings and those of others as a truly remarkable man.[34] Three of his elder brothers – Æthelbald, Æthelberht and Æthelred – had held the throne before him. All had died before the age of thirty, leaving Alfred with the unenviable task of dealing with the Viking invaders. In the year of his accession, a second Viking army landed in England. Bowing to ugly reality, the Witan counselled suing for peace and King Alfred heeded their advice.

Three years later, a Viking warlord called Guthrum, who had established himself as de facto King of the Danelaw (the area of England occupied by the Vikings), broke the peace and attacked Wessex. By 878, the kingdom was nearly finished and Alfred was forced to flee in the depth of winter with a small band of followers. They made for the appropriately-named little isle of Athelney, which translates into Anglo-Saxon as 'the island of princes'. Surrounded by marshes and bog lands, Athelney was an island in the loosest possible sense of the word, but it served as the base needed by Alfred and his court-in-exile. There they could re-group. The men of Somerset joined him and helped build a defensive fort on Athelney, from which they could launch retaliatory raids on the Vikings.

Monarchy was, and is, far more than a selfish pageant centring on an individual. Some of the worst kings in history have made the mistake of assuming it is, as have many of their opponents. Loyalty is reciprocal; duty is rendered in return for leadership and protection. A good king needed good servants with many different skills. Alfred, one of England's finest monarchs, knew this. In his own words, a throne relied on 'praying men, fighting men and working men' – priests, warriors and administrators to help with the sacral, military and legislative duties of the increasingly complex monarchies being forged by the Anglo-Saxon kings. Luckily for Alfred he was able to attract the support of all three and by May, he was ready to strike at Guthrum. It was a fortuitous time, not just because of the change in weather that comes with each new spring, but also because of the arrival of Easter, the Christian season of resurrection. The religious element was especially important in this conflict, more so than most, because Alfred's piety, coupled with the bloody paganism of his Viking enemies, enabled him to be cast in the role of 'Leader of the Christians', as one of his earliest biographers dubbed him. This was a fight for the country's soul, as much as its land.

Alfred would no doubt have seen his subsequent victory against Guthrum as a manifestation of Divine Providence. God had spoken through the actions of men and blessed Alfred, His faithful lieutenant on Earth. The Vikings were defeated and Guthrum fled, with Alfred in hot pursuit. When they captured him, Alfred was determined to submit Guthrum to his religion with more gentility than the sacrificed kings of Northumbria and East Anglia had been incorporated into the Vikings'. Guthrum's conversion to Christianity was one of Alfred's conditions of peace, with Alfred standing as godfather at the baptismal ceremony – an indicator of Alfred's magnanimity on the one hand and his seniority to Guthrum (now re-christened Æthelstan) on the other. Guthrum/Æthelstan was allowed to return to his home in East Anglia, with drastically reduced power and a new faith, where he lived as Alfred's subordinate until his death a decade later. Alfred, meanwhile, set about making sure that Wessex would never again fall prey to a foreign invader. To give thanks where thanks was due, the King paid for the construction and endowment of a monastery on Athelney, which was to last right the way down to the Reformation and in the ruins of which the famous 'Alfred Jewel' was unearthed in 1693.† Having taken care of spiritual obligations, Alfred turned his attention to more temporal considerations. The army was reorganised and expanded, a series of forts were built and Alfred helped found the navy that would one day enjoy a symbiotic relationship with British power. Separated by nearly a millennium though they were, there was an understanding shared by Alfred the Great and the eighteenth-

† The Alfred Jewel is a beautiful piece of jewellery crafted from enamel, quartz and gold, showing Christ enthroned in Majesty and bearing the inscription in gold, *AELFRED MEC HEHT GEWYCRAN* ('Alfred ordered me made'). It is believed to have been part of a series of royal gifts sent to bishops and high-ranking clergy in Alfred's kingdom, possibly functioning as a handle for a bejewelled pointer stick to help the bishop or abbot trace his progress as they read religious manuscripts. The Jewel is a fascinating relic not just of Wessex's wealth, but also its artistic vitality. It was discovered in the ruins of the Athelney monastery in the reign of William III, by which point the land was owned by a local gentleman called Sir Thomas Wroth. The Alfred Jewel now resides in the wonderful Ashmolean Museum in Oxford.

century composer, Thomas Arne, about the role the navy could fulfil as a guarantor of British independence, that if an island nation could defend herself by sea, then her population 'never, ever, ever shall be slaves'.

After Alfred, who died in October 899, there was a succession of four kings of his line who expanded the borders of Wessex and the authority of its Crown. Alfred's son, King Edward the Elder, was acknowledged as overlord of sizable portions of the country by 920. Like his father, he styled himself King of the Anglo-Saxons, rather than solely of Wessex, a telling indicator of their family's growing power. It was his son, and Alfred's grandson, Æthelstan, who could justifiably claim to be the first King of England by conquering the last of the Viking kingdoms at York. He also forced the Welsh and Scottish royals to acknowledge him, reluctantly, as their overlord and the chroniclers gave him the rather magnificent Tolkein-sounding epithet of 'lord of warriors and ring-giver of men'.[35] His successor and younger brother, King Edmund the Just, was called 'lord of the English, guardian of kinsmen, loved doer of deeds'.[36] It was a strong line of Christian warrior-kings who, from Alfred the Great to Edmund the Just, took a small kingdom on the brink of annihilation to be conqueror and liberator of an entire nation. It was this family, and their followers, who gave birth to the kingdom of England.

In 946, King Edmund was murdered by a crazed ex-thief, shortly after attending Mass for Saint Augustine's Day. Edmund was succeeded by his brother Eadred, who died in 955 and bequeathed the crown to Edmund's handsome teenage son Eadwig, nicknamed Eadwig the Fair due to his good looks. Young and lusty Eadwig had other things on his mind than the piety and conquest of his forebears. He was determined to enjoy his kingship, not endure it. Things got off to a decidedly rocky start when the young monarch skipped-out on his own coronation banquet, an event at which his absence was rather likely to be noted. Wondering where the star of the show had gone, his courtiers made the horrible (in hindsight) decision of sending the saintly Dunstan to find him. Dunstan, abbot of the great monastery at Glastonbury, found the King romping in bed with a young woman – according to some sources, with two. To say that the leading champion of monastic reform in England did not see the funny side of the King's actions would be something of an understatement. Later stories suggested that one of the women had been the young King's future mother-in-law and that an enraged Dunstan had dared drag the King, possibly mid-coitus, out of bed and back to the banquet. Eadwig's intermission performance at his coronation set the tone for the rest of the reign, marked as it was by deteriorating relations between throne and Church.

Eadwig died before his twentieth birthday and he was succeeded by his younger brother Edgar, who was made of more conventionally holy stuff. Dunstan was back in royal favour as Edgar's new Archbishop of Canterbury. Together, the two men organised a magnificent pageant of royal power at Bath in 973. It was an innovative coronation ceremony, which helped set the tone for nearly all that followed. As Edgar was enthroned as 'Eadgar Rex Anglo' ('Edgar, King of the English'), the choir sang the story of Zadok the Priest and Nathan the Prophet anointing King Solomon in the Old Testament.[37] Today, those words still ring out at British coronations, albeit to the splendid music of Handel. Edgar was invested with the crown, the ring, the rod, the sceptre and the sword as symbols of his political, spiritual, judicial and military duties. These too are still part of the insignia of a British monarch.[38]

However, all the pomp and circumstance could not change the fact that the Vikings had not entirely gone away. They may have been temporarily crushed in England, but they thrived in their Scandinavian homelands. Nor had they forgotten their humiliation and as the Wessex line weakened, they prepared to return. After Edgar's death, his son and successor, King Edward ('the Martyr'), was assassinated in Dorset to pave the way for the succession of his younger half-brother, Æthelred the Unready. 'Unready' more closely translates as 'badly-advised', which Æthelred certainly was, although the responsibility for listening to that advice still rests squarely on his shoulders. A perfectly competent, if not exactly an inspiring, monarch for the first part of his long reign, Æthelred the Unready's reign ended in ignominy when he failed to respond to the resurgent Vikings with the heroism of his ancestors. This time, the Vikings were better organised, better trained and converted to Christianity. Under the leadership of King Harald Bluetooth, they struck hard as the tenth century gave way to the eleventh.

The English fought valiantly against them, but sustained heavy losses. All that Æthelred could do was to try to buy them off with increasingly enormous payments in 991, 994, 1002 and 1007.

With each payment, England became poorer and her weakness was confirmed. Surrounded by unpopular favourites, Æthelred was no match for Swein Forkbeard, the Danish King who attacked England in 1013. England's King sought refuge in London, but uninspired by his leadership and reared on stories of the ferocity of Viking vengeance, the Londoners surrendered to Swein and Æthelred fled across the Channel to Normandy. Luckily for him, Swein died in February 1014 and, although the Danes wanted to proclaim Swein's son Canute as the new King, the English seized the opportunity to invite Æthelred back from exile. Cleverly, they also imposed enough conditions to prevent any repetition of the worst mistakes of his earlier reign. Thus curtailed, Æthelred died two years later and was followed by his stern and self-disciplined son Edmund, nicknamed the Ironside, who along with his irrepressible stepmother, Emma of Normandy, had provided some of the much-needed backbone of Æthelred's regime. Edmund died at the age of twenty-three and the throne passed to the Danish King, Canute. Some of the surviving princes of the Wessex line sought refuge at the court of the King of Hungary, while Æthelred the Unready's widow, the Dowager Queen Emma, pragmatically made peace with the conquerors and married Canute herself, becoming Queen of England for the second time in her life. Her two sons by Æthelred sensibly chose to stay with their mother's family in Normandy until she could negotiate their return.

Canute, who was immortalised in the probably apocryphal legend that has him vainly trying to halt the tides to illustrate the mortal limitations of Christian kingship against the divine monarchies of the pagan past, was a capable, sometimes a brilliant, king. However, from necessity he spent at least half of his reign abroad, tending to his other kingdoms in Denmark and Norway, and this had a significant impact on how government was handled in England. To ensure stability, Canute cultivated the support of the native aristocracy, who were essential to the exercising of royal authority while he was overseas. One of his most trusted noblemen was Leofric, Earl of Mercia, whose wife, Godiva, is more famous than her husband because of the legend that she rode naked through the streets of Coventry to persuade her husband to lower the taxes on the suffering poor. Out of respect for her decision to sacrifice her dignity for the common good, the people of Coventry gallantly left the streets and shut their windows, rather than gawk at Godiva's nudity, apart from one young boy called Thomas, who dared to sneak a glance, thus creating the term 'peeping Tom'. Another of Canute's most important English liegemen was Godwin, whom he created Earl of Wessex and who was allowed to marry into the extended royal family by taking Canute's kinswoman Gytha as his wife. Over the course of Canute's reign, Godwin of Wessex became the most powerful man in England after the King and when Canute died in November 1035, it was Earl Godwin who played a crucial role in deciding who should be the next ruler.

There were two choices – Canute's son by Queen Emma, Harthacanute, or Harold Harefoot, the elder of the two boys, who had been born from a marriage of contested legitimacy earlier in Canute's life. Queen Emma loudly insisted to anyone who would listen that Harold Harefoot's mother had legally been nothing more than Canute's concubine, which meant that he could not succeed. Godwin of Wessex agreed with her, but he was in the minority. Harthacanute was currently in Denmark and Harold Harefoot, legitimate or not, had the home-field advantage of being in England. Lady Godiva's husband, Leofric of Mercia, hastened to support Harefoot, as did the majority of the men of the aristocracy, the thegns, as they had been dubbed under Danish rule.

Godwin and Leofric may both have favoured different heirs, but they and their inferiors were united in determination to prevent a war. As had ever been the way in Anglo-Saxon England, the Witan were called in the hope that deliberation and compromise might prevent a succession settled in blood on the battlefield. A dual monarchy was proposed. Both Harefoot and Harthacanute were recognised as Canute's heirs in England, both would therefore take the throne, but to prevent a personal clash between the two brothers the Witan proposed that Harthacanute could stay in his newly-inherited kingdom of Denmark, while his mother could reside in Winchester, exercising power on his behalf, in partnership with Harefoot.

Unfortunately, neither Emma nor Harefoot were exactly thrilled with this proposal and cracks appeared within weeks. Two of Queen Emma's sons from her first marriage to Æthelred the Unready were still living with her relatives in Normandy. Even their mother's marriage to Canute could not remove the unease the Danes felt about the threat these young Wessex princes posed and while their stepfather lived, they had remained abroad. Now, they both chose to return to aid their mother's quest to wrest power from Harold Harefoot.

Luckily for him, the elder of the two, Edward, never made it across the Channel thanks to bad weather that forced him to retreat back to Normandy. The younger brother, with the thoroughly Wessex-sounding name of Alfred, made it safely to Dover in Kent, where he was set upon by Harefoot's thugs. His servants were either killed or tortured and he was dragged away to have his eyes stabbed out. The blinding went wrong and Alfred died as a result of his wounds. In the ensuing chaos, Harefoot expelled a grief-stricken Queen Emma, who made the perilous winter crossing to Bruges in modern-day Belgium. She was given sanctuary by the local Count, Baldwin V, and help by her daughter, Godgifu, Countess of Boulogne. Four years later, Harefoot died at Oxford and Emma returned to England like a Fury. In retribution for his role in the mutilation and manslaughter of her son, Emma had the body of King Harold Harefoot torn from its tomb in Westminster, beheaded and thrown into a swamp.[39] With her other son Harthacanute now securely on the throne as she had always wanted, Emma was the first Queen in English history to be given the honorific of mater regis, or 'queen mother'.

Emma of Normandy was no fool. Like Charles II six centuries later, she was determined to never again endure exile. She knew better than anyone what the vagaries of tenth- and eleventh-century monarchy could bring. If Harthacanute died without sons, Emma did not want to see a repeat of 1035 or 1036, during which she had been shunted to one side, robbed of a child, impoverished and driven into exile. With this in mind, she carefully schooled her elder son Edward to succeed if Harthacanute should die prematurely. She enlisted the King's support for naming his Anglo-Saxon half-brother as his heir and commissioned works of art and literature that showed all three of them – Emma and her two surviving sons – wearing crowns.[40] In 1042, Harthacanute died at the age of twenty-three. At the time, some put his death down to poison; it was later suggested that he had actually suffered an enormous stroke. However, his mother's feverish obsession with securing the succession and Harthacanute's remarkable acquiescence to her plan to elevate his half-brother to king-in-waiting during his own lifetime would suggest that Harthacanute had probably been unwell for most of his life and that both the King and the Queen Mother expected him to die prematurely – hence their joint grooming of Edward as his replacement. By a remarkable turn of events, the Wessex line that had fallen with Æthelred the Unready returned to the throne of England in 1042, thanks to the tenacity of the Norman Queen who had married both the Anglo-Saxon loser and Viking victor of England's Danish monarchy.

EDWARD THE CONFESSOR

THE SURVIVING son of Æthelred the Unready and Emma of Normandy was Saint Edward the Confessor – both the halo and the sobriquet were added by later generations. When he came to the throne, Edward had already spent much of his life in exile. After the triumph of Canute, he lived in Europe, spending most of his formative years with his mother's family in Normandy. There, Edward had acquired many Norman sympathies, as well as a passion for their architecture. It was during his reign that the famous abbey at Westminster, now so integral to our image of the British monarchy, was built.[41] Like most of the Norman aristocracy, Edward possessed an enthusiasm for hunting that bordered on mania. He was also, as his nickname suggests, devoutly religious, but how far his faith influenced his reign is hotly debated by modern scholars, with at least two of Edward's biographers suggesting that he was a far more effective Sovereign than the later image of a gentle man of God who was too pure for the sordid world of politics might suggest.

A key issue in the discussion is the extent to which Edward's piety influenced his sexuality and, by extension, the crises of 1066. In order to secure his throne, Edward reluctantly married the Lady Edith of Wessex, a daughter of the Godwin family, who had once been stalwart supporters of Edward's mother, Emma. However, the Godwins had eventually betrayed her, and Edith's father had played a key role in handing over Edward's brother Alfred to be blinded and killed in 1036. Edward the Confessor's antipathy towards his wife's family is therefore understandable, but he could not rule without their support and so Edith became his Queen. Whether she also became a wife in anything more than name is another matter.

Since Christianity taught that both Christ and the Virgin Mary had lived and died undefiled by sexual intercourse, there was very little doubt in many medieval Christians' minds that sex was an abomination. That was certainly how the clergy saw it. Christ's Incarnation in human form had been a sign that Divinity wished to share in the totality of the human experience, yet Christ had not married. Needless to say, neither had He taken a lover. Faced with this stark biographical fact, it seemed a matter of inescapable logic that sex was not therefore an acceptable or desirable part of the human experience. It was only reproductive necessity that made it anything other than the grossest sin and, even then, only just. The teachings of a dozen saints shored up this belief and, despite our later image of the double standard of medieval sexuality, the fathers of Christian thought were as emphatic in their praise of male virginity as they were of females'.[†]

Nor was this view the product of a morbid and superstitious medieval Catholicism; its obsession with sexual chastity had a firm biblical footing, which has been all-but excised from modern-day Bible-heavy Christianity as part of the problem verses nobody likes to talk about. Saint Paul, the author of at least seven books in the New Testament, believed that virginity was preferable to marriage: 'It is good for a man not to touch a woman.'[42] Saint Ambrose of Milan taught that losing one's virginity was 'to deface the work of the creator', since all humans were born as virgins, in God's own image.[43] Saint Jerome, he who had wept at the gaudy wealth of the new Church, proclaimed that even sex within marriage was only just about tolerable because it would lead to the birth of more virgins. Saint Augustine held up the chaste marriage of Joseph and Mary as the supreme example of marital felicity for Christians, particularly its vow of abstinence. The culture of the Church too was full of stories, by turns excruciating and inspiring, of Christian virgins who had endured martyrdom in the days of paganism rather than abandon their sexual purity.

Given that King Edward and Queen Edith's marriage remained childless, it has been suggested that Edward took a vow of celibacy in order to imitate Christ, Mary and the legion of virgin-saints who had sought to honour them. However, the theory of the virginal marriage of Queen Edith has been dismissed as lacking 'authority, plausibility and diagnostic value' by Edward's twentieth-century biographer, Frank Barlow.[44] A sexless union between the two is certainly a possibility, but that does not necessarily make it a probability. The results, however, were the same whatever their cause and twenty years into Edward's reign, a crisis of the succession was looming because of the couple's childlessness. Disastrously for the realm, there were four possible contenders: Edward's brother-in-law, Harold, Earl of Wessex, who carried a necessary dash of royal blood in his veins and had the added bonus of being the most powerful aristocrat in England;

†   Their contemporaries' application of this teaching, of course, was not quite so egalitarian.

Edward's distant kinsman, William, Duke of Normandy; King Harald II of Norway, who wanted to re-unite the empire of Edward's stepfather, Canute, and Edward's young nephew, Edgar the Ætheling (an Anglo-Saxon word for a prince who was eligible to inherit the throne), who had only recently returned from his childhood in Hungary where his family had fled during the Danish invasion. Both William and Harald had the advantage of being proven warriors with sizeable fleets and armies at their disposal. Edgar, who lost a lot by being so young, would undoubtedly have been the chosen if England operated strictly by the rules of primogeniture – inheritance by the next in line in the family. Harold of Wessex was the most popular choice with King Edward's subjects. It boiled down to a difficult choice between bloodlines, military strength and popularity, with no candidate having the winning combination of all three; stories that Edward himself favoured the claim of William were probably manufactured or exaggerated after 1066.[45] As the 1050s wore into the 1060s, the four claimants were working behind the scenes to prepare themselves for the inevitable struggle once King Edward died.

In 1064, Harold of Wessex was shipwrecked in the English Channel and taken prisoner by the Count of Ponthieu. The Count intended to ransom Harold for an enormous sum of money, but before he could do so, William of Normandy turned up on his doorstep and demanded he hand Harold over. William was not a man one refused lightly and so the Count wisely bent the knee. Harold was taken back to Normandy by his erstwhile rival, where he was treated to the lavish hospitality of William's charming Duchess, Matilda of Flanders. A diminutive woman with an impeccable bloodline who counted the King and Queen of France as her grandparents and who could trace her ancestry back to the great Christian Emperor Charlemagne, chroniclers judged Matilda 'even more distinguished for the purity of her mind and manners than for her illustrious lineage [...] She united beauty with gentle breeding and all the graces of Christian holiness'.[46] However, if Matilda was a thoroughbred in medieval eyes, then her husband William qualified as a mongrel – born of a violent Duke's illicit liaison with an unmarried commoner. William the Bastard, as he was known before victory gave him a more flattering nickname, lacked both his wife's family tree and her delicacy. As Matilda charmed Harold, William leaned on him. His liberation from Ponthieu had not come gratis. No matter how comfortable his stay in Normandy was, Harold knew that he would never see home again if he did not agree to renounce his own claim to the English throne in order to support William's.

At this point, the Anglo-Saxon and Norman versions of events diverge. According to Harold, he submitted to William's conditions under duress, while William claimed that Harold not only swore, but did so with his hand on holy relics. If you believed Harold, then the oath he pledged in Normandy hardly merited the name. However, if you believed William, then Harold had entered into a contract with God and the presence of the relics made breaking that promise akin to blasphemy. Both parties appeared satisfied at the time, with Harold agreeing to give-up his common-law wife, the gloriously-named and ravishing Edith Swan-Neck, to marry one of William and Matilda's younger daughters, once she came of age. Harold was allowed to sail back to England in 1064 and, in hindsight, it does seem unlikely that a man as canny as William would not have incorporated something binding like holy relics when extracting an oath as important as the one he elicited from Harold. Letting him go suggested confidence in his loyalty.

In the first week of January 1066, as the country was celebrating the penultimate of the twelve days of Christmas, Edward the Confessor died in London. He was in his early sixties and was buried in the abbey he had commissioned at Westminster. Less than a century later, he was elevated to the sainthood by Pope Alexander III, becoming England's most famous royal saint. At the time, what mattered was not the dead King's holiness but who would follow him on the throne. In Rouen, William of Normandy confidently awaited the invitation that never came. Twenty-four hours after Edward the Confessor died, the Witan met in London on the Feast of the Epiphany, when the Church commemorated the visit of the Wise Men to the Infant Christ. Like the Magi, this Anglo-Saxon gathering of learned men had come to proclaim a new King and, as in the Bible, their decision unintentionally led to a massacre. They nominated Harold of Wessex and, to William of Normandy's fury, he consented to be crowned at Westminster immediately. It was a controversial start to what is arguably still the most famous year in English history.

GOD, LIFE AND VICTORY

THE COMING OF THE NORMANS

'It is shameful to record it, but it did not
seem shameful for him to do ...'

The Anglo-Saxon Chronicle

WHEN EDWARD Longshanks succeeded to the throne in
1272, he went down in the annals of history as King Edward I,
despite the fact that there had already been several king Edwards in
England. The reasons for this slightly misleading numeracy lie in
the fact that Longshanks was the first Edward to sit on the throne
since the conquest of 1066 and it was from there that everything
was subsequently dated, with William the Conqueror's arrival
retrospectively serving as the English monarchy's year zero. Even
today, 1066 looms large in the imagination as the beginning of our
national story, with everything before relegated to a kind of prologue,
the tellingly-nicknamed 'Dark Ages', occasionally lit-up despite itself
by men like Alfred the Great or Edward the Confessor. For years,
British schoolchildren were taught that the Middle Ages in their
country had been birthed at Hastings and buried at Bosworth.

It might be fashionable now to suggest that such a view was both
silly and reductive – it was certainly simplistic – but the importance

endowed by hindsight on William I's victory at Hastings is only-just exaggerated. Without that victory, England would not have been tied as closely to the continent and it was that relationship that defined much of England's subsequent experience of the medieval period. Without the conquest, ruthless military organisation might not have come to the British Isles in quite the same way and, without that, English domination in Ireland and Wales might never have reached the levels it did. The personalities of the kings supplied by the Norman dynasty, hungry for glory and intolerant of dissent, mattered greatly in defining what England did and, crucially, where England fought. It was in the Middle Ages that England acquired the taste for expansion that did not leave it until the middle of the twentieth century. What happened in 1066 could not have mattered more.

THE CONQUEROR

WILLIAM I, known variably as William of Normandy, William the Conqueror or William the Bastard, was a hard man forged in the fires of a brutal and merciless generation. Even in the context of the eleventh century, William stood out as a man to be feared. Or, as he might have seen it, respected. Dragged to maturity in a world that possessed all the security of quicksand and with companions that might have made a seasoned mafioso blush, William was the illegitimate son of Robert, the Viking-descended Duke of Normandy, and his mistress Herleva of Falaise. Herleva's origins are disputed, with some claiming that she was the daughter of a tanner, a skinner of animals or a town official. She was certainly not a member of the nobility and William remained touchy about both his birth out of wedlock and his mother's ancestry. When the townsfolk of Alençon pelted his army with animal skins, as a mean-spirited joke about Herleva's family, William responded by lopping off their hands and feet.

His father died when William was seven, leaving his bastard boy to inherit a region notorious for its quarrelsome and disobedient nobility. William's youthfulness meant that whoever controlled his person also held the reins of power, a recurring problem for medieval kingships, since the wellbeing and happiness of the prince was usually far down the list of their guardians' priorities. In William's case, the instability and greed he was exposed to at such a young age seems to have permanently warped his character. In one grisly incident, William's protector had his throat slit by a rival as he slept in a château at Vaudreuil, in the same bedroom as a slumbering William. He learned early that power lay at the edge of the sharpest sword wielded by the strongest man. Insubordination was not to be tolerated. Open defiance was to be punished efficiently and viciously. Freeing himself from the fetters of his guardians, William scored his first major military victory at the Battle of Val-ès-Dunes, aged nineteen. By 1052, he had married Matilda of Flanders, 'a very beautiful and noble girl of royal stock', whose father ruled the nearby province of Flanders and who dutifully provided William with a small tribe of children.[1] Matilda's royal pedigree helped cancel out the stigma that came from William's mother and, apart from a politically useful alliance with

Flanders, the new Duchess added a respectability to William's rule that had previously been lacking.[†] William's power grew further when his only two significant rivals in the region, Geoffrey, Count of Anjou, nicknamed Geoffrey the Hammer, and King Henri I of France, died and were respectively succeeded by Geoffrey's incompetent nephew and Henri's eight-year-old son. Without anyone there to check him, William annexed the county of Maine in 1062, on the pretext that its previous ruler had nominated him as his rightful heir before dying. It was not the last time he employed that justification.

By 1065, William the Bastard had been Duke of Normandy for thirty years. He was about thirty-seven years-old, five feet ten inches tall, with cropped hair, a clean-shaven face, and he was fastidious about his personal hygiene. He had successfully suppressed all challenges to his rule and expanded his family's influence. Norman towns like Rouen, Caen and Bayeux were growing; the region's economy was healthy, thanks in part to the industry of Jewish settlers in its towns and the money yielded by Normandy's excellent vineyards. William and Matilda were sufficiently wealthy to devote substantial resources to the building of monasteries, nunneries and churches, as was expected of successful medieval rulers. Then, in January 1066, William received the news that Edward the Confessor had died and Harold, Earl of Wessex, had reneged on his promise to help William succeed to the English throne. Almost immediately, preparations began for an invasion of England. Even gentle Matilda seemed incensed and paid for a new warship, the *Mora*, to speed her husband's army across the Channel.

It took the best part of a year to prepare the soldiers, the fleet and then to wait for good weather to start their journey. A Papal blessing for the Norman war effort came from Pope Alexander II, who was carried away by stories of Anglo-Saxon promiscuity, gleefully related to him by William's emissaries in Rome, who also fed the Pope (not entirely untrue) tales of Anglo-Saxon clerics' aversion to celibacy, their lacklustre implementation of the reforms currently being promoted

---

[†] Matilda had initially been unenthusiastic about the marriage herself, due to her disdain for William's illegitimacy. Contemporary chronicles reported that he had beaten her in front of her servants in rage and, overcome at this display of masculine determination, Matilda had changed her mind. An even less agreeable version of their courtship held that William had raped her and thereby forced the deflowered Matilda to marry him, since she could not now marry anybody else. William's own concerns with sexual propriety and the apparently happy nature of their marriage subsequently make this story doubtful, but by no means impossible.

by Rome and their toleration for rampant simony (the practise of buying and selling well-paying Church offices to the highest bidder). William, good and faithful servant of His Holiness, vowed to bring the ecclesiastical reforms of the eleventh century across the Channel with his armies and whip the errant Anglo-Saxon Church into line. A particular bug-bear of the Papacy's was the news that the so-called Danish marriages were still being tolerated in England – a sort of common law or secular marriage that did not feel a priest was necessary to solemnise a union. William and Matilda had actually married without Papal permission themselves. Their marriage had only been retrospectively legitimised by their friend Pope Nicholas II in return for each of them promising to build an abbey with their own money, but in the Anglo-Saxon-bashing craze of 1066, nobody felt the need to remind them of such inconvenient facts.

When William set sail for England, he left Matilda behind as regent, which was a tribute to her capabilities and his confidence in them. Before William set foot in England, another of the four claimants to the throne had landed in the north of the country: Harald Hardrada, King of Norway, came with three hundred ships and the treacherous support of King Harold's estranged brother Tostig. Together they scored an early victory in the Battle of Gate Fulford, where they defeated and killed two of the English King's most loyal supporters, the earls of Mercia and Northumbria. King Harold moved north to retaliate and the two armies clashed at the Battle of Stamford Bridge on 20 September. Harald Hardrada and Tostig were both killed in combat and the Norwegians fled home, having sustained such heavy casualties that they only filled twenty-four of their original three hundred ships.

Stamford Bridge displayed King Harold's skill as a warrior and the seriousness with which he took the task of defending his newly-won throne. However, he was also facing several problems that weakened his ability to respond to the second invasion of that autumn: William's. The first was a question of energy. His men were exhausted from the swift march northwards for their subsequent battle with Hardrada. Now, Harold expected them to march with equal speed to the southern end of the kingdom to score another victory against another large and well-trained army. Secondly, the size of his army had also been reduced and not just by the deaths of two loyal and powerful supports like the earls of Mercia and Northumbria. Harold had no choice but to release thousands of soldiers known as the fyrd, because they were farmers who could legally be temporarily co-opted into royal military service but who had to be allowed to go home again in time for harvest. Harold could not, or would not, face the chance of famine if the crops were not properly collected. Thus his army shrank significantly between Stamford Bridge and Hastings. Tired and with far fewer men, the King marched south to face William.

As soon as the Normans arrived in England, they lived up to their dire reputation. William had the area around him scorched, ruining the common people's livelihoods and forcing Harold to hurry into battle. It was actually in Harold's interests to avoid open battle for as long as possible. William had destroyed the countryside, limiting his own access to resources and food supplies. If Harold waited in the north, or in London, he could allow dissatisfaction and malnourishment to undermine William's army. Instead, an under-pressure Harold rushed towards his ruin. Perhaps he was panicked by reports of William's cruelty in southern England and wanted it to end. Maybe he was buoyed up by his victory against Hardrada and hoped he could do the same thing again. Whatever the reason, and like most things in history, it is likely to have been a combination, Harold and his army arrived, exhausted by their travels, in southern England on 14 October 1066.

Initially it looked like the King was about to win a second victory, despite his difficulties. An assault by the Norman infantry was rebuffed by the English shields. A later charge by the cavalry saw William unhorsed and momentarily presumed dead. In the ensuing confusion, the Normans appeared to retreat and the English broke rank, and thus their wall of shields, to pursue them. As they chased, the Normans suddenly rounded on them in what looked suspiciously like a premeditated ambush. Pathetic fallacy played its part as Harold and his entourage were seen charging into the sunset to face an archery attack that included the arrow that allegedly pierced King Harold's eye.[2] Incredibly, both the Bayeux Tapestry, that great artistic tribute to the Norman victory, and a later chronicler, Henry of Huntingdon, seem to confirm the story that Harold kept fighting, even after his horrific injury, and it was only when he was ridden down and hacked to pieces that he finally died. Most of his companions perished alongside him, either from the arrows or the swords of the Norman cavalry. The Anglo-Saxon Chronicle, a monastic history bitterly hostile to the Normans, wrote later, 'The King fought very hard against him with those men who wanted to support him, and there was great slaughter on either side. There was killed King Harold and Earl Leofwine his brother, and Earl Gyrth his brother and many good men. And the French had possession of the place of slaughter.'[3] Another chronicler, Orderic Vitalis, was more poetic, calling Hastings 'a scene of destruction so terrible that it must have moved any beholder to pity [...] the mangled bodies that had been the flower of the English nobility and youth covered the ground as far as the eye could see'.[4] Tradition has it that Harold's body was eventually identified by his beautiful companion, Edith Swan-Neck, who waded through the dead to find the King's mutilated corpse by identifying marks on his chest known only to her. It was apparently thanks to her efforts that the dead monarch's body was found and taken to nearby Waltham Abbey to receive a decent Christian burial.[5] A later tale had William chivalrously honouring his dead foe by having Harold buried 'near to the sea shore, which in life he had defended so long'.[6] But that seems unlikely, not least because Harold was buried miles inland.

From 'the place of slaughter', a triumphant William proceeded to London, where he repeated the tactic of laying waste to the country by fire and sword until the civic leaders of the city came outside its walls to participate in a humiliating ceremony of surrender. A king was supposed to protect his subjects from harm and unfair destruction of their property, unless they had rebelled against him, but William wanted to terrorise on arrival. Like a teacher hoping to stamp his authority over a new classroom early on, William acted firmly (psychotically, some might say) in the first few weeks after his seizure of power in England. Until his coronation, he maintained the legal fiction that a *publicum bellum* ('state of war') still existed between Normandy and England, meaning that he and his knights could behave as marauding invaders until it ceased. On Christmas Day he was crowned in Westminster Abbey as England's new 'great and peace-giving King, crowned by God, life and victory'.[7] As his virtues as a peace-giving monarch were proclaimed inside the abbey, outside, local homes were burned to the ground by William's ham-fisted soldiers who thought the crowd's cheers sounded suspiciously like cries of protest and decided it was better to punish first and ask questions later. As the sounds of the screaming, burning, panicking and rioting reached the abbey, it was said later that William displayed a rare moment of public weakness, 'trembling from head to toe' as the bishops rushed through the task of anointing him.[8]

His wife Matilda and their now-royal children were brought over to England later, where Matilda received her own coronation as Queen consort in the summer of 1068. She had maintained a close financial relationship with many of the more successful segments of the Jewish community in Normandy and it has been suggested that Judaism in England can trace its origins to those Jews who migrated to England under the protection of Queen Matilda in the 1060s.[9]

Edgar the Ætheling was now the last of William's three counter-claimants still alive. He, his mother and his two sisters chose exile, fleeing north to the court of Scotland's King Malcolm III, whom readers of Shakespeare may recognise as the victorious Prince Malcolm in *Macbeth*. The family's safety from William's clutches was soon guaranteed when Edgar's eldest sister, Margaret of Wessex, caught the eye of their protector and became Queen of Scots by marriage. She had initially wanted to become a nun, but Malcolm's persistence and no doubt a trace of familial pressure reconciled her to the idea of marriage. Edward the Confessor's widow, the Dowager Queen Edith, managed to save her fortune by testifying that William was her husband's true heir and King Harold's bereaved Edith Swan-Neck led dozens of well-born Anglo-Saxon girls, widows and heiresses seeking to avoid rape or forced marriages with the invaders by seeking sanctuary behind convent walls.

Not all of the old elite went so quietly, nor did the ordinary people look upon the invasion kindly. There were numerous rebellions against Norman rule, most of which were punished with the mass blinding and mutilation of their leaders. The most serious of the uprisings captured York, the premier city in the north, proclaimed Edgar the Ætheling the rightful king and wrote to Denmark inviting them to invade. William paid the Danes off and his gold clearly weighed more than their scruples, since the absconding allies abandoned the northerners to their fate. Even by William's precedents, it proved to be a harrowing one, retrospectively referred to as the Harrying of the North. The Anglo-Norman monk, Orderic Vitalis, whose family was among the thousands victimised by the harrying, recalled that to William's 'lasting disgrace, he yielded to his worst impulse and set no bounds to his fury, condemning the innocent and guilty to die by slow starvation.'[10] The King burned most of York, ordered every adult male in the region to be executed, and had all the crops, fields and harbours in the surrounding area torched. Like the after-effects of a nuclear bomb, those who did not perish in the immediate slaughter were left to die from the consequences, as plague and starvation swept the north, helped along by the piles of unburied and rotting cadavers, ruined crops and lack of shelter. William's actions were so depraved in their viciousness that a century later Yorkshire had still not recovered in terms of agriculture, economy or population.

So many insurrections over the course of five years had unsettled the King. In the remaining years of his rule, dozens of castles were built across the country to intimidate the populace, beginning with the makeshift motte and baileys that bought time until their more permanent replacements could be raised in stone - the most famous of which was the Tower of London, built to subdue the capital. The judicial system was manipulated to discriminate against the old aristocracy in favour of the new to the extent that the Anglo-Saxon nobility as a class had all-but ceased to exist by the end of William's reign. Their titles and estates were handed over to William's followers who, speaking French and hiding behind stone walls, formed an alien ruling class, indifferent to, and generally loathed by, the native population. The native minor nobility, the landowners of small- or medium-sized estates, fared better, but only just. Some were able to buy back their family estates at extortionate rates set by the Normans or found some kind of security in serving the new elite as their feudal dependents. Taxation records from the final year of William's reign reveal that of all the substantial landowners in England, only two were actually English. One monk expressed the national unhappiness when he wrote, 'foreigners grew wealthy with the spoils of England, whilst her own sons were either shamefully slain or driven as exiles to wander helplessly through foreign kingdoms'.[11]

The Church was treated much as the aristocracy was, with the promotion of Normans and the eradication of the native English. William's spiritual adviser, Lanfranc, was installed as Archbishop of Canterbury and quickly made good on his master's promise to bring the recent Papal reforms to England. The historian Frank Barlow called the eleventh century 'perhaps one of the most religious periods of all time', and William, with his scrupulous attendance of Mass and interest in reform of the Church, won plaudits from Pope Gregory VII, who was normally convinced that royal rulers were more hindrance than help when it came to safeguarding Holy Mother Church.[12] Celibacy as a job requirement for Christian priests was a relatively new innovation and the English branch of the Church had resisted it for as long as they could. Under William and Archbishop Lanfranc, it became mandatory. Lanfranc also protected monasticism, tackled financial corruption in the Church hierarchy and oversaw a massive architectural regeneration of the country's churches. He had less success in persuading the English to abandon their secular form of marriage, which seems to have persisted in certain parts of the country for at least the next century-and-a-half. He also presided over the systematic eviction of English men from any significant positions of authority within the Church until, by 1096, there was not a single bishopric or abbey in England that was under the control of someone who was ethnically English. The legacy of the conquest's ecclesiastical policy was more nuanced than its legacy with the nobility or wider population, but it was no less thorough in asserting Norman interests over England's.

While the English were being reduced to living as second-class citizens in their own country, if that, William faced problems from his own family. His second son Richard, Duke of Bernay, was killed in a hunting accident to the sorrow of Queen Matilda, who was a devoted mother. Her maternal instincts were further put to the test when their eldest boy, Robert, rebelled against his father in an almighty strop when he felt he was not being given enough share in the government of Normandy, which he was one day due to inherit. As with so many medieval royal quarrels, this family squabble unfortunately took on all the characteristics of a civil war, as Robert treacherously fled to seek help from his father's foe, the King of France. When attempts to heal the rift between father and son broke down, Matilda was 'choked by tears and could not speak'.[13] Despite her previous devotion to William's interests, the Queen could not bear the thought of her firstborn being cut off and she secretly used one of her servants, a man from Brittany called Samson, to deliver money to the exiled Robert. When William discovered what she had done, he was furious and threatened to have Samson blinded. It says something for the depth of his affection for his wife that he eventually relented and allowed Samson, eyes intact, to retire to a monastery, to take the cowl as penitence for aiding a traitor. Defending her actions towards the son that everyone but her seemed to regard as an entitled and spineless nuisance, Matilda allegedly told her husband, 'O, my lord, do not wonder that I love my first-born with such tender affection. By the power of the Most High, if my son Robert were dead and buried seven feet in the earth and I could bring him back to life with my own blood, I would shed my lifeblood for him!'[14]

The sting of Robert's rebellion was supplemented when the King's half-brother Odo also betrayed him. The details of Odo's treachery are lost to us, but he had once been William's right hand. Whatever he did, or tried to do, it must have been serious to result in the loss of royal favour and seven years imprisonment. Odo was not just Earl of Kent as one of the chief recipients of the conquest's decimation of the English aristocracy, but he was also Bishop of the Norman episcopacy of Bayeux. He was an unconventional prelate, best-remembered for the colourful tale that he used to ride into battle with an enormous club in order to avoid disobeying Christ's command that His apostles should not spill blood by the sword.[15] So his Grace of Bayeux apparently went through his life gleefully clubbing people to death and, eventually, betraying his royal brother. William quailed at arresting a priest, before Archbishop Lanfranc told him to arrest Odo in his capacity as an earl rather than as a bishop. A convenient loophole that soothed the royal conscience.

The final years of the Conqueror's reign saw him grow corpulent and lose much of his hair. The Queen died in 1083 and she was buried in an abbey she had founded in Normandy, where her eldest daughter Cecilia was the abbess. William had stayed by his wife's side during her final illness and did not remarry. Without Matilda's mediation, the King's relationship with his eldest son Robert never recovered. In England, William's government introduced the famous Domesday Book, a meticulous record of the wealth, land and property of all William's subjects for which historians remain eternally grateful and that his contemporary subjects roundly cursed, because the survey enabled higher and more efficient levels of taxation. The Anglo-Saxon Chronicle was particularly snippy about the great book's avaricious attention to detail: 'so very thoroughly did he have the enquiry carried out that there was not a single hide, not one vigrate of land, not even – it is shameful to record it, but it did not seem shameful for him to do – not even one ox, nor one cow, nor one pig which escaped notice in his survey. And all surveys were subsequently brought to him.'[16]

Goethe once said, 'At the close of life, thoughts hitherto unthinkable rise into the mind of one who meets his fate with resignation; they are like good spirits that diffuse their radiance upon the summits of the past.' Such was the case with William as he lay dying in September 1087. That summer he had gone campaigning against King Philippe the Amorous of France. As his armies were laying waste to the city of Mantes, William rode through the destruction, urging his men to further acts of violence. It was the last city he destroyed. His horse stumbled on a burning ember and William was thrown violently against the iron pommel of his saddle. A mortal injury was sustained and William's attendants rushed him back to his castle in Rouen. As life ebbed out of him at an excruciating pace, his two youngest sons, William and Henry, joined him. William seems to have been his father's favourite and while it was unwise to contemplate disinheriting his firstborn, the disgraced Robert, it was William who was to inherit the throne of England. Robert would get Normandy. The youngest, Henry, wept bitterly in front of his dying father and loudly complained that he was inheriting nothing. This was not exactly true. He had already inherited all of his mother's estates in England and the Conqueror planned to leave his youngest the enormous sum of five thousand pounds in silver. Still, for a man who wanted power, money with no land was a bitter pill to swallow. The younger William, meanwhile, left his father's deathbed with a parting letter for Archbishop Lanfranc, commanding him to place the crown of England on the prince's head. With his affairs in order, King William asked to be moved from the castle. The sounds from the streets were too noisy and he wished to die in the way he had denied to so many thousands of others – in peace.

His servants carried him to the priory of Saint Gervais, a picturesque little monastery overlooking Rouen from a hill beyond its western walls. There, in a monk's cell, William the Conqueror began to reflect aloud on the extraordinary journey that had taken him from bastard boy to one of the most powerful and feared leaders in Christendom. His final musings were long and eloquent to the point that later writers suspected embellishment. It is certainly possible, but equally possible that this culture of loquacious deathbed testimonials was self-perpetuating. By extolling their virtues in art and chronicles, the writers of the period actually created a trend that men and women began to imitate in life. Certainly the chroniclers edited out the blood, guts, stench, hesitations and deathbed vomiting, but we need not believe they made the whole thing up or that human beings are not capable of great speeches, even in extremis.

William lived through the Feast of the Nativity of the Blessèd Virgin Mary. The next day he was woken by the sound of church bells summoning the faithful to morning prayers. His last words, apparently, were, 'I commend my soul to the holy Mary, Mother of God, that by her prayers she may reconcile me with her Son, Our Lord Jesus Christ.'[17] Fearful of retribution from his many enemies, William's servants fled, abandoning his corpse as panic seized the streets of Rouen. It was left to the local Archbishop to calm the situation by processing out to Saint Gervais' to take possession of the dead King's body and make arrangements for his funeral. His remains lay in Saint Étienne's, a monastery he had founded in Normandy, until France's sixteenth-century Wars of Religion when, in a burst of Protestant iconoclasm, the monastery was attacked in the onslaught against everything that they perceived to be idolatry, and William's sarcophagus was destroyed, along with numerous works of Catholic art. The only part of his body ever recovered was his thigh bone, which was re-interred at Saint Étienne's beneath a new tombstone in 1987, nine hundred years after his death.

THE RED KING

THE STORY of the Anglo-Norman dynasty now shifts to William the Conqueror's three surviving sons – Robert, William and Henry. Their father's intention to split his realm into two, leaving Normandy and England under the control of the two eldest boys, had some merits. It would hopefully prevent the princes from warring with each other. Even William's lavish financial bequests to Henry, the only son who did not receive a title under the terms of his father's will, seem to have been motivated by a desire to buy Henry's loyalty to the succession settlement. This division of thrones, however, did not take into account the machinations of the Anglo-Norman nobility, most of whom held estates on both sides of the Channel, which left them perfectly positioned to cause mischief now that the realms were divided. Many of them would have preferred to see weak and malleable Robert on the throne, since he was susceptible to advice and buckled under pressure. In contrast, his brother William II was strong, clever, decisive and, like his late father, he expected to be obeyed. Faced with the choice between him and a monarch who would do whatever they wanted, the Anglo-Norman magnates unsurprisingly preferred Robert. The reign of William II thus began with an unsuccessful aristocratic rebellion that aimed to topple the new King from his throne and re-unite England and Normandy under one conveniently pliable ruler.

That rebellion failed, but the treachery of so many Norman lords led to a tentative change in the monarchy's attitude towards its English subjects. In order to keep his throne, William II had been compelled to rely on the support of the English, who were liable to endorse anyone who would prevent their detested aristocracy further expanding its power. This support in his hour of need resulted in William promising to alleviate his subjects' lot by lifting many of the legal discriminations put in place against them by his father. Like most medieval kings and modern politicians, William did not keep all of his promises, but he kept enough of them to mark a tentative rapprochement between Crown and country.

Despite this, until very recently William II had a fairly dire historical reputation. Nicknamed William Rufus from the Latin word for red, a tribute either to his complexion or his hair, William had the bad historiographical luck to be both a homosexual and to quarrel with the Church. Since most of the surviving chronicles from his era were written by monks, it is unsurprising to find William emerging so unfavourably – only in recent years has the hysteria of their denunciations attracted suspicion. One scribe claimed that under William II 'everything that was hateful to God and to righteous men was the daily practice in this land during his reign'.[18] Homosexuality had not yet attracted the opprobrium in Christian countries that it was to acquire in later centuries – there is substantial evidence to suggest that the real witch-hunt did not begin until the century after William – nonetheless, it was still something the clergy generally disapproved of and William, quite clearly, did not care one fig for that disapproval. There was no "don't ask, don't tell" with this soldier-King. Gifted with great physical presence, William II was vital and muscular, with a physique that one of his enemies likened to that of a strong bull. Although he lacked the regal demeanour expected of a King, he evidently had scads of the charisma needed for a successful general. He lacked his father's vindictiveness, letting several of Robert's rebels sail into exile rather than murdering or mutilating them; he was funny and easygoing in private, but apparently far less gifted as a public orator. He peppered his conversation with a soldier's oaths and he was always dressed in the height of fashion. Once, when he discovered that the boots he was wearing had only cost three shillings, he rounded on his chamberlain and exclaimed, 'You son of a whore! Since when has a king worn boots of so paltry a price? Go, and buy me a pair worth a mark of silver.'[19] For inexplicable and obscure reasons, a few monks took particular umbrage at William's introduction of pointed shoes for men, now such an integral part of our popular image of medieval fashion. Why they felt so moved to fury by his shoes is unclear, but royalty's accessories often seemed to provoke clerical ire. In the next century, the famous preacher Saint Bernard of Clairvaux would wax apoplectic about Eleanor of Aquitaine's earrings, which he considered too long to be seemly.

Less than two years after he became King, William had to deal with the death of his father's trusted Archbishop of Canterbury, Lanfranc. Lanfranc and William II had enjoyed an amicable working relationship, but the King seemed in no hurry to replace him. The Crown enjoyed significant powers of clerical appointment, meaning that no major episcopal or monastic appointments could be made without the King's permission. The Papacy was working hard to end this practice and William II's actions showed why. As long as the see remained vacant, its incomes went to the royal household and Canterbury was by far the best-endowed see in England. For four years, William left the country without an archbishop in Canterbury, as he pocketed the archbishopric's numerous incomes for himself. The clergy were appalled at his actions and it is interesting to surmise how long this would have continued had William II not fallen deathly ill at Gloucester in 1093. Frightened by his brush with mortality, the King hurriedly tried to appease the Almighty's wrath by making good his wrongs at Canterbury and appointing one of Lanfranc's former students as the new Archbishop. He chose the intellectual and deeply devout Anselm, who is today venerated as a saint in the Roman Catholic communion.

As soon as William felt better, he regretted his decision. Anselm was unquestionably one of his generation's most gifted theologians, but he lacked tact and all sense of flexibility. He was determined to limit the monarchy's power over the Church and to implement yet another set of ecclesiastical changes, known as the Gregorian Reforms, the brainchild of Pope Gregory VII. Anselm and William were two strong-minded men, both used to getting their own way and determined to see their respective institutions emerge as the dominant power in England. The Gregorian Reforms that Anselm was championing in England declared that the Roman Catholic Church was supreme among earthly bodies and that no other terrestrial power could hold any kind of authority over it. The reforms wanted to see all important religious matters decided in Rome, not locally, and they also wanted to end the involvement of kings, princes and emperors in clerical appointments. For William, these reforms were tantamount to making the Church politically equal with the monarchy, if not superior to it. The Church held a significant amount of land in England and to have such a sizable segment of the country operating under the authority of an institution that was completely independent of the Crown was something William would not tolerate.

In 1095, William tried to resolve the dispute by summoning a council at Rockingham, where he expected the priests and bishops who owed so much to him to pressure Anselm into abandoning the implementation of Pope Gregory's reforms. Anselm, in a magnificent piece of defiance, proclaimed he would cling to the rock of his faith, conjuring images of Saint Peter, Christ's chief apostle, the rock of the Church and, so tradition claimed, the first Pope. Church-state relations deteriorated further after the impasse at Rockingham, with William famously declaring of Anselm, 'Yesterday, I hated him with great hatred, today I hate him with yet greater hatred and he can be certain that tomorrow and thereafter I shall hate him continually with ever fiercer and more bitter hatred.'[20] In 1097, Anselm voluntarily chose exile in Europe and William, no doubt overjoyed by his rival's departure, began collecting the archiepiscopate's income once again. Many grumbled, but few complained openly.

Outside the issue of the Church, William Rufus was a much more successful King. The feud with the last sprigs of the Wessex family tree was finally resolved, with two of Edgar the Ætheling's Scottish nieces completing their education at nunneries in England. That did not stop William smashing an invading army led by their father, King Malcolm III, in 1093. To his credit, he continued to treat the Scottish princesses with every kindness and they remained in England, where they were treated with great honour. He increased his country's presence in Wales, continued his father's wars in Europe and allegedly had designs on Ireland and the Aquitaine. Apart from his feud with Anselm, he was a generous patron of certain monasteries and helped fund the completion of the wonderful cathedral in Winchester, where he was later buried. In contrast to his abysmal brother Robert, William II also managed to control the aristocracy, suppress rebellions and hold onto his inheritance. In 1089, a cash-strapped Robert effectively sold most of western Normandy to their youngest brother, Henry, then relied on Henry to suppress a rebellion against his rule, while he hid in terror at the church of Notre Dame du Pré in Rouen. Two years later, William invaded Normandy in retribution for Robert's interference in England. The King walloped the Duke and forced Robert to cede half the duchy to England. In 1096, Robert pawned what little was left of his realm and used the money to 'take the Cross', an expression for going on Crusade.

With Robert off fighting in Palestine, the two remaining brothers established a friendly relationship at last, with the clever and ambitious Henry rising high in his brother's court. Unusually for medieval kings, even homosexual or bisexual ones, William II showed no intention of marrying and so Henry was widely regarded as the heir-apparent, even though he was younger than Robert. During his time at Robert's court in Normandy, Henry had wisely built up a network of allies and friends among the Anglo-Norman magnates, attracting the support of men who had estates in both Normandy and England, men like Hugh d'Avranches, nicknamed Hugh Lupus ('Hugh the Wolf') due to his crest or, less kindly, Hugh le Gros ('Hugh the Fat'), who was Earl of Chester in England and vicomte d'Avranches in Normandy. Like Henry, these men were intelligent and tenacious, and they formed the backbone of the political career he forged in the decade after his father's death.

On 2 August 1100, William II was killed on a hunting trip in the New Forest. The forest had been one of his father's creations and a deeply unpopular one. To indulge his passion for hunting, the Conqueror ordered the creation of many royal hunting demesnes, for which the penalty for poaching in was to have one's eyes put out. Creating these vast pleasure fields had not been easy. Henry of Huntingdon disapprovingly remembered, 'so as to form the hunting ground of the New Forest he [William I] caused churches and villages to be destroyed, and, driving out the people, made it an habitation for deer'.[21] During a trip there, William II was hit by a stray arrow and died almost instantly. His death at the height of his political and military success, coupled with his brother's alacrity in accepting the throne, caused a suspicion that William's death had been deliberate. It is certainly possible, but by no means certain. Henry's swift consolidation of power may have looked premeditated, but it is also worth remembering that Henry was a seasoned political operator who knew the importance of establishing one's authority quickly. In this he was no different to Harold of Wessex in the days after Edward the Confessor's death, or even William Rufus, rushing to join forces with Archbishop Lanfranc before William the Conqueror was cold. A lengthy grieving process was something a medieval monarch could not afford and Henry I's political savvy should not necessarily be construed as proof of pre-meditated fratricide.

William Rufus remains one of England's most interesting Sovereigns, if for no other reason than his reign showcased the mounting tensions between an absolute monarchy that, by its very nature, could brook no organised opposition to its authority, and an increasingly imperial Papacy that sought to liberate the Church from secular interference. Yet William's larger-than-life personality and the contradictions posed by his promiscuous lifestyle, his magnanimity, his success as a soldier, his hatred of Archbishop Anselm but close political partnership with Ranulf, Bishop of Durham, his coarse speech but quick brain, his humour and his towering temper, make him interesting in his own right, as do the ways in which his private life and his quarrel with Anselm shaped his subsequent reputation. Perhaps the fairest and most nuanced assessment of William II comes from his modern biographer, Frank Barlow, who wrote of him:

> William Rufus became a scandalous figure, the subject of much gossip. His outrageous remarks were collected and even monastic writers could not always conceal their delight. A rumbustious, devil-may-care soldier, without natural dignity or social graces, with no cultivated tastes and little show of conventional religious piety or morality – indeed according to his critics addicted to every vice, particularly lust and especially sodomy – he nevertheless could not simply be written off as a degenerate wastrel. His chivalrous virtues and achievements were all too obvious. He had maintained good order and satisfactory justice in England and restored good peace to Normandy. He had extended Anglo-Norman rule in Wales, brought Scotland firmly under his lordship, recovered Maine, and kept up the pressure on the Vexin. His wars had been costly and not all had been cost effective; but he impressed contemporaries as being a victorious general [...] Even the clergy did not expect a king to be a saint. They were quite happy with a hero.[22]

BEAUCLERC

A S THE youngest of four brothers, Henry I should never have become King. His father's over-generous financial provisions for him and his mother's bequest of all her English estates indicate that his parents were trying to provide for a child who they never expected to wear the crown. Circumstance had other ideas, as each of his brothers exited life's stage prematurely – Richard was killed in a hunting accident as a young man, William Rufus met a similar fate in the New Forest in 1100 and Robert performed the eleventh-century Christian equivalent of seppuku on his political credibility – until Henry was left standing alone beneath the spotlight, outliving all of them and reigning for thirty-five years, the longest reign, thus far, in English history.

He was the only one of William the Conqueror's sons to be born in England. Unlike his brothers, he had spent most of his childhood there as well and his education had been excellent. Contemporary chroniclers like William of Malmesbury and Orderic Vitalis praised his intellect and he was later given the nickname Beauclerc, in homage to his love of learning. Centuries later, Henry's reputation for cleverness had survived and he was said to have been the first royal to gain a degree from Cambridge – an interesting achievement, given that the university was not founded until the century after his death. During his brothers' reigns, Henry had used the money left by his father to establish himself as a powerful magnate in Normandy. As has been mentioned, he managed to suppress a rebellion against Robert's rule, while Robert himself hid in the safety of a nearby church. It was during that turmoil that Henry showed he could be just as brutal as his father. Coming across Conan, one of the rebellion's teenaged leaders, Henry frogmarched the boy up to the top of a castle tower and kicked him off. He could be kind and considerate as well, especially to the priesthood. While hunting, the Bishop of Lincoln felt ill and collapsed, Henry caught the old man in his arms and carried him to the nearest shelter. He fathered at least two dozen illegitimate children, but the monastic historians who adored him for ending the homosexual, archbishop-feuding free-for-all of his brother's reign could not quite bring themselves to criticise his rampant promiscuity. William of Malmesbury quite seriously described the man who fathered more bastard children than any other English monarch as a King who was 'free during his whole life from impure desires' and claimed that it was only 'female blandishments' that led Henry astray.[23]

His coronation took place three days after the Red King's death. He was in his early thirties, already beginning to bald, muscular and barrel-chested like his late brother, but with darker hair. He ate simple food and drank very little, he was well-spoken and a calm sleeper, but with a rather regrettable tendency to snore. His crowning was accompanied by an unfilial charter that shredded William II's legacy by vowing that the Crown would never again abuse the Church's finances. The document was dispatched to the country's bishops and the shire courts, ensuring a swift and efficient distribution of the Sovereign's promises. A grovelling letter was sent to the exiled Archbishop Anselm while William II's favourite adviser, Ranulf, Bishop of Durham, was imprisoned in the Tower of London. The court was given a makeover, with Henry publicly renouncing the fashions, haircuts and even the beards favoured by his late brother. Not to go clean-shaven, a bishop warned him, would be tantamount to condoning the 'fornicators and sodomites' who had peopled the royal court during William's time.[24]

All this may sound unpleasant, ridiculous or both. At the time, there were aristocrats within the court who thought the attempt to set fashion back by a generation was tiresome and silly. However, Henry I wanted a strong and united country and he knew that this could only be achieved by re-establishing good relations between the monarchy and the Church. Equally astute was his choice of a bride, Matilda of Scotland, who he married within three months of his accession. The marriage was popular, because Matilda was Edgar the Ætheling's niece and, in marrying her, Henry united the bloodline of the conquering Normans with that of the old royal family. Like Henry, the Queen was preoccupied with etiquette and deferential to the Church, but she was also frumpy, badly dressed and, when it came to her looks, the best that even her supporters could manage was to claim that her appearance was 'not entirely to be despised' – an underwhelming conclusion that the courtiers in the palace would doubtless have giggled at, since they seem to have enjoyed mocking Matilda for her dowdy fashion and barbarian ancestry, meaning Scottish and Anglo-Saxon.[25]

The very same qualities that made the worthy Matilda such an easy target for courtiers' malice were what made her so popular with the wider population. The people did not care if she was badly dressed. What mattered to them was that she seemed so unashamedly and unrelentingly good. During her childhood in Scotland, Matilda had learned from the example of her mother Queen Margaret, who instilled good manners and a love of religion in her children. Charity was a major preoccupation for the Scottish royal family; Matilda grew up witnessing her mother wash the feet of poor people in imitation of Christ bathing the feet of His apostles at the Last Supper, reading aloud from the Bible every night and going out into the streets to feed the children of the local poor. The royal children were beaten if they misbehaved and rudeness to their servants was not tolerated. Evidently, Margaret's style of parenting worked. During her time as Queen consort, Matilda personally financed the building of several monasteries and convents in England, served as patroness for two leprosy hospitals in Chichester and Westminster, made lavish bequests to churches and cathedrals in England and on the continent, improved the roads, bridges and sanitation on her estates (one bridge, built over the River Lea to help her tenants cross it safely, survived until the reign of William IV, seven centuries later), and promoted trade in the city of London. The Queenshithe Docks, which still exist today, were founded by Matilda of Scotland and carefully nurtured to increase economic opportunities both for the city and for the Queen's household, which derived part of its income from them. Her surviving correspondence reveals a sophisticated understanding of complex theology that was 'rare among laymen and quite exceptional amongst laywomen' in the twelfth century.[26] Her religious zeal won her many admirers; her brother David was stunned to find her bathing and kissing the feet of a crowd of lepers, a move she defended as inspired by Christ's example. Her one brief dip in popularity came in the middle of her time as Queen, when her charitable expenditures were so numerous that she tried to hike-up rent on her properties, before her advisers managed to explain why that would have a negative impact on her relationship with the people. Henry I adored her and, although compulsively unfaithful to her sexually, he relied on her advice and trusted her implicitly.

Yet this successful royal marriage very nearly did not happen at all. As a young girl, Matilda had spent some time in the care of her aunt Cristina, the abbess of the English convent at Romney. At various stages of her childhood and adolescence, Matilda had been seen by numerous witnesses wearing the habit of a nun. Committing a child to a vocation in the Church before they were old enough to make the decision for themselves was common enough in the eleventh and twelfth centuries, with the children known as the oblati and their committal to the Church regarded as legally binding as if they had taken the vows as adults. There was Biblical precedent for the custom, since tradition held that both Samuel the Prophet and the Holy Virgin Mary had been placed in the Temple in Jerusalem as infants to be raised in the service of God; William I's eldest daughter Cecilia had been an oblate.[27] However, when confronted by a marriage proposal from the King of England, Matilda of Scotland insisted that she had been forced to wear the veil by her tyrannical aunt and that this coercion invalidated her obligation. Archbishop Anselm, who had referred to her as 'the prodigal daughter of the King of Scots whom the devil made to cast off the veil', was returning to England after three years in exile, in no mood to pander on the issue of the Church's rights.[28] He forbade Matilda to marry Henry and warned that he would 'not be induced by any pleading to take from God His Bride and join her to any earthly husband'.[29] Then a few weeks later, it was Anslem himself who stood on the steps of Westminster Abbey to officiate at Henry and Matilda's wedding. Why had this man, notorious for his obstinacy, changed his mind?

It was Matilda herself who headed Anselm off by arranging a private meeting before the Archbishop had a chance to reunite with Henry. The pair met in Salisbury and despite the fact that there were numerous holes in Matilda's claim that she had been forced to wear the veil, chief among them being the fact that she had continued wearing it long after she left her aunt Cristina's company, Anselm managed to invoke a suitably obscure piece of ecclesiastical legislation that allowed girls to renounce the cloister if they had only fled to it at a time when their life or virginity was at risk. This patently did not apply to Matilda of Scotland but, with rare flexibility on his part, Anselm decided to believe that it did.

The role of a queen consort was an enormously important one in the medieval polity. Later queens in England are more famous than the Anglo-Norman queens, but they were certainly not more powerful. The influence of earlier royal women like Emma of Normandy, who had played a central role in the reigns of two husbands, two stepsons and two sons, as well as the trust placed in their queens by kings like William the Conqueror, show that medieval queens consort were anything but the doe-eyed breeding machines of popular assumption. Queens possessed huge economic clout, with vast estates signed over to them at the time of their marriages to generate the rents and revenues needed to fund the Queen's household. They also played a vital ceremonial role in medieval monarchy. Just as Catholicism taught that God was the font of justice, stern and firm, with the Virgin Mary serving as the mediatrix between a just God and a weak humanity, kings and queens were expected to conform to these cultural tropes. Kings were to bring fairness to their people and being fair often required being strict. If kings symbolised justice, queens served as the conduits of mercy. A queen was supposed to ask the king to show clemency and grant pardons. If a king granted mercy because of the entreaties of his female relatives, there was no shame in that, but if he acted too kindly of his own volition, then he was perceived as weak and rebellion or disobedience inevitability ensued. Sometimes, if a king wished to show mercy but did not want to seem feeble in initiating it, his wife would publicly beseech him to do so, thus enabling the king to embark upon a course of action he had already decided on. This accepted function of queens, whose role as guarantors of the succession entitled them to gorgeous coronations of their own in which their position as earthly handmaidens of the Virgin Mary was clearly advertised, often produced fine moments of political theatre. Queens were integral to the mechanics of a successful monarchy and William II's failure to marry may very well be one of the reasons why there was no possibility of him climbing down during his feud with the Church.

Looked at from this perspective, it is easy to see why a mixture of piety and pragmatism resulted in Anselm changing his mind about Matilda of Scotland becoming Queen of England. We should not discount Matilda's own personality, since Anselm evidently began to soften on the issue after their first meeting at Salisbury. He was impressed both by her character and her eloquence. Perhaps, although this might seem unduly cynical, a deal of sorts was struck. Anselm had seen the difficulties that William II's bachelor state created. Now, God had provided Anselm with a potential Queen who would owe her crown to the Church. If Anselm helped her, he would have a useful ally at the King's side.

If that was Anselm's plan, it proved fortuitous, because although neither the Archbishop nor King Henry wanted more secular-ecclesiastical tensions, they re-surfaced despite their best intentions, and in 1103 Anselm again went into exile. The dispute this time centred on lay investiture. The Church's wealth derived from the amount of land it held, nearly one-third of the country, most of which had either been given to it by the royal family or bequeathed to it in the final wills and testaments of landowners who had themselves previously received their land from the King. Under a feudal monarchy, it was vital that the Sovereign receive homage from the land's custodians, with their public obeisance guaranteeing future loyalty to him. This requirement had resulted in two ceremonies that were a fixture of court life before Henry I – lay investiture and lay homage, in which members of the Church hierarchy would be invested in their new office by the King then perform homage to him in return for the land their office controlled. Hitherto, the Church had tolerated this but in 1099, at the Council of Rome, Pope Urban II banned both lay investiture and the custom of ecclesiastics bending the knee to swear fealty to a secular ruler. Archbishop Anselm was not particularly enthusiastic about this decision and tried to persuade the new Pope, Paschal II, to grant England an exemption, but the pontiff refused. Henry, who had been more than prepared to compromise on ecclesiastical demesnes, vacant sees and finances, absolutely could not bring himself to relinquish what he saw as the monarchy's feudal prerogatives. An impasse was reached and Anselm left for Rome.

During his absence, he was in constant secret correspondence with the Queen. Matilda, who had taken to signing herself as 'reginæ et filiæ Anselmi archiepiscopi' ('queen and daughter of archbishop Anselm'), was told to persuade the King 'publicly and privately' to accept the Pope's decision.[30] At times a stressed Matilda had to remind Anselm that she had a loyalty to her husband and that she could not work miracles. The situation dragged on for four years, during which Matilda was often the only point of communication. Finally, a meeting was organised with the help of another interceding royal female, Henry's sister Adela, and a compromise was reached with Henry agreeing to give up the right to actually invest the clergy, in return for which Anselm and the Papacy would look the other way by allowing English clerics to do homage to the monarchy for the land their bishoprics held. It was a rare moment of flexibility from both Henry and Anselm, and Matilda, rightly, received most of the credit from their contemporaries for saving the country from another four years of religious gridlock.

Henry I was also lucky to rule during what historians dubbed the renaissance of the twelfth century, a revival of interest in Latin and the legacy of the Roman Empire, as well as significant cultural, economic, technological and social changes. Although most of the era's scientific or technological innovations occurred after Henry, his reign did benefit greatly from the increased levels of literacy, the birth of Europe's first universities, and developments in law and philosophy. With these Henry was able to build up a professional bureaucracy, whose success depended on their successful implementation of the King's laws not their own grand connections, as had been the case with the feudal underlings of William I. With these men raised from the dust by his favour and nothing else, the King was able to preside over a period of domestic stability fuelled by governmental reform. He had an encyclopaedic memory and could delegate to those around him while remaining firmly in control of the situation. Orderic Vitalis wrote that Henry, 'inquired into everything, and retained all he heard in his tenacious memory. He wished to know all the businesses of officials and dignitaries; and, since he was an assiduous ruler, he kept an eye on all the happenings in England and Normandy.'[31] He was fanatical about the importance of due process and judicial fairness. The shire courts went into decline as Henry appointed itinerant royal justices who travelled the kingdom implementing royal law as fairly in one part of the country as they would in the next. Two surviving documents, the *Leges Henrici primi* and *Quadripartitus*, written by two of his administrators, give us an idea of the intricacy and sophistication of England's legal code during Henry's reign. These laws were ruthlessly applied and harsh penalties were in place for those who broke them. The punishment must fit the crime and, just as castration had been the penalty for rape under William the Conqueror, Henry's laws mandated that the scourge of his time, counterfeit coiners, should lose their hands for their misdeeds. It was (half) joked that by the end of Henry's reign, every forger in the country had been mutilated in one way or the other.

Henry I's financial innovations were no less remarkable or important than his legal reforms, but predictably they were a good deal less popular. As has ever been the case in British history, taxes were high and they got higher when Henry's eldest surviving daughter was betrothed to Heinrich V, ruler of most of central Europe. The princess's dowry was astronomically high and it has plausibly been suggested that the Exchequer, which remains the bedrock of the British government's finances, was set up by Henry I and his minister, the Bishop of Salisbury, to create an efficient way to raise the dowry.[32] The Exchequer survived the wedding and instituted annual audits, known as the pipe rolls, which gives us a fascinating insight into the sophistication of royal finances in the early twelfth century. By the time Henry died, the monarchy was not only solvent but financially stable. As many of his successors were to discover, this was no small accomplishment.

The final half of Henry I's long reign witnessed several catastrophes in the King's private life. Queen Matilda died at Westminster in 1118, aged only thirty-eight. Her last political act had been to issue a charter protecting the rights of a group of religious recluses in Oxford. She was given a stately funeral, with grandiose plans for an eternal flame at her tomb in Westminster. Two years later her only son William drowned at the age of seventeen when he was returning from a visit to France. The *White Ship* left Barfleur harbour in the middle of a storm and collided with submerged rocks moments after its departure. The sole survivors were the captain and a butcher's son from Rouen. Making it to the surface, the captain deliberately drowned himself when he realised the prince was dead. The news was brought to the King who 'fell to the ground overcome with anguish, and after being helped to his feet by friends and led into a private room, gave way to bitter laments'.[33]

The *White Ship* disaster was not just a personal tragedy for Henry I, it completely changed the political environment around him. At the time of his son's death, Henry had already finalised plans to take a second wife, the adolescent Adeliza of Louvain, whose father Godfrey held land in modern-day France and Germany. Adeliza, nicknamed 'the Fair Maid of Brabant', arrived in England shortly after the sinking and the couple were married at Windsor Castle in January 1121. The new Queen was young and very beautiful – Latin poems and flattering comments from the Archbishop of Canterbury attest to her loveliness – she was also kind, elegant, generous and artistic, with a fondness for music and poetry. However, what had perhaps initially intended to be a winter-spring marriage to bring the King comfort as he reached his twilight had been transformed by Prince William's death. From the moment she was married, Adeliza was under immediate and undisguised pressure to produce an heir to replace the one lost off the coast of Normandy.

Initially, Henry was smitten with Queen Adeliza and she was showered with gifts, grants of land, tax exemptions and financial perks that even her esteemed predecessor had not enjoyed. She massaged her irascible husband's ego by having poets write flattering accounts of his reign, then paying for them to be set to music and performed in front of him. However, unlike the first two Norman queens, she had no political authority and, despite the wealth of her household and charm of her personality, Adeliza of Louvain's fourteen-year career as Queen of England ultimately serves as a study of grace under fire.

Years passed and as Adeliza kept the trim waist of her childhood, Henry's expanded. His health began to suffer. Those around him blamed the Queen. William of Malmesbury cruelly wrote that Henry's later life was spent 'in grief that the woman did not conceive and in fear that she would always be barren'.[34] 'The woman' also felt the pain and turned to religion, entreating Hildebert, Archbishop of Tours, for advice. The good Archbishop did not exactly write back with words of comfort, unhelpfully musing that it may not have 'been granted to you from Heaven that you should bear a child to the King of the English', before suggesting that Adeliza might like to throw herself into charitable enterprises instead since 'it is more blessed to be fertile in the spirit than the flesh'.[35] Adeliza's response, sadly, has not survived.

In 1126, five years into the marriage, Henry's only surviving legitimate child, Maud, returned to England.[†] She had been living in Germany and Italy since childhood, but the recent death of her husband Emperor Heinrich V had left her a childless widow. With her brother's death and stepmother's childlessness, Maud had the best blood claim to the English throne. She was hampered, of course, by her gender but during her time as Empress she had shown herself to be a gracious and competent leader, often exercising power as regent

---

[†] The Empress is usually referred to as Matilda and far less frequently as Maud, the Anglo-Saxon version of her name. In a chapter that already has three Queens Matilda, I have opted to refer to her as Maud for clarity's sake.

during her husband's travels. Impressed by Maud, Henry's illegitimate son Robert and his brother-in-law, the King of Scots, were among those who urged the King to take the unprecedented step of naming a woman as his heir. On the first day of January 1127, a ceremony was held at Windsor Castle at which the Scottish King, the Archbishop of Canterbury and Henry's favourite nephew Stephen led the lords of the realm in swearing to uphold Maud's claim to the throne once Henry passed away. Queen Adeliza also attended and it is difficult not to sympathise with her humiliation at witnessing this unfortunate necessity. To her fury, Maud was quickly married-off to Geoffrey Plantagenet, the Count of Anjou; it was a far cry below the rank of her first husband and Geoffrey was still in his early teens, while Maud was in her late twenties. Packed off to Anjou, she laid back and thought of England, producing her first son, Henry, in 1133.

In the same year, there was a solar eclipse, interpreted as an evil omen. Henry I died on 2 December 1135 at Lyons-le-Forêt in Normandy, allegedly as the result of accidental food poisoning brought on by eating a batch of lamprey eels. On his deathbed, he exhorted those around him to uphold the stability he had brought to England and Normandy, to defend the rule of law and the rights of the poor, then he made his last confession and received absolution. One of his courtiers reflected, 'God grant him peace, for peace he loved.'[36] It perhaps serves as a fair epitaph for a personally unpleasant but politically successful monarch who had spent years trying to safeguard peace only to have the last, and greatest, of his ploys to fail. Twenty-four days after his death, his successor was crowned in Westminster Abbey. But it was not Maud, currently incapacitated by pregnancy on the other side of the English Channel. Instead it was Henry's nephew Stephen, who had helped lead the acclamations of loyalty to Maud in 1127. He had organised a swift and bloodless coup, followed by a long and vicious civil war.

WHEN CHRIST AND HIS SAINTS SLEPT

STEPHEN OF Blois, who was crowned on his patron saint's feast day in 1135, was one of history's most pleasant usurpers. He was exceptionally handsome, tall, rich, chivalrous, faithful to his wife, friendly with his servants, well-mannered and brave.[37] His father Étienne was killed at the Battle of Ramlah on the First Crusade and his mother Adela, one of William the Conqueror's daughters, had raised her children to love God as much as she did. She sent Stephen to make a career in his uncle's service in England where he eventually married Matilda of Scotland's niece, yet another Matilda, the daughter and heiress of the Count of Boulogne. After their marriage, Matilda of Boulogne handed her county over to Stephen to rule in her name, since a woman could not exercise power in her own right. Seemingly a common view on their side of the family.

Stephen had actually been due to board the fateful *White Ship* with his cousin William in 1120, but had to cancel his journey at the last minute when he was laid low by a providential bout of crippling diarrhoea.[38] Stephen and Matilda had five children together: Baldwin, Eustace, William, Matilda and Mary. The Empress Maud was the couple's mutual first cousin and yet both seemed curiously untroubled at robbing her of her inheritance.[39] The simplest explanation for their actions in 1135 is that ambition can make even the worthiest of souls do things they might ordinarily consider reprehensible. Even during Henry I's lifetime, Stephen had nursed the ambition to one day be king. He had gone so far as to consult a hermit rumoured to have the gift of prophecy, who had correctly predicted that Adeliza of Louvain would remain childless during her time as Queen of England, that the King would die in the land of his ancestors and that it would be Stephen, not Maud, who succeeded him. At the time of his death, Henry had been mid-quarrel with the fiery Maud and her husband, allowing Stephen's supporters to claim that the King had changed his mind at the last minute, preferring succession in the male line through Stephen, who reacted with lightning-fast speed and made it back to England before Maud had even heard her father was dead. Stephen's brother Henry, Bishop of Winchester, had been lobbying hard to win over the last of Maud's adherents, including the

Archbishop of Canterbury, who was one of the few men to display any qualms about abandoning the woman they had all sworn to serve. The Pope blessed the usurpation and formally recognised Stephen as Henry I's heir. A coronation was a mystical ritual of consecration that involved anointing with holy oil; it permanently elevated kings from the ranks of the rest of humanity. Through it, Stephen was crowned, blessed and proclaimed before the heavily-pregnant Maud had the chance to react.

A successful monarchy excels in participatory splendour, whereby elaborate displays of pomp and pageantry invite elite or populace to feel that the throne is part of their cultural identity, rather than ruling remotely from above. Extravagant panoply also projects an image of wealth, confidence and, above all, stability. Shortly after their coronations, Stephen and his Queen held a summer court at Oxford, which witnesses described as the most splendid seen in years, with their eldest surviving son Eustace on prominent display as the heir-apparent. The lords temporal and spiritual danced in attendance, suggesting that loyalty to the new order had successfully been established. Yet the few absences from Stephen's celebrations were nonetheless conspicuous ones, including Henry I's favourite bastard son Robert, Earl of Gloucester, and his widow, the Dowager Queen Adeliza. The impeccably proper Gloucester formally severed his ties to Stephen by sending him a diffidatio, a written notification of a removal of allegiance. Etiquette mattered, even on the brink of civil war. At Easter of the following year, rebellion returned to England, with the Stephenite loyalist Henry of Huntingdon bewailing that 'the abominable madness of the traitors flared up'.[40] The Empress, safely delivered of her third child, decided to join the faithful who remained obedient to her late father's wishes. She sailed to England to pursue the conflict in person and made immediately for the safety of Arundel Castle, where the gates were opened to her by her stepmother, Adeliza.

There were now two would-be monarchs in England and Stephen began to haemorrhage allies. Queen Adeliza's support for the Empress indicated that the Stephenite story of Henry I's last-minute change of heart was a fabrication and the walls of Arundel Castle allowed the rightful Queen to incite further uprisings against Stephen. She was backed by many members of the nobility who saw their own cause in hers, specifically families who had inherited any or most of their land through the female line, and who therefore had good reason to see

Maud's cause triumph. In a world based on precedent, a strike against the King's daughter was a strike against them all. Those clans who were unaffected by the principle of succession via a woman, or who simply chose to ignore its implications, flocked to Stephen's banner, but their loyalty was a double-edged sword. The King's goodness and kindness counted against him. When one of Stephen's lords, John Marshal, betrayed him, the King besieged Marshal's castle at Newbury, but pardoned him and took Marshal's infant son William as his ward-cum-hostage for his father's future good behaviour. Callously indifferent to his son's wellbeing, John Marshal was soon up to his old rebellious tricks and everybody expected Stephen to execute the child, even the boy's father, who cruelly jested he had the ability to father replacement sons. However, at the last minute Stephen was so moved by the young boy's playful trust in him that he could not go through with the hanging.[†]

This clemency won Stephen much praise for his decency, particularly when contrasted to the repulsive behaviour of the child's father, but it did not encourage the other aristocrats to think of him of as their feared overlord. William of Malmesbury wrote that 'by his good nature and the way he jested [Stephen] earned an affection that can hardly be imagined', but the Anglo-Saxon Chronicle gave a more depressing assessment: because the lords 'saw that he was a mild man, and soft, and good, and did not exact the full penalties of the law, they perpetrated every enormity'.[41] In the next generation, the writer and priest Walter Map considered Stephen 'adept at the martial arts but in other respects little more than a simpleton'.[42] Another writer said it best, though, when he wrote of Stephen, 'If he had legitimately acquired the kingdom and had administered it without trusting ears to the whispers of malevolent men, he would have lacked little which adorns the royal character'.[43]

There were some successes for Stephen. His clever and loyal wife negotiated a treaty that stayed Scottish support for the Empress, three bishops of doubtful loyalty were successfully apprehended and the Second Lateran Council did not reverse the Pope's earlier decision in Stephen's favour, despite the impassioned pleas of the Empress's representatives. However, in 1141 Stephen suffered an eviscerating defeat at the Battle of Lincoln. The skirmish took place at Candlemas,

---

† William Marshal went on to become one of the most celebrated knights in history and closely involved with the royal family, ultimately serving as regent of England during the childhood of King Henry III.

the feast that marked the anniversary of the infant Jesus being formally presented by His mother and stepfather at the Temple in Jerusalem. The day also marked when the Virgin Mary had been ritually purified by the rites of the Jewish faith, removing the stain of childbirth from her. Thus known variably as Candlemas, the Presentation of Jesus or the Feast of the Purification of the Virgin, the day was celebrated by a festival of light within Christian churches and it was during Mass that King Stephen's Candlemas candle broke in his hands. If it was an omen, as many at the time assumed, it was an accurate one. In the ensuing carnage, Stephen fought bravely in hand-to-hand combat, but was eventually knocked unconscious by one of the Empress's knights.

With Stephen in her clutches, the Empress moved to London, where she was granted the interim title of *domina Anglorum* – 'lady of the English'. Rather than win hearts, however, the Empress preferred to step on toes. Her haughtiness, her petty vindictiveness, her demands for tribute, her heavy fines and her overbearing arrogance alienated the capital until the Londoners rose up against her, forcing her to flee before she could be crowned. The riots happened so abruptly that the Empress fled mid-dinner, plates still on the table. Stephen's wife Matilda was encamped on the south bank of the Thames with mercenaries from her native Boulogne, perfectly situated to take advantage of the Empress's incompetence. The latter's biographer, Marjorie Chibnall, is certainly correct in stating that the Empress was excoriated for displaying the same kind of dictatorial behaviour that had been tolerated in her father and it is curious that a woman who had won such praise for her behaviour in Italy and Germany during her first marriage could have behaved with such belligerent idiocy in England, but people change, and rage at her disinheritance by Stephen, and the ease with which he had done it, may have permanently shocked and embittered her. Either way, the loss of London in 1141 was the closest the Empress ever came to winning the crown. After that, the war between the cousins settled into a long and vicious campaign of attrition.

The chronicles of the time record the agony endured by the population. Normandy, invaded by the armies of the Empress's husband Geoffrey, 'suffered continually from terrible disasters and daily feared still worse […] the whole province was without an effective ruler'.[44] The *Gesta Stephani*, a chronicle sympathetic to King Stephen, wrote of 'villages […] standing solitary and almost empty because the peasants of both sexes and all ages were dead'.[45] Henry of Huntingdon remembered an England full of 'slaughter, fire and rapine, cries of anguish and horror on every side'.[46] The rich men filled their castles 'with devils and evil men', and with royal justice in the doldrums, the common folk bore the brunt of the aristocracy's lawless depravity. 'They put them in prison,' the Anglo-Saxon Chronicle wrote, 'and tortured them with indescribable torture to extort silver and gold [...] They were hung by the thumbs or by the head, and chains were hung on their feet. Knotted ropes were put round their heads and twisted till they penetrated to the brains. They put them in prisons where there were adders and snakes and toads, and killed them like that. Some they put in an instrument of torture, that is in a chest which was short and narrow and not deep, and they put sharp stones in it and pressed the man so that he had all his limbs broken.'[47] The vicious, bloody and selfish upper class installed by the first Norman King helped lose it for the last. Many of those nobles had pressured Stephen into taking the throne in the first place, but abandoned him when war came. Little wonder that Stephen cried, 'When they have chosen me king, why do they abandon me?'[48] It was a time of anarchy, misery and unanswered prayers: 'To till the ground was to plough the sea; the earth bare no corn, for the lands were all laid waste by such deeds; and [men] said openly that Christ slept and his saints.'[49]

Stephen, released from captivity in a hostage exchange in 1142, suffered from intermittent depression for the rest of his life. The Empress was besieged at Oxford and escaped by scaling the city walls during a snowstorm, dressed all in white for camouflage, and making for nearby Abingdon with the help of four faithful knights. She spent the next few years carrying on the struggle from her base at Devizes Castle in Cornwall, but she had no real hope of victory. Equally, Stephen had clearly underestimated his cousin's tenacity when he first moved against her in 1135. Neither she nor her sons were prepared to surrender. Even the Papacy had now qualified its support for Stephen with a succession of popes deigning to recognise him only as de facto King of England, suggesting a degree of uncertainty about his future prospects.

Gradually, the struggle started to move to the next generation. In 1143, the Earl of Hereford was killed in a hunting accident; he had been one of the Empress's most stalwart supporters and even the hostile *Gesta Stephani* said that he had 'always behaved to her like a father in deed and counsel'.[50] In 1147, another of her inner circle, her half-brother the Earl of Gloucester, died and a year later the Empress returned to Normandy. Her husband died in 1151, as did her stepmother Adeliza of Louvain, who had been the first person in England to open her doors to the Empress and her soldiers.[†] A year later, Stephen's Queen, Matilda of Boulogne, died while visiting her friend Euphemia, Countess of Oxford, and on 17 August 1153, their son Eustace died on the very same day that the Empress's new daughter-in-law, Eleanor of Aquitaine, gave birth to a healthy son. It is not difficult to guess what a providentialist society made of these developments. God, it seemed, had spoken. In that vein, reactions to Prince Eustace's death were insultingly relieved.[51,‡] His passing made the possibility of the war lasting into the next generation a good deal less likely. Perhaps Stephen, devout to the end, did see the hand of God in his son's death; given his generation's attitudes to the Almighty, it would have been curious if he did not. Sickened by bloodshed, weary of conflict and broken by the deaths of his wife and son, Stephen brokered the Winchester Agreement, whereby he would keep the crown until his death, but after that it would pass to the Empress's son, Henry. To the Empress's credit, she took the deal and won her son's undying gratitude in doing so.

Eleven months after the deal was made, Stephen's bowels began to haemorrhage and he received the Last Rites from Prior Ralph, his late wife's trusted confessor. He died on 25 October 1154, after a nineteen-year reign that was one of the most spectacularly unsuccessful in English history. His body was taken to nearby Faversham Abbey, where it was buried next to his wife and son. Across the Channel, the Empress's son was notified of his change in fortune and a new dynasty, variably called the Angevins, the House of Anjou or the House of Plantagenet, succeeded to the throne.

[†] Adeliza's is one of the few genuinely uplifting stories from the period. During her widowhood, she married a man called William d'Aubigny, the future Earl of Arundel, and a man known for his good looks and skills as a knight. He had allegedly once spurned the advances of the unfortunate-looking Queen Mother of France, Adélaïde of Maurienne, but his marriage to Adeliza was a happy one that produced seven children – making it likely that Henry I had suffered from fertility issues in his old age, hence the succession crisis.

[‡] Reactions to Eustace's death, which occurred after he choked to death at a banquet, helped form part of the inspiration for the universally-unlamented death of the fictional horror, King Joffrey, in George R. R. Martin's modern and hugely popular *A Song of Ice and Fire* series of novels, filmed as *Game of Thrones*.

THE LIONESS IN WINTER

THE ANGLO-NORMAN monarchy began as it ended – with a claimant in Normandy. Maud, the Lady of the English, spent the last thirteen years of her life as a widow, dividing her time between practical responsibilities as a great landowner and retreats to the Norman abbey of Notre Dame du Pré. There was a brush with illness, which prompted her to sell her prized silk mattress and give the proceeds to a leper hospital in Rouen, in gratitude to God for her recovery. Religion in general increasingly dominated her life. She was a generous benefactress of the Church and particularly devoted to the Virgin Mary. A knight called Drogo, who had fought in her service, took religious vows and became the first abbot of a new monastery founded by the Empress for the Premonstratensian order of monks at Silly-en-Gouffern. She paid for the construction of accommodation for pilgrims journeying to Mortemer, a religious house founded by her late father, but something of her century's social views were evident in her bequest when she stipulated that there should be different types of shelter for wealthy pilgrims, poor pilgrims, military pilgrims and clerical pilgrims. She continued to exert some political influence through her son and apparently counselled against a proposed invasion of Ireland. When she died in 1167, she left most of her treasures and jewels to monastic foundations in England, Normandy and Germany. It was a glittering haul that shimmered in tribute to the exalted positions Maud had held, or aspired to hold, in life. One of her crowns was so heavy that servants had to carry it in procession on two solid silver rods; the family had come a long way from the days when the little bastard William had been pelted with animal skins at the walls of Alençon. Like the Conqueror, Maud had been ambitious and determined, but unlike him she never succeeded in winning a ruler's crown. In the end, she had to suppress personal ambition to ensure the continuity of the dynasty and her tomb paid tribute to her sacrifice, its inscription described her as 'ortu magna, viro major, sed maxima partu' – 'great by birth, greater by marriage, greatest in her offspring'.

Yet the Empress's political career in many ways reads less as a story of greatness and more like a cautionary tale about the dangers to, and of, monarchy when it deviated from exercising the power expected of it. On the one hand, Stephen's usurpation of the throne in 1135 and the subsequent disintegration of royal authority showed how vulnerable the Crown was to aristocratic intrigue. The magnates of England had glibly broken the oaths they swore to Henry I and even the good and honourable Stephen had shown almost no remorse at disinheriting the cousin he had sworn to serve. Stephen's personal virtues, particularly his mercy and his kindness, were used against him and enabled the nobility to abandon or manipulate him with the same alacrity with which they had abandoned the Empress. The power of the monarchy had grown under Henry I to the extent that, when the institution imploded, the results were catastrophic, leading to a period in which Christ and His saints slept, as the chroniclers put it. At the opposite extreme, it was the Empress's personal unpopularity and her tactlessness that saw the city of London rise against her in 1141. No monarchy, even one as absolute as the Normans', could afford to alienate the people if it wished to remain in power. Despite William the Conqueror's best efforts, the people's spirit of resistance in England had not been permanently crushed.

FROM SCOTLAND
TO SPAIN

THE EMPIRE OF THE PLANTAGENETS

'In all parts of his realm the king won the renown of a monarch who ruled over a wider empire than all who had previously reigned in England, for it extended from the border of Scotland to the Pyrenees.'

William of Newburgh on Henry II

HENRY OF Anjou and Eleanor of Aquitaine emerged from the cathedral of St Pierre de Poitiers as man and wife on 18 May 1152. It was the groom's first marriage and the bride's second. Having been shunted aside by her first husband, who blamed her for their lack of sons, Eleanor needed this marriage to restore her reputation and safeguard her inheritance. Henry, at nineteen years old about a decade younger than his new wife, is often referred to as Henry Plantagenet, the surname given to his family by Posterity; his late father had apparently worn a sprig of *planta genista* in his helmet, hence the nickname. However, it was not until the fifteenth century that members of the family began to refer to themselves as Plantagenets, and apparently not until the histories of the seventeenth century that it came into wider use. At the time, Henry had little to gain from emphasising his paternal ancestry. He was much more concerned with his mother's family, from whom he derived his claim to the English throne. His contemporaries often called him Henry FitzEmpress ('son of the Empress'). Irish chroniclers were still referring to Henry as 'the son of the Empress' decades into his reign.[1] At the time of her son's wedding, Maud, the daughter and granddaughter of kings, widow of an Emperor and Lady of the English, was preparing to pass the struggle for the crown to the next generation – Henry. A marriage, particularly to someone so wealthy, would greatly benefit their cause.

ELEANOR

ELEANOR WAS the reigning Duchess of the Aquitaine, a picturesque province covering much of central and south-western France. Born in the first half of the 1120s, the premature death of her only brother left Eleanor heiress to one of the most prosperous lordships in medieval Europe. She came from a good-looking, if unconventional, family – her grandfather William IX was a witty man with a penchant for writing erotic poetry. He spent most of his married life ignoring his worthy wife and cavorting with the deliciously named courtesan, Dangerosa. Eleanor's paternal uncle Raymond lived in the Holy Land, ruling over the principality of Antioch, one of the four constituent parts of Outremer, a Christian federation established to keep Palestine in the hands of the faithful after the First Crusade. In 1137, while she was still a young teenager, Eleanor's father died on pilgrimage to the shrine of Santiago de Compostela in Spain, the reputed burial place of Saint James the Apostle. Fearing that she might be kidnapped, raped and forced into marriage, Eleanor fled to the safety of her family's walled palace in Bordeaux and flung herself on the protection of the French royal family, begging them to provide her with a husband. Aquitaine was technically in France's political orbit and its dukes traditionally pledged allegiance to the French monarchy, but in practice the Aquitaine operated more like an independent principality and in normal circumstances paid nothing more than lip service to the feudal system that made the uncultured French their overlords. The Aquitinians had an innate sense of their own superiority, particularly in relation to the French; an insight into their political thought process comes from their mantra, 'No good ever came from a king who lives north of the Loire.'[2] But the fragility of Eleanor's position after her father's death meant that she had very few alternatives to seeking the help of her Capetian overlords. Aside from being honour-bound to help her, France also saw an opportunity to turn the theory of the Aquitaine's subservience into a reality by marrying its heiress into the French royal family and thus appropriating her inheritance for themselves. The unimaginatively but accurately nicknamed King Louis the Fat dispatched his handsome and pious seventeen-year-old son Louis to fetch Eleanor and the couple were married at the local cathedral in July 1137.[†] The marriage was not without controversy in the Aquitaine since Eleanor's union with Louis very likely meant the duchy's union with France, certainly if Eleanor produced a son who would one day rule in both, thus potentially permanently uniting the two regions under one crown. One especially disgruntled seigneur refused to take the expected oath of loyalty to the newlyweds and added insult to injury by stealing two of Eleanor's prized white hunting falcons. The gallant bridegroom hunted the errant lord down and cut off his hands, indicating how much the concept of romantic gestures has changed in the last nine hundred years.

Shortly after her marriage, King Louis died and Eleanor's husband succeeded to the throne as Louis VII. Arriving in Paris for their coronation, Eleanor quickly discovered that she was no more popular with the French than Louis was with the Aquitinians. Her respected mother-in-law, Adélaïde of Maurienne, was ugly and pious; Eleanor was extravagant and said to be very beautiful. France hardly has a heart-warming history when it comes to its foreign-born queens consort, particularly if they happened to be pretty and had so much as a spark of a personality. It has already been mentioned that powerful clerics like Bernard of Clairvaux took issue with their new Queen's pendulous earrings, but they also disliked her expensive jewellery, fur-trimmed silks and the long sleeves of her gowns. To them, and for whatever reason, the Queen's wardrobe seemed indecent. She had been raised in a court that was comparatively more sophisticated and far wealthier than that of France. One contemporary noted that from childhood Eleanor had acquired 'a taste for luxury and refinement'.[3] Now that she was Queen, she saw absolutely no reason to tailor her whims to soothe the outrage of a few troublesome priests.

More damaging by far than her extravagance was Queen Eleanor's passion for intrigue. Her younger sister Petronilla came to Paris with her and embarked upon an affair with the Comte de Vermandois, who was married. His wife, Éleonore, was King Stephen of England's younger sister. That the Count was married to the sister of a King and that she had numerous powerful relatives at the French court should

---

[†] The French monarchy certainly wins points for the originality of its kingly sobriquets, which seem to have been far more imaginative than England's. Along with Louis the Fat, there was also Pepin the Short, Louis the Debonair, Charles the Bald, Louis the Stammerer, Charles the Simple, Louis the Lazy, Philippe the Amorous, Philippe the Fair, Louis the Headstrong, Jean the Posthumous, Philippe the Tall, Philippe the Fortunate, Jean the Good and Louis the Universal Spider.

have warned Petronilla off her course of action. It should certainly have dissuaded Eleanor from stepping in to help her. However, Eleanor was close to her sister and she had a score to settle with the Comte de Champagne, King Stephen's brother, who had recently opposed a French invasion of Toulouse, part of Eleanor's patrimony, which she felt was being kept from her illegally. When news of the affair between Vermandois and Petronilla broke, Eleanor persuaded her husband to support Vermandois divorcing his wife to marry Petronilla. The clergy were appalled at the Queen's actions and she gained a lifelong enemy in the Comte de Champagne, who regarded the divorce of his sister as a slight on his entire family. Champagne subsequently rebelled and many blamed Eleanor for provoking it. Criticised on all sides, the Queen brazenly refused to apologise and even publicly quarrelled with Bernard of Clairvaux when he declined to intercede with the Pope on Petronilla's behalf. It was only when Eleanor began to fear that her continued childlessness was a sign of God's displeasure that she began to improve her relationship with the Church.

It was during her first pregnancy, which she and those around her attributed to the intercession of the Blessèd Virgin, that news reached France that Edessa had fallen to the armies of Imad al-Din Zengi, the Islamic Emir of Mosul and Aleppo. Edessa was part of Outremer and its collapse prompted Pope Eugenius III to issue the Papal bull *Quantum praedecessores*, exhorting the Christian knights of Europe to 'take the Cross' and go east to defend the holiest sites of Christianity from falling into the hands of the non-believers. Both Louis and Eleanor were caught-up in the crusading fever and at Bernard of Clairvaux's Easter sermon in praise of the sanctity of the Crusade, Eleanor knelt at her former opponent's feet and pledged that the knights of the Aquitaine would take up their swords in the service of Christ. She, as their Duchess, would go with them.

It was not quite what Bernard had wanted from her. Like many of his contemporaries, the famous preacher neither liked nor trusted the idea of women anywhere near an army and Eleanor in particular worried him. However, the Queen had sworn publicly and she could not therefore be gainsaid. If she did not go, there was also every chance that the men of the Aquitaine would not go either, since going without their Duchess would mean submitting themselves entirely to the control of the French. One is tempted to think that Eleanor's public gesture of commitment to the Crusade may therefore have been a deliberate ploy to bounce Bernard and her clerical opponents into giving their reluctant blessing to her participation. In any case, the Pope was keen to encourage maximum royal involvement in the holy war and his office formally blessed Eleanor and Louis in a ceremony at the basilica of St Denis shortly before they set off for Palestine. Having won a place for herself, Eleanor did nothing to dispel fears that she would prove a disruptive influence. She took nearly three hundred female servants with her and turned up for the army's departure on a silver horse, saddle encrusted with golden fleurs-de-lis and a dress glistening with jewels. She had many strengths. Minimalism was not one of them.

French participation in the Second Crusade was an unmitigated disaster, largely because of the distrust between the European armies fighting on the same side and the tactical incompetence of Eleanor's husband. Yet it was Eleanor who was subsequently blamed for the first serious French loss in the conflict, when they were ambushed by the Turks at Cadmos. Later sources claimed that the Queen demanded taking a more scenic route where she and her women got into difficulty, which necessitated the French riding out to rescue her and into a trap. This story does not have so much as a shred of contemporary evidence to back it up.[4] Indeed, any advice Eleanor did give during the Crusade seems to have been both wise and usually ignored. It was she, along with her uncle Raymond, who advised against Louis's terrible decision to launch an attack on the city of Damascus. Louis would not listen, marched on Damascus and suffered a defeat so total that it resulted in the effective collapse of the Second Crusade.

Louis VII's reasons for ignoring the advice of his wife and uncle-by-marriage may not have been entirely political. It could have been hurt pride. Rumour speculated that Eleanor had embarked upon an incestuous and adulterous fling with her uncle, who was described by one contemporary as 'the handsomest of the princes of the earth'.[5] So much nonsense has attached itself to Eleanor's legend that it is tempting to dismiss this too as misogynist bunkum. However, something evidently did happen in Antioch and Eleanor constantly took her uncle's side over her husband's. Raymond had been living and ruling in Palestine for years, so it could be that Eleanor chose to side with the superior warrior who had a better working knowledge of the terrain they were in and the enemies they were facing. However, uncle and niece, who were close in age, also got on very well and the possibility that they succumbed to genetic sexual attraction, brought on by the fact that they had never met prior to Eleanor's arrival in the Holy Land, cannot lightly be dismissed. Evidence from the time is conflicting. One contemporary heard that 'the attentions paid by the Prince to the Queen, and his constant, indeed almost continuous conversation with her, aroused the King's suspicions.'[6] This assessment of their relationship sounds deliberately ambiguous – the King was suspicious, and with good reason, but that suspicion does not necessarily mean adultery actually took place. More explicit is the testimony of William of Tyre, a chronicler stationed in the Holy Land and ordinarily an admirer of Raymond's, who stated quite categorically that Eleanor 'disregarded her marriage vows and was unfaithful to her husband'.[7]

Whatever happened between Raymond and Eleanor, her marriage to Louis reached a nadir during the Crusade and there were rumours of impending divorce. Things did not improve after the French retreated home and Eleanor received the news that her uncle Raymond had been killed fighting the enemy that Louis had left him to face alone. He fell at the Battle of Inab. As a final humiliation his head was hacked off to be sent as a gift to the Caliph of Baghdad in a solid silver case. Louis and Eleanor reached Italy, where the Pope tried to mediate between them, even giving them a gift of an expensive bed to encourage renewed intimacy. Another baby, another daughter, followed this pontifical gift and talk of divorce grew louder.

Louis VII summoned an ecclesiastical conference at Beaugency to try the validity of his marriage and the bishops found in the King's favour, declaring that the marriage was null on grounds of consanguinity (too close a genetic relationship), but the couple's two daughters could remain legitimate because they had been born in 'good faith', meaning before anyone realised the marriage was void.[†]

In the aftermath of the verdict, Eleanor asked for leave to go on retreat, Louis granted her request and she dashed across the countryside in disguise, narrowly avoiding being kidnapped by her old enemy the Comte de Champagne. She made it to the safety of

† Consanguinity was a wonderful excuse to be dragged out when a marriage was failing in the Middle Ages. Eleanor and Louis VII were not closely related by any stretch of the imagination. They were third cousins, once removed. However, the Church prohibited any unions within seven degrees of affinity. Impediments were thus conveniently discovered on a regular occurrence to enable *de facto* divorces.

the abbey at Fontevraud where Henry Plantagenet swiftly arrived to marry her. Prior to the wedding, she revoked all charters issued in her husband's name in the Aquitaine, re-issued most of them in hers and thus ensured that the French monarchy would not be able to maintain its control over the region without her. Louis was livid at his ex-wife's actions. She had handed Aquitaine over to another power, she had clearly been in league with Henry before the divorce and she had told anyone who would care to listen that Louis was so bad in bed that it was more like being married to a monk than a King. Louis tried to exact revenge by declaring war on the newlyweds with a coalition of the many lords Eleanor had managed to offend during her career as Queen of France. Louis's military prowess had not improved since Damascus and Henry proved his usefulness by smashing the forces of Eleanor's ex in the space of six weeks. After an already scandalous life, Eleanor of Aquitaine, the woman who 'abounded in riches of every kind', had just ditched the current King of France and married the future King of England.[8]

HENRY

ELEANOR OF Aquitaine's second husband looked far more like a Norman than he did an Angevin. Like his grandfather and great-grandfather, Henry was of medium height, barrel-chested, muscular and physically robust. He was obsessed with physical fitness, monitoring his weight (many of his male ancestors had grown fat in later life) and controlling his diet.[9] He had the red hair of his great-uncle William Rufus, which he wore short, and blue-grey eyes that flashed 'like fire' when he was angry.[10] He enjoyed teasing his courtiers to the point of torment, either by endlessly pacing the room and forcing them via etiquette to stand for as long as he did or by altering his itinerary at the last minute, resulting in total confusion as courtiers fought for the meanest and most uncomfortable lodgings because the King's sudden change to the schedule had taken them to a place where there was only enough shelter for the royals and their closest servants.[11] One of his secretaries, Peter of Blois, told the Archbishop of Palermo, 'I believe in truth he took a delight in seeing what a fix he put us in.'[12]

Like all the Norman kings, his temper could be terrifying. He was admittedly better at controlling it than William I or William II, but enraging him was still akin to waking a dragon. Once, when a courtier unwisely praised the rival King of Scots, the King 'fell out of bed screaming, tore up his coverlet, cramming his mouth with the stuffing of his mattress'.[13] He was a man of boundless energy, capable of riding several horses to the point of exhaustion to cover as much ground as possible in a single day. More than once his enemies were surprised to find him on their doorsteps when they had believed he was still several days' march away. The King of France grimly joked that Henry 'must fly rather than travel by horse or ship'.[14] Unlike his glamorous wife, he had no interest in pomp and luxury, beyond the political purposes they served. He was personally frugal, rarely stood on ceremony, a good linguist, well-read and intelligent – one courtier recalled the King 'in constant conversation with the best scholars and discussion of intellectual problems' – and, again like most of his mother's family, he enjoyed hunting.[15]

Born in 1133, the first of the Empress's children, he was named in honour of his grandfather, King Henry I. Because of his success in taking the English throne where his mother had failed and his policy of conciliation where she tried brute force, Henry is often seen as his mother's opposite, but in fact it was Maud who oversaw much of his education and instilled in him his political morals, such as they were. His second cousin's usurpation of the throne in 1135 changed the young boy's life and he grew up quickly. In December 1149, when he was sixteen years old, he assumed control of Normandy while his mother fought in England. In summer 1151, he met his future wife for the first time when he and his father visited Paris to try to persuade the French royal family to abandon their support for King Stephen. He was eighteen and she, thanks to her exploits on Crusade, was already notorious. Rumours of a divorce between the King and Queen of France were rife and it does not seem unduly speculative, given the speed with which they married later, to suggest that Eleanor and Henry may instantly have sparked with one another, sexually or politically.

Unlike her first marriage with the obsessively pious Louis, whose childhood desire to become a priest seems to have left him with a lifelong distaste for sex, Eleanor conceived quickly and often with Henry. Her first son, born on the same day as Stephen's son Eustace died, arrived fourteen months after the marriage. Christened William, he was styled the Count of Poitiers. She was pregnant again when news reached her that Stephen had died at Dover and her husband was now King Henry II. Pregnant or not, Eleanor did not intend to miss her coronation and the couple crossed the Channel in time for a ceremony at Westminster Abbey, six days before Christmas 1154. Nine weeks later, she gave birth to a second son, Henry, at Bermondsey Palace in Surrey and just over a year later, he was joined by a little sister, Matilda. At the same time, probably within the space of a few weeks, the eldest of the royal children, the Count of Poitiers, died shortly before his third birthday, meaning that young Henry became heir to his father's throne. Another boy, Richard, born at Oxford on the Feast of the Nativity of the Blessèd Virgin Mary in 1157, was followed by his brother Geoffrey a year later.[16] Meanwhile, Eleanor's first husband Louis VII and his new wife Constanza had produced two daughters. Queen Constanza died giving birth to the second child and, panicking about his continued lack of a son, Louis remarried five weeks later to Adèle of Champagne. That marriage produced another daughter, Agnès, and, at long last, a son, the future King Philippe II, who came into the world with the French proclaiming 'there is born to us this night a King who shall be the hammer of the English'.[17] It was optimistic but not entirely inaccurate. Back in England, Eleanor had a brief respite after Geoffrey's birth and her final three children, Eleanor, Joanna and John, were born in 1161, 1165 and 1166 respectively. In total, she had ten children, including the two daughters born to her first marriage with Louis, who she seldom saw after losing custody of them to their father during the divorce. Time would show that from having a dearth of sons, Eleanor of Aquitaine had actually ended up producing far more than was good for the monarchy's stability, but at the time she could bask in the contrast between her sprawling family and Louis VII's sparsely populated nursery.

From the moment he became King, Henry II wanted to expand his kingdoms. At first glance this seems nothing but greedy to the modern eye. The land he had inherited from his mother's family gave him England and Normandy, further land in the north and east of France was given by his father's territories and thanks to his marriage to Eleanor, he controlled much of western and southern France. The boast that Henry had an empire that stretched from Scotland to Spain, from the Pennines to the Pyrenees, is only a marginal exaggeration; he ruled more land than any king of England before him. His wealth won him admiration from as far afield as Byzantium and envy from closer to home; in a fit of patriotic pique, Eleanor's ex-husband told an English visitor, 'Your lord, the king of England, who lacks nothing, has men, horses, gold, silks, jewels, fruit, game and everything else [...] We in France have nothing but bread and wine and gaiety.'[18] But it was not enough for Henry. According to his contemporaries, 'the whole world was too small a prize' for his ego.[19] He wanted glory as well as power and from the earliest days of his reign he wanted to preside over a monarchy that was both expansionist and absolute. John of Salisbury wrote that Henry intended to be 'king in his own land, Papal legate, patriarch, emperor, and everything he wished'.[20] Shortly after his coronation, he briefly toyed with resurrecting William II's plan to bring Norman rule to Ireland, but his advisers were unconvinced and, as we have seen, his mother also counselled against it. The cost of invading Ireland would be high and the chance of a return on the investment was slim. Henry ditched the proposal. A decade later, events on that island transformed the idea of intervention into an imperative.

DIARMAIT NA NGALL

NO PART of the British monarchy's history has caused more controversy than its involvement in Ireland. Even today, with the northern third of the island still part of the United Kingdom, the monarchy often provokes the extremities of reaction in Ireland. For the majority of unionists, the throne is an integral part of their cultural heritage and the lynchpin of their national identity as British citizens. Long-dead kings like William III have acquired near-iconic status for Irish Protestants and there is a deep well of affection for current members of the royal house. For unionists, there is little trust in the elected British government at Westminster, but paradoxically almost boundless faith in the monarchy. For many Irish nationalists and republicans, the monarchy is a foreign institution that has brought little or no benefit to Ireland over the last nine hundred years. British-orchestrated massacres at Irish towns like Drogheda and Dundalk in the seventeenth century (ironically carried out on the orders of Oliver Cromwell, one of the staunchest anti-monarchists in British history), the suppression of the Irish language, the anti-Catholic Penal Laws that held sway for most of the eighteenth century and the grim horrors of the great Potato Famine in the 1840s have all created the impression of an institution that was, at best, callously indifferent and, at worst, wantonly bloodthirsty in its treatment of the Irish people.

The story of how the English Crown first invaded Ireland is therefore understandably a vexatious one, with the exact sequence of events and the apportioning of blame fiercely contested by the opposing sides. Part of the problem in trying to judge the actions of Henry II, Dermot of Leinster, Adrian IV, the Irish princes and the Plantagenets' warriors is that any standards we impose upon them will be anachronistic. Even the concept of nationhood, so central to the Anglo-Irish debate, is problematic here. We are aware, almost painfully, that there are four countries in the British Isles – England, Scotland, Wales and Ireland. However, in the twelfth century, regional identities were far more important than national ones; a person from Ulster was as likely to distrust someone from Munster as he was an Englishman, a person from southern England might regard a northerner with equal distaste as they viewed a Scot or a Frenchman. Beyond that, the ties of feudalism meant that one's local lord and, through him, one's monarch was the theoretical summit of a person's loyalty, rather than what country you were born in. Witness, for instance, the fact that so many knights of the Aquitaine went on Crusade with the French because their Duchess Eleanor had pledged to go. There were certainly concepts of being English as opposed to being Norman, Welsh, French or Irish, but they were not yet of primary importance. So when Henry II arrived in Ireland, it was seen very much as the actions of a powerful King, not necessarily the expansion of a powerful country.

Furthermore, while hindsight has created the impression that England had been created by Henry II's era, that may not have been so obvious to people at the time. The story of Anglo-Saxon England had been the story of the coalescing of the seven kingdoms of Kent, Essex, East Anglia, Wessex, Sussex, Mercia and Northumbria into a single political entity. We tend to think that the job had been done by the time of King Æthelstan, but for the Norman and Plantagenet kings, the process appeared ongoing. Power in the Middle Ages was based on dynasty, violence or both. The princes, chieftains and kings in Scotland, Wales or Ireland were not much different in the eyes of William Rufus and Henry II than Guthrum had been to Alfred the Great, or Offa had been to Egbert of Wessex. Ireland, or what was later patronisingly dubbed 'the Celtic fringe', had been on the agenda right from the beginning. At the first recorded coronation in English history, King Edgar's at Bath in 793, part of the ceremony had involved the new King being rowed across a lake by princes sent from Wales, Ireland and Scotland, symbolising his throne's supremacy over theirs. The modus operandi of a successful medieval monarchy was expansion and consolidation. Its neighbours must either be conquered or forced into submission by acknowledging its king as their feudal overlord. In return, the suppliant lords would be allowed to hold onto their ancestral lands, their wealth and some of their former power. That the conquest and colonisation of Ireland was spectacularly badly handled, both then and later, does not take away from the fact that at some point in their history, geography and medieval concepts of power made it inevitable that the two countries would collide. If Henry II had not intervened in Ireland, one of his successors would have.

The short-term countdown to the intervention followed the assassination of Muircheartach Mac Lochlainn, ruler of Cinéal nEoghain, an area that roughly correlates to most of what is now western Northern Ireland. He had been Ireland's High King, the chief of its local royalty, and his murder spelled disaster for those allies who shared his support for the modernisation of the island. Central to that idea was increasing Ireland's links with foreign lands, a policy warmly supported by Dermot MacMurrough (Diarmait Mac Murchada, in Irish), the ruler of most of Leinster, the easternmost of Ireland's four provinces, who, in the aftermath of the assassination, found himself surrounded when isolationists and conservatives gained the upper-hand as Rory O'Conor (in Irish, Ruaidhri Ua Conchobhair), King of the western region of Connacht, rose to take the butchered Muircheartach's place as high king.

Like most rulers in the Middle Ages, Dermot was forceful and ambitious. He does not seem to have been a popular ruler, except perhaps with the Benedictine and Cistercian monastic orders who he patronised in Leinster. He had previously blinded seventeen noblemen who rebelled against him and one contemporary chronicle, the Annals of Clonmacnoise, refers to him as a man of 'insatiable, carnal and adulterous lust'.[21] In the course of his career, two of his sons, Donncha and Conor, were killed by their father's enemies and a third, Éanna, was captured and blinded. As Rory O'Conor attacked, chroniclers claimed that Dermot's own people helped the invaders because they detested Dermot 'na chintaib fein' ('for his own misdeeds').[22] Before he fled, a defiant Dermot burned down his own fort rather than let it fall into Rory's hands. He set sail from Bannow in County Wexford, reached Bristol and travelled south to the Aquitaine, where Henry II was holding court.

Initially, Henry regarded Dermot's pleas for help as the unbearably banal whinging of a backwater nobody. Yet his request could not go totally unaided and while the King had no interest in helping him personally, he did allow Dermot to network among the English knights then at court to see if any were interested in joining his enterprise. He found another down on his luck has-been, Richard de Clare, the thirty-seven-year-old former Earl of Pembroke, who had been demoted from his title for clinging too tenaciously to the cause of King Stephen. With no future in England, de Clare decided to seize the opportunity of one in Ireland with both hands. Those hands proved capable. As his men returned with Dermot to the shores of Ireland, the ex-earl's archers earned him the sobriquet of 'Strongbow'.

They quickly recaptured Dublin, Wexford and Waterford, the key towns of Leinster.

Strongbow's marriage to Dermot's daughter Aoife sealed the alliance between the Anglo-Norman invaders and the Irish who supported them. Another daughter, Órla, was already married. However, Dermot did not long enjoy his homecoming. According to his contemporaries, he died eighteen months later, 'iar cind bliadne do galar etualaing' ('after a year of insufferable illness').[23] He died piously, having time to make his peace through a priest.[24] For his role in facilitating the English invasion, Dermot was remembered as 'fer buaidhirtha na Banba ocus aidhmillti Erenn' by the contemporary Annals of Tigernach – 'the disturber and destroyer of Ireland'.[25] The exact fate of his only surviving son, Donal, is unclear; he either predeceased his father or died shortly afterwards, at which point Strongbow laid claim to his father-in-law's throne.

Strongbow's attempts to make himself King in Leinster prompted Henry II to take decisive action. He could not afford to allow a subject to acquire such power for himself so close to England. He had to act quickly to crush Strongbow's upwardly mobile pretensions. He landed on the island with a force of his own, Dermot's old bête noire, Rory O'Conor, submitted to him and Henry became feudal Lord of Ireland. He wisely cloaked his arrival in holy intent by announcing his intention to modernise and reform the Irish Church, which he did, giving rise to the story that Pope Adrian IV had issued a document explicitly blessing the invasion, which he probably did not.[26]

At the end of the King's six-month stay in Ireland, the majority of the island's native princes, chiefs and newly arrived invaders swore fealty to him, recognising him as their overlord. He was helped along, at least according to some scholars, by the differences in the two countries' political systems – the rigid organisation and slick efficiency of feudalism allowed it to occupy and dominate with a lot more uniformity than alternative systems of government, like Ireland's Brehon laws, which had feudalism's preoccupation with status but tended to localise and devolve all issues of justice, power and authority. In a sense, the Brehon laws meant that Ireland was disunited when it faced invasion in the twelfth century and this lack of central political authority helps explain the speed with which it fell, much as had been the case with Britannia to the Romans a millennium before. Or perhaps it was not so much a story of clashing cultures as it was of brute superior military strength helped along by enough Irishmen to make victory possible. Either way, it was a swift beginning to a very long and very fraught relationship.

MURDER IN THE CATHEDRAL

HENRY II'S VISIT to Ireland came in the middle of the first great crisis of his reign and it is entirely possible that part of his reason for going there was to escape the fallout of his actions in England.[27] Thomas Becket was the brilliant and theatrical son of a London merchant who symbolised better than anybody else the elevation of talented new men in Plantagenet service. Henry II adored him and for the first part of his reign, Becket was his most trusted adviser, rising to become chancellor. He worked hard to expand the remit of his office and his ambition was almost matched by his capabilities. Like Queen Eleanor, he had a flair for display and he understood the impact of the visual and the gesture in medieval politics. Henry II trusted him completely to the extent of sending his son and heir, young Henry, to be raised in Becket's household. The relationship between King and commoner soured when Henry nominated Becket to succeed the late Theobold as Archbishop of Canterbury. Becket was not even a member of the priesthood until he was rushed into clerical orders after his nomination, so it is difficult to escape the conclusion that Henry II favoured his appointment because he hoped Becket would continue to place the monarchy first, by bringing the Church in England more firmly under royal control.

It was one of the greatest misjudgements of Henry II's career. Thomas Becket rapidly transformed himself into a spectacularly unappealing example of a born-again Christian. Henry II seemed more astonished than anybody by the transformation of his former friend into a stiff-necked fanatic. The clash between the two men was not just over the century-old tensions between Church and state, but it was also a personal struggle between a King who felt grossly betrayed by his one-time servant and an Archbishop who was determined not to betray the organisation he felt God had called on him to serve.

During the civil war between King Stephen and Henry II's mother, the power of the Church in England had swollen to enormous proportions. The ecclesiastical courts, which had the right to try certain morality charges, had stepped far beyond what previous monarchs had allowed and this subsequently formed one of the central points of contention between Henry and Becket. Unhappily, the twenty-first century is no stranger to charges that the Catholic

Church was guilty of being unduly lenient when it came to punishing priests or to accusations that the reputation of the institution was made a priority over the proper pursuit of justice and the corresponding rights of the victims. Whatever the validity of these charges, there was a similar set of views in twelfth-century England. The issue then was not paedophilia, but other acts of criminality committed by men who hoped their orders would shield their sins, namely murder. The ecclesiastical courts maintained that they alone could prosecute errant members of the priesthood and Becket protected that right on the grounds that to abandon it would be to allow too great a deal of secular interference in the Church. Then as now this led to accusations of cover-ups and punishments hardly worthy of the name. Under Becket's leadership, priests, monks and clerics found guilty of rape and murder were sentenced only to isolation or imprisonment, when a layman would have been castrated, mutilated or executed by the secular courts. With a tenacity worthy of a better cause, Archbishop Becket refused to negotiate.

Henry confiscated properties from the see of Canterbury, trying to dent its income. Becket retaliated by prohibiting the proposed marriage between the King's younger brother William and Isabella de Warenne, Countess of Surrey in her own right. What was intended as a deliberate insult to the royal family quickly assumed the attributes of a blood feud when William died in Normandy in January 1164, shortly after Becket prevented his wedding. The King was devastated by his younger brother's passing and both he and many of his courtiers blamed the Archbishop for breaking William's heart, thus hastening his death.

Pope Alexander III tried to induce Becket to flexibility, but even the Holy Father could not get Becket to bend. Alexander had problems of his own, faced with two rival claimants to the Papacy, styling themselves 'Victor IV' and 'Paschal III', and with the Holy Roman Emperor Frederick using the Papacy's weakness to his own advantage.[†] Henry made it known that he was considering marrying some of his children to Frederick's and the possibility of yet another monarchy abandoning the troubled Roman see was enough to bring

---

[†] The Holy Roman Empire constituted most of what is now Germany, but took its name from the claims of its first Emperor, Charlemagne, that it was the custodian of the legacy of the Christianised Roman Empire. The Emperor was usually elected by a batch of German princes and after the thirteenth century they nearly always chose the head of the House of Hapsburg until the empire was overthrown during the Napoleonic Wars. In German history the Holy Roman Empire was subsequently referred to as the First Reich.

Alexander III into the quarrel with Becket, tentatively on Henry's side. Twisting the screw further, Henry found or manufactured evidence that Becket had been guilty of embezzlement during his time as chancellor. Becket fled abroad and sought asylum from the King of France, where he spent much of his time in tireless and shameless networking with Henry's numerous enemies. When Becket was allowed back to England, no sooner had he returned than he resumed his policy of belligerence by issuing excommunications left, right and centre to those who had sided with Henry, including the Archbishop of York, the Bishop of Salisbury and the Bishop of London, all of whom had incurred Becket's ire by presiding at the coronation of young Prince Henry, his former ward, as heir-apparent at York.[28] The only people who seemed happy to see him again were the poor of Canterbury, to whom he had always been a generous benefactor.

Hearing of Becket's arrogance and the excommunications, which made Henry look like a fool for trying to negotiate with him, the King apparently exploded with the now-infamous roar of 'Who will rid me of this turbulent priest?' In fact, the wording of Henry's rage was slightly different, but the effect was the same. He apparently said, 'What miserable drones and traitors have I nourished and promoted in my household, who let their lord be treated with such shameful contempt by a low-born clerk!' Four knights in his service were stung by their King's words and crossed the Channel from Normandy to take revenge. Reginald FitzUrse, Hugh de Monville, Richard de Brito and William de Tracy made it to Canterbury on 29 December 1170. After an altercation with Becket, in which he refused to come to Winchester to give an account of his actions, they returned to the cathedral with their weapons while the monks were celebrating the evening service of Vespers. Becket had a chance to flee, as some of those around him urged him to, but perhaps he had always known it would end like this. Perhaps, in his own way, he wanted martyrdom or felt that it would be wrong to run from it.

The knights hacked him to pieces in the flickering candlelight. One of his killers, Richard de Brito, taunted Becket, screaming that he was murdering him 'for the love of my lord William, the king's brother!'[29] In the most magnificent moment of his life, Becket faced death by saying calmly, 'For the name of Jesus and the protection of the Church, I am ready to embrace death.'[30]

When the news of Becket's death was brought to Henry, he was apparently so convulsed with shock that he went into seclusion for three days. Like Elizabeth I with Mary, Queen of Scots four centuries later, it is likely that Henry wanted Becket out of the way, but in any way bar the one that transpired. The murder of the Archbishop in the consecrated ground of his own cathedral struck right to the heart of medieval Europe's concept of mortal sin. There was no doubt in anyone's mind that whatever his faults in life, Becket had died a martyr for the holy Catholic faith and scenes of his horrible death were replicated in manuscripts, reliquaries and jewellery throughout Western Europe. The Pope was so disgusted that he refused to speak to anyone from England for days after hearing of the murder; Henry closed all the ports to prevent any excommunications or interdicts arriving from Rome. He went to Ireland not just to frustrate Strongbow's ambitions, but also to escape the Papal legates sent to remonstrate against him. By the time he did meet with them in May 1172, strict conditions were set for the King to receive Papal forgiveness. He must perform penance, appeal any laws passed blocking judicial appeals to the Roman see, publicly reaffirm his obedience to Pope Alexander as the one true pontiff and prosecute none of Becket's surviving friends in England. Within three years of his death, Becket had been formally canonised and a magnificent jewel-bedecked shrine was built over his tomb in Canterbury. It soon became one of medieval Christianity's busiest pilgrimage centres. However, a letter from Henry II in 1173 to the monks of Winchester Cathedral priory shows what he continued to think of too much ecclesiastical independence: 'I order you to hold a free election, but nevertheless, I forbid you to elect anyone but Richard my clerk, the archdeacon of Poitiers'.[31]

FAMILY STRIFE

NO SOONER had Henry quelled the fallout from Becket's death than he was faced with a betrayal even closer to home: his wife and most of his children masterminded a rebellion against him. The birth of Henry and Eleanor's youngest child John in 1167 brought the number of surviving royal children to seven. In an amusing quirk of fate, their eldest surviving son and heir, Henry, married Louis VII's daughter from his second marriage, Marguerite, and there was talk of cementing the French alliance by betrothing Richard to Marguerite's sister, Alys. Their daughter Matilda was married at the age of twelve to Heinrich the Lion, Duke of Saxony and Bavaria. Plans were made for the other children's marriages and to start preparing various parts of the empire for the boys. As it stood, young Henry, styled 'the Young King', was expected to inherit England, Normandy and Anjou. Richard, Eleanor's favourite son, would get the Aquitaine. Geoffrey married Constance, the sole heiress to the duchy of Brittany, and John would get Ireland. Henry II, looking confidently into the future, saw nothing but a game of happy families. He was utterly oblivious to the resentment brewing all around him, particularly in his wife and his eldest son, but what happened to turn resentment into rebellion?

For a long time, the explanation was personal, particularly in guessing at why Queen Eleanor decided to take up arms against her husband. In 1165, when she was pregnant with their last child, Henry had taken a mistress called Rosamund de Clifford. Rosamund, the daughter of a minor country squire, was said to be very pretty and unlike many royal mistresses she was neither greedy nor ambitious. This, coupled with her beauty, earned her the nickname 'Fair Rosamund' in later romantic stories, in which she was pitted against an imperious and manipulative Queen Eleanor. In these fables, Rosamund appears as a kind of Snow White, hounded to death by poison at the hands of an evil Queen consumed with jealous resentment at the poor girl's loveliness. The story that Henry protected Rosamund from Eleanor in a beautiful country house surrounded by a maze are fanciful legends based on the fact that the house Henry built for Rosamund was encircled by pools and flowering gardens, like the Norman palaces in Sicily. Allegations that Eleanor had Rosamund killed are defeated by basic chronology, since Rosamund lived until 1176, three years after the latest possible date she could have been in the Queen's company.

More recently, historians like John Gillingham and Lisa Hilton have dismissed personal motivation for Eleanor's treason and, in particular, the idea that his liaison with Rosamund played a part in it. Henry had been persistently unfaithful to her for most of their marriage. He had fathered nearly half-a-dozen illegitimate children with a variety of mistresses. Why should Rosamund de Clifford be any different? Henry was certainly besotted with his new lover, far more so than he had been with any of her numerous predecessors, but even if personal rancour played a part in alienating Eleanor's affections, it was politics and concern over the future of the Aquitaine that seemed to push her into rebellion.

The Aquitaine had spent the last three decades being ruled by the French and then the English. By 1168, two years after John's birth, Henry allowed Eleanor to journey home to resume semi-independent life there as its ruling Duchess. In December 1168, Eleanor held a lavish Christmas court in Poitiers to celebrate her return. Although she was still technically under her husband's control, Eleanor threw herself into the day-to-day business of governing and she was close to Raoul de Faye, her chief adviser. The seigneurs of the Aquitaine journeyed to her glittering court to perform homage at her feet. In 1170, the forty-something Queen was joined by her cherished son Richard. It was time for him to gain some experience of his intended inheritance. This time, however, Eleanor was determined to hold onto her power. At Richard's investiture ceremony as Duke of the Aquitaine, carried out in Saint Hilaire's Cathedral, Eleanor appeared next to him, wearing the crown jewels of both England and the Aquitaine, and set the ducal coronet on her son's head before placing it back on her own, as a clear indicator to the crowds of who was the dominant partner. Two years later, she stopped addressing her official documents as 'fidelibus regis et suis' and instead they now began 'fidelibus suis'. It was no longer 'to the king's faithful followers and hers', it was only 'to her faithful followers'. A year after that, the rebellion began.

The enormously complex military and tactical manoeuvres of the family uprising against Henry II in 1173 can be reduced for simplicity's sake to saying that the Queen and her sons finally cracked under the pressure of living in Henry's shadow and that they no longer trusted him. Eleanor and Richard distrusted his plans for the Aquitaine. Young Henry feared he was going to remain excluded from government while his father lived and all of them worried that their own inheritances were going to be diminished to provide for John. An exceptionally good-looking prince, young Henry had been promised more of a say in affairs of state as he grew older, but while his younger brother Richard actually got to experience that when he joined their mother in the Aquitaine, the King kept young Henry shut out in England. On 5 March 1173, he fled under cover of darkness from the château at Chinon where he and his father were staying. It was daylight before his father realised he was gone and by that point his son was halfway to Paris. There, like Becket before him, he sought asylum with his mother's ex-husband, King Louis.

To his father's distress, young Henry was joined there by his brothers Richard and Geoffrey. In May, Eleanor attempted to reach them. Once again, she travelled in disguise, but this time she was betrayed by her own servants, some of whom were spies in the pay of her husband. She was captured before she reached Paris and Henry set about crushing their sons' supporters. The children's rebellion had grown to include alliances with the kings of France and Scotland, both of whom were eager to exploit this epic familial dysfunction in the hope of weakening the Plantagenet empire. The Counts of Blois, Boulogne, Champagne and Flanders also joined them. With such a formidable cabal of enemies ranged against him, surrounded and betrayed by his closest loved ones, it is nothing short of miraculous that Henry II scored such a resounding victory. Miraculous indeed, because most incredibly of all is the strong possibility that Henry accredited his victory to the heavenly intercession of the murdered Becket.[32] At the very hour he was performing his penance for the slaying, which involved him walking barefoot before his people to the cathedral, publicly confessing his sins, allowing the Bishop of London to beat him five times with a rod on the back, then all eighty of the Canterbury monks to beat him three times, before keeping vigil at Becket's grave, King William of Scotland was captured. Shortly after that, the boys' rebellion collapsed entirely. God had spoken; the King of England had been forgiven.

Relatively magnanimous in victory he pardoned his sons and even, within reason, tentatively increased their power. Queen Eleanor alone was never pardoned. She was taken to Winchester, stripped of most of her jewels, separated from her servants and placed under effective house arrest. Her skeleton staff was eventually increased in number, but the only female attendant who was in regular attendance on her was a young maid called Amaria. Henry could not, or would not, forgive her. Many of the King's closest friends did not believe that Eleanor had simply joined in a rebellion devised by her sons. They suspected, perhaps quite rightly, that she had planted the seed. At one point, Henry wanted to divorce her, but doing so ran the risk of losing the Aquitaine, and in any case, the Pope refused to allow it. The disgraced Queen spent the next fifteen years of her life as her husband's prisoner, occasionally trotted out for public displays of the farcical unity of the royal family. Her eldest surviving son, young Henry, dared to rebel again a decade later. Midway through the campaign, he contracted dysentery and had to be rushed to the house of a local merchant in the town of Quercy in France, where he died screaming for his father's forgiveness. When told of his son's death, Henry II wept, 'He cost me so much, but I wish he had cost me more.'[33] Since young Henry died childless, the next-in-line was Eleanor's favourite son Richard, who had already acquired a reputation as one of the finest warriors of his generation.

Richard's impatience with his brilliant but egotistical father reached breaking point again in the months before Henry II's death in July 1189. The two men were estranged when Henry passed away, his once impressive vigour reduced to an exhausted and embittered shell of a man being carried in a litter by his servants. In England, William Marshal, esteemed as one of Richard's most valiant knights, broke the news to Queen Eleanor, who had the pleasure of both her freedom and seeing her favourite son succeed to the throne.[†]

---

† Marshal was the boy whose life had been spared by the mercy of King Stephen when he was held hostage as a guarantor of his father's obedience.

COME, AND SEE THE PLACE

RICHARD I'S LIFE and legacy were defined by the winds that blew westward from Jerusalem. The holy city was the summit of Christendom's longing to defend and touch the Divine, and the grandest incarnation of medieval Christianity's belief in the importance of a religion wedded to actions. To this mentality, which saw synchronicity between spiritual renewal and sacred location, the land where God had spoken through His prophets, Mary had wept in her seven sorrows and Abraham was promised descendants more numerous than the stars was the supreme guarantor of their own revitalisation, the chance to expiate their sins through action, to reach an ecstasy by paying tribute to the God they believed in with such fervour. The energy of the faithful was vital, never more so than when it felt itself under threat as it did in the face of Islamic armies encircling Christ and Mary's patrimony. The Crusaders and the unarmed believers were united as *peregrini Christi*, pilgrims of Christ, and they came from every social background, mortgaging their estates to finance the long and arduous journey that took years as they progressed to the city where their Saviour had been fêted, betrayed, martyred, buried and Resurrected. As the angel had said to Saint Mary Magdalene in the gospel account of Christ's resurrection, 'He is risen, as he said. Come, and see the place where the Lord was laid', and ever since the Empress Helena had a church built on the site, the Christians of the world had endeavoured to heed the angelic dictum.[34]

A Persian invasion of 614 had ransacked the original structure. It was the destruction of a site that had witnessed the supreme interaction between humanity and the world beyond, and Christendom held a collective determination that it must not be repeated, that the restored Church of the Holy Sepulchre, its jewels, icons and votive candles and the redemption they represented should never again endure a similar horror. The sacred allure of the mission to keep the pilgrim trails open, the *peregrini* unmolested and the holy sites untainted by the hands of heathens entered into Christian hearts. The prayers for Jerusalem were the medieval era's greatest *cri de guerre*, and for centuries Europe's cultural imagination held fast to the belief that there was no glory comparable to that of a Crusade.

No wonder then that Richard I, England's Crusader-King, was remembered as 'the Lionheart', the 'triumphal and bright shining star of chivalry' for centuries to come.[35] Later, his reputation does not glow with the same lustre. David Hume sniffily concluded that Richard was 'better calculated to dazzle men by the splendour of his enterprises than either to promote their happiness or his own grandeur by sound and well-regulated policy'.[36] And modern filmmakers who grew to maturity in an era disgusted by the slaughter of war and suspicious of its legitimacy in the long cultural aftermath of Vietnam tend to depict Richard I as an unlikable warmonger, focussing on his brutality towards Muslim prisoners during a massacre at Acre.[37] He may also have been a homosexual, rebuked for his 'sodomy' by an irate hermit whose spiritual counsel Richard sought en route to the Holy Land, and that perhaps dents the traditional or imperialist view of him, even if the term sodomy was a catch-all term for any kind of non-procreative sex, or even blasphemy. It was only subsequent generations that narrowed its use and claimed it had ever been thus.[38] His enemy King Philippe II of France and his own brother-in-law King Sancho VII ('the Strong') of Navarre have both featured in hypothetical scenarios as the Lionheart's lovers, as has the devoted and possibly semi-fictitious musician Blondel. Richard's marriage to Berengaria of Navarre was childless, but most of his modern biographers err on the side of caution by pointing out that theories concerning Richard's sexuality are based upon modern interpretations of highly fragmentary evidence and 'in the final analysis his sexuality must remain unknown'.[39]

He was arrogant, alienating his allies on the Crusade until, as he tried to return home, Leopold, Duke of Austria, kidnapped him to hold him prisoner in return for a ransom so ruinous it almost bankrupt the English Exchequer. He was belligerent too, abstaining from taking Communion because he was so consumed by hatred for Philippe II that he could not bring himself to partake of the Sacrament while nurturing such an un-Christian feeling.

However, Richard I was also clever, brave and an excellent military commander who shared his men's hardships and dangers. He once said, 'I sent these men there. If any die without me, may I never again be called a king.'[40] His soldiers idolised him, helping to birth the legend that grew in his own lifetime. Scotland too esteemed him highly, referring to him as 'that noble king so friendly to the

Scots' and his mother, who ruled England during his long absence pursuing the dreams of Jerusalem, was devoted to him.[41] His martial record was impressive – he crushed a usurpation to the throne of Sicily which threatened to rob his sister Joanna of her dower, defeated a network of pirates in the Mediterranean, toppled the government of Cyprus, where he married Berengaria, and all of these achievements read almost as an afterthought, a postscript that he scribbled onto the pages of History as he journeyed towards the Holy Land. These victories, which would have been the high point of many another prince's career, were entr'actes for Richard I. The Islamic elite who posed his greatest threat in Palestine respected him greatly, despite his compulsive dishonesty, bouts of rage and terrible cruelty towards their people. It was a brutal time and they knew that as much as Richard did.

He had the Plantagenet-Norman strength coupled with the tall, lusty handsomeness of the dukes of the Aquitaine, which contrasted painfully with his only surviving brother John, who betrayed him numerous times as they had once betrayed their father. John's attempts to exploit his brother's long absence from England extended to yet another alliance with Philippe II and collusion with the men who had imprisoned Richard in Austria. When Queen Eleanor, using fair means and foul, even hand-bagging the Pope into blessing her raising of loans at the expense of ecclesiastical foundations in England, scraped together enough of the ransom to set Richard free, Philippe broke the news to John in a letter that contained the phrase, 'the devil is loosed'.[42] John, however, could not be punished for his treachery because with all three of their brothers already in the grave, their nephew Arthur a dubious candidate and Queen Berengaria still without child, he remained next in line. The wisdom in keeping him alive, at least from Queen Eleanor's point of view, came in 1199 when Richard was hit by an assassin's arrow while on military campaign against rebels in France. He forgave his killer, requested to be buried at his father's feet in penance for rebelling against his overlord, and then died in his mother's arms at sunset on 6 April 1199, shortly after his chaplain, Brother Miles, heard his last Confession.

Richard, the King whose career had held back but not prevented the eventual loss of Jerusalem, the disobedient son who became a betrayed brother, the hero, the murderer, the man who tried and failed to prevent mounting violence against his Jewish subjects in

England, died cradled in the arms of a mother who was to become almost as famous as he. The figure to be immortalised in *Ivanhoe*, the lead in a thousand chivalric romances and *Robin Hood*'s 'good King Richard' emerged from the suppurating bowels and tortured deal of the real Richard I. His deathbed pardon for his killer went unheeded as his entourage, demented with grief mixed with fury caught the young Frenchman and had him flayed alive for regicide. The tensions between chivalric ideal and ugly realpolitik were never quite fully resolved.

SIC GLORIA TRANSIT MUNDI

RICHARD THE Lionheart lies today in effigy in the vast whitewashed knave of what was once the abbey church of the Fontevraud nunnery, a magnificent convent founded and expanded by his mother's family, where she chose to construct the early Plantagenets' necropolis at the centre of what was then an empire that straddled both sides of the English Channel. The bright artwork, clouds of fragrant incense and kaleidoscope of splendid colour designed to tremble the knee and swell the heart is long gone. In the centuries after the region was claimed by the kings of France, Fontevraud retained its association with royalty and nobility. In the seventeenth century, its abbess was a favourite of Louis XIV and ties to Versailles lasted until 1792, when the Revolution's hurtling mania towards enforced secularisation saw the last of the nuns, led by Abbess Julie-Gilette de Pardaillan d'Antin, take flight as the abbey was ransacked within weeks of the monarchy itself imploding in a hail of blood, bullets and fire on the cobblestones of the Tuileries Palace courtyard. The bright new world of de-Christianised republican France had no use for places like Fontevraud and the damage done was so extensive that even after Louis XVIII and Charles X were restored to the thrones of their forebears, the broken abbey retained the purpose assigned to it by the revolution, a prison, until 1963. To amuse themselves, the souls trapped in terrible conditions within its walls, some poor and victimised, others criminal and malign, vandalised what was left of Fontevraud's once-splendid interiors. The *misérables* hacked off the nose of Richard's effigy and whittled away in boredom at his carved joints.

Today his tomb is a small splash of colour alongside his mother's, father's and sister-in-law Isabelle's, in the vast white emptiness of the disused chapel, where the grave of the abbey's saintly founder, Robert of Arbrissel, is covered by nothing more than glass so that people can glibly walk across it. The sounds of tourists have replaced the pilgrims and the knights, the faintly discordant notes of their conversations and even their whistling echoes of the walls in place of hymns, chants and prayers. The bodies of Richard I and his relatives have long since vanished, torn from their tombs with every other set of royal bones in revolutionary France, no matter how antique. The outward shell of the tombs remain. Whether it was the result of her design or vandalism after the 1790s is hard to tell, but it is amusing that Eleanor of Aquitaine's effigy today rests a few slight but very definite inches higher than her estranged husband's.

Emerging up the steps and into the light of the museum's gardens, one's mind flutters to one of medieval Christianity's sternest enjoinders – 'Sic Gloria Transit Mundi'. ('Thus passes all the glories of the world'.) In the end, all that remains of Eleanor's ambitions for her improbable family's eternal memorial are four fading effigies in a defunct church. And, of course, the very faint possibility that her grave is deliberately a little higher than everyone else's. Perhaps it is just the failed poeticism of the place, but it encourages the happy thought that through vanished magnificence a kernel of humanity, a reminder of our eternal foibles, lasts intact. There is some comfort in that.

DILUTED MAGNIFICENCE

THE BIRTH OF PARLIAMENT

'The English will never love and honour
their king unless he be victorious and a lover of
arms and war...'

Jean Froissart, merchant, clerk and chronicler
(died 1259)

RICHARD I'S DEATH posed a great problem to the major
statesmen of England. He left behind two potential heirs – his
younger brother John and their twelve-year-old nephew Arthur.
Neither inspired much confidence. Arthur was a foreign-born child
and John was an unsavoury incompetent. 'I can see no successor
able to defend the kingdom,' said Hubert Walter, the Archbishop of
Canterbury, with depressing prescience.

Both William Marshal and the Queen Mother preferred the
claim of John and their support proved decisive. Eleanor of Aquitaine,
now in her seventies, had never shown much faith in her youngest
son, but she detested her widowed daughter-in-law, Constance of
Brittany, and did not want to see Constance's power grow if Arthur
became King. Marshal's support for the native-born and more mature
John carried the Archbishop of Canterbury and the influential Earl

of Essex, so that by the time John landed in England to be crowned King at Westminster Abbey on the Feast of the Ascension, he was supported by the majority of the magnates.

THE WRATH OF GOD
ABIDETH UPON HIM

JOHN WAS thirty-one at the time of his succession and his early career can generously be described as uninspiring. Born in Oxford on Christmas Eve 1167, John had been Henry II's youngest son and, for reasons passing understanding, his apparent favourite. Unlike another famous birth at Yuletide, no cherubim sang at John's nativity and precious few angelic influences were subsequently felt in his life. It had been Henry II's attempts to provide an inheritance for John, cruelly nicknamed John Lackland by courtiers, which helped alienate the elder princes from their father. Undaunted by their opposition, when John was seventeen his father made him Lord of Ireland and dispatched him across the Irish Sea, where the young prince delivered an eight-month virtuoso performance in governmental incompetence. The chronicler Gerald of Wales recorded that John listened to his advisers 'who were utterly unknown in Ireland and themselves knew nothing'.[1] He insensitively laughed at the beards and costumes of the Irish chieftains who came to perform homage to him and he managed to offend both the Irish and the Anglo-Norman settlers before returning to England to repay his father's unstinting efforts on his behalf by siding with the latest rebellion against him.

In 1189, a month after his father's death, he married his second cousin Isobel of Gloucester in a small ceremony at Marlborough Castle.[2] Isobel, the eldest daughter of William FitzRobert, Earl of Gloucester, and his wife, Hawisa de Beaumont, was co-heiress to her father's estates and titles. It was a substantial inheritance and, as her husband, John could hope to exercise it *suo uxoris* (on his wife's behalf). Even at his wedding, John managed to offend people. Bride and groom were both great-grandchildren of Henry I.[3] This relationship put them within the prohibited degrees of affinity and they therefore needed a Papal dispensation to make their union canonically valid. John went ahead without permission from Rome, raising suspicions that he was marrying Isobel to get his hands on her money, but in deliberately murky circumstances so that when a more advantageous bride came along, he would have no difficulty in securing an annulment.

These suspicions proved justified. When John became King in 1199, poor Isobel was almost immediately ditched on the miraculously convenient grounds that her marriage had proceeded without a Papal dispensation and was thus incestuous. Married or not, John could not let her, or rather her lands and castles, go. He demoted Isobel from wife to ward and became her legal guardian, despite the fact that she was in her early twenties. In 1200, he took a new wife by kidnapping the Count of Angoulême's daughter Isabelle, to prevent her marrying young Hugh de Lusignan, whose family exercised significant influence in the Aquitaine. An alliance between the Angoulêmes and the Lusignans would have posed a problem for the English empire in France; both families had raised insurrections against John's predecessors but they had risen independently of one another, making them relatively easy to defeat. The spectre of a marriage between Isabelle and Hugh indicated that the two clans were prepared to ally to ensure that their next rebellion was a success and so King John absconded with the lynchpin before a problem became a crisis.

However, by abducting and marrying a girl who was quite possibly below the canonical age of consent (then twelve years old), John had once again opened himself up to allegations of lechery and impropriety. Isabelle of Angoulême's exact date of birth is unknown, guesses range from 1185 to 1191, meaning that at the time of her marriage she was, at the very most, fifteen.[4] However, her contemporary Roger of Howden claimed that Isabelle's proposed marriage to Hugh de Lusignan had not gone ahead by 1200 because she was underage and the Lusignans wanted to wait for decency's sake.[5] The fact that her first child was born in 1207, seven years after her wedding, supports the theory that she must have been very young when John married her. In total, Isabelle of Angoulême gave birth to sixteen children and so the logical conclusion is that, prior to 1207, she was simply unable to conceive.

John found a use for his first wife in ordering her to take care of his second, who was young enough to require a chaperone. Once Isabelle was old enough to join the royal court on a more permanent basis, John slashed his ex-wife's income and moved her out of the way to a small castle in Dorset. When he eventually found her a new husband in the shape of Geoffrey de Mandeville, Earl of Essex, previously one of King John's most stalwart supporters, it was fifteen years after their divorce and Isobel was well-past the average age of childbearing for a medieval lady. He sold Isobel's hand to an allegedly reluctant Geoffrey for the titanic sum of twenty thousand marks, only to add injury to insult by handing over all of Isobel's inheritance to her new husband with the exception of Bristol Castle, the most prestigious and valuable part of it. When a rebellion against John came the following year, it is unsurprising to find Geoffrey and Isobel among the insurgents.

John also displayed a similarly repulsive combination of ruthlessness and stupidity when it came to his main rival for the crown. As the son of John's elder brother Geoffrey, the strictest interpretation of primogeniture favoured Arthur's claim over John. But as with Edward V and Richard III three centuries later, King John proved tireless and inventive in his quest to disinherit his nephew. John captured the boy in 1202 and shortly afterwards, Arthur disappeared. One version of events, uncorroborated but also impossible to dismiss because it originated from a chronicler writing at the Cistercian abbey at Margam, one of the places where Arthur was briefly kept prisoner, stated that John had murdered Arthur with his own hands:

> After King John had captured Arthur and
> kept him alive in prison for some time, at length,
> in the castle of Rouen, after dinner on the
> Thursday before Easter, when he was drunk and
> possessed by the devil he slew him with his own
> hand, and tying a heavy stone to the body cast it
> into the Seine. It was discovered by a fisherman
> in his net, and being dragged to the bank and
> recognised, was taken for secret burial, in fear
> of the tyrant, to the priory of Bec called Notre
> Dame des Prés.[6]

Shortly after Arthur's murder, Eleanor of Aquitaine passed away in her late seventies or early eighties. Her last few years had been blighted by dementia and after her political retirement this most unconventional of queens took the veil as a nun at the abbey at Fontevraud.[7] Prior to that, she had grown old with delicious disgracefulness. During the struggles to put John on the throne, Eleanor had been seen on the battlements of a castle under siege, daring the enemy soldiers to fire on her. She had been an energetic and capable adviser during Richard I's rule, but it is doubtful that even she could have saved John from himself. His reign read almost like an exemplum of how a medieval monarchy should not have operated.

The Lusignans, enraged at his abduction of Isabelle of Angoulême, pledged allegiance to the French Crown, which proved as troublesome to John as he had once sought to make it for his brother Richard. Philippe II launched an invasion of Normandy, eventually taking Falaise, where William the Conqueror's mother had hailed from, and then Caen, where the Conqueror himself was buried. At the same time as the dynasty's ancestral heartlands were being pillaged from the south and east, Brittany, outraged at John's murder of the half-Breton Arthur, invaded Normandy from the west and captured the hilltop monastery of Mont St Michel. English possessions in Anjou, from which the royal family derived their name, were also taken. By 1204, five years into his reign, John had presided over the loss of one-third of the English empire.

Desperate to recapture it, John raised taxes as high as he could, torturing England's persecuted Jewish community for more money, turning the screws on the aristocracy and driving those who could not pay into exile. Hatred for the royal family grew with each new tax hike. The presence of Queen Isabelle's jilted in-laws in the armies that were ransacking Normandy resulted in her being unfairly characterised as a latter-day Helen of Troy. Having blossomed into a devastatingly beautiful young woman, the Queen was accused of enslaving her husband with her sexual wiles and when she invited her half-brother, Pierre de Joigny, to join her in England, they were accused of an incestuous affair. Stories ran rife that Isabelle enjoyed numerous lovers and that a jealous King John had tormented her by hanging four of them from the four posts of her bed. Even one of John's own ambassadors claimed that the Queen 'had often been found guilty of incest, adultery and witchcraft'.[8] A generation later, rumours still circulated that one of the Queen's bastard children by her brother was living secretly in County Cavan in Ireland.

Demonising a royal woman by accusing her of unnatural sexual passions was not new to the Middle Ages, nor did it die with them. The ludicrous if memorable canard of Catherine the Great's equestrian fetish, the Empress Alexandra's fictitious affair with the unwashed Rasputin and the torrent of perversions attributed to the unlucky Marie-Antoinette were in no way reflective of the real woman, but rather of a need to discredit the monarchy by suggesting that its leading lady, and thus by extension the institution itself, was inherently unnatural. How could one respect, let alone obey, a system that was influenced by such monsters? The idea that the royal wife could corrupt the body politic with her femininity and her proximity to the monarch was a paranoiac fear that plagued the later Plantagenets. It was an inversion of the reverence for the perfect queen consort – the chaste yet fecund font of mercy who could use her position to elicit mercy from the king for his people. If the Queen could use her influence for good, surely she could also use it for evil? She needed to be watched. A queen, foreign-born and very wealthy, could easily be blamed for everything that went wrong, particularly if the monarchy entered a prolonged period of crisis and failure.

John's own behaviour certainly did nothing to ameliorate fears that he was a slave to his baser instincts. There were stories that his nobles were so afraid of his predilection for other men's wives that when they knew he was planning to visit them they would dress prostitutes as their ladies in the hope of tricking him. Along with the possibly true story that John had murdered his nephew Arthur with his bare hands, there were allegations that he had maliciously ordered the boy to be tortured, blinded and castrated in the hours before his death.

His contempt for Christianity was as pronounced as it was damaging and during a Requiem Mass for his father and brother, John's eye-rolling and ostentatiously bored tutting resulted in the officiating priest losing his temper and tossing the King out of the chapel. As his reign progressed, John managed to go even further in his feud with the Church than his father or great-great-uncle ever had. This, in fairness, was not entirely his fault. Pope Innocent III, young, determined and an organisational genius, was so zealous in his defence of Papal authority that he was quicker to reach for the institution's equivalent of the red button than any of his predecessors. When John refused to accept Stephen Langton, Innocent's nomination for the archiepiscopacy of Canterbury, because he wanted his secretary John de Gray to get it instead, Innocent retaliated by laying a general sentence of interdict on John's domains, under which all religious services except baptism and the Last Rites were temporarily prohibited. When John threatened to hang Langton if he ever returned to England, Innocent excommunicated the King and absolved his subjects of loyalty to him.

Unrest began almost immediately in Ireland and along the Welsh border, English bishops refugeed to the continent rather than serve an excommunicated Sovereign, religious hermits like Peter of Wakefield were executed for making dire prophecies against the King, the aristocracy grew restless and Innocent issued letters of deposition, removing John from his throne and legitimising a proposed French invasion of England. Frightened by the unravelling of his rule, John backtracked and Innocent exacted a humiliating set of conditions in return for forgiveness – the King must do public penance for his wrongs, he must accept Langton as the rightful Archbishop, he must pardon all those who had chosen exile during his excommunication, he must financially compensate the Church for the trouble he had caused it and he must acknowledge the Pope as overlord of England and Ireland. Even Archbishop Langton thought the last clause was excessive and by giving in to it, John appeared craven.

By the time the feud with the Papacy had been resolved, John's relations with the nobility had reached a nadir. Long-festering resentments about the Plantagenet monarchy's extortionately expensive foreign policy and concerns that the landowning class were finding it too hard to pay the sums demanded of them were exacerbated by the fact that John kept creating new and legally dubious taxes, he unevenly distributed royal largesse, he confiscated aristocratic land arbitrarily and all the money he was demanding from his people seemed wasted, since it had bought nothing but defeats. At least when Richard I bled them dry, he had come home with victories. In August 1212, a plot to murder John had been uncovered and foiled. In 1214, open rebellion erupted and John realised too late how widespread it was. He was outnumbered and outmanoeuvred into meeting with the rebels at Runnymede in June 1215, where they forced him to accept a charter limiting the power of the monarchy.

That great charter, better known by its Latin name of Magna Carta, was devised purely by the aristocracy and the Church, and it therefore naturally served their interests first. However, clause twenty did mention men and women of all social classes. It also defined the principle that taxes could not fairly be levied to the point where they mitigated the taxpayers' livelihood and included the famous phrase, 'no man shall be seized or imprisoned or stripped of his goods or possessions save by lawful judgement of his peers or equals or by the laws of the land'. It also asked for a reduction in the size of William the Conqueror's private forests and a reform of the judicial system. Magna Carta was subsequently seen as the symbolic birth not just of England's future constitutional monarchy but also of the nation's much-vaunted sense of jurisprudence and commitment to due process. Seven centuries later, journeying from London to Windsor Castle during the Second World War, King George VI pointed at the fields of Runnymede and said, 'That is where it all started.'[9]

After he signed it, King John spent much of his time trying to consign it to the dustbin of History as he could. He was helped in this by his one-time enemy the Pope, who thought the charter's attempt to legitimise future rebellions constituted a monstrous attack on social stability. Knowing the King's revulsion for the charter, some of its original architects committed the ultimate betrayal in inviting Philippe II's son, Louis, to invade England and claim the throne. The plan might just have succeeded had 'Bad King John' lived any longer. By the autumn of 1216, he was in poor health and en route from Swineshead Abbey he gorged himself on peaches and cider at supper one evening. The next day, he felt far worse. The journey continued and in a moment rich with symbolism, John quite literally lost his crown. The royal baggage train became trapped in quicksand and swamped by incoming tides. One contemporary wrote that 'the ground opened in the midst of the waters and whirlpools sucked in everything, men and horses'.[10] By the time the King reached shelter, he was dying. The abbot, who had some medical training, could do no more than administer the Last Rites. John reached nearby Newark Castle, where his will asked that his executors look after his infant son and make amends to the Church and Almighty God for the wrongs he had done to them during his lifetime. He died at Newark either late on the night of 18 October 1216 or in the early hours of the nineteenth. When he heard of the King's death, the monk Matthew Paris wrote with memorable turn-of-phrase and a total lack of charity, 'Foul as it is, Hell itself is made fouler by the presence of King John.'[11] Whispers that the peaches and cider had been poisoned to save the dynasty from annihilation by the French, the Scots, the Welsh or the numerous rebels flocking to all three were probably untrue. John's body was taken to Worcester, where it still lies in its splendid tomb.

CROWNED WITH A BRACELET

KING JOHN'S son Henry III is traditionally seen as a weak King, whose incompetence brought the same kind of misfortune to the monarchy as his father's malevolence - a pious bibliophile and art lover, who was manipulated by his self-indulgent wife and the foreigners she allowed to infest his court. A slightly more critical take on the reign holds that the birth of Parliament, which occurred despite Henry III's best efforts over the course of his fifty-six year reign, was rendered necessary because the King reached adulthood determined to undo Magna Carta and in the process prompted further rebellions to protect the great charter's legacy.

Henry was crowned, so legend has it, with his mother's bracelet. The coronation ceremony for the nine-year-old had to be carried out with maximum speed so that anti-Plantagenet rebels did not exploit the opportunity presented by King John's fortuitous death to advance their cause further. The child was rushed to Gloucester Cathedral to a sparsely attended service at which, because so many of the crown jewels had been lost in the destruction of his father's baggage train, the officiating bishops had to crown him with Queen Isabelle's bracelet. The anecdote is not quite accurate – it was actually one of the Queen Mother's hair ornaments, what might be called a tiara nowadays – but the rest of the story, including the climate of panic, is true. The monarchy was in a weaker position than it had been at any point since the Viking invasions. William Marshal, the heroic old Earl of Pembroke, whose destiny had been inextricably tied to the royal family's ever since King Stephen spared his life as a child, had risen far from the son of a disgraced rebel lord and it was he who took the reins as Henry III's first regent. The boy's unpopular mother was prevented from taking part in politics and she eventually went back to France, where she married Hugh de Lusignan, the fiancé John had stolen her from seventeen years earlier.

Age had not withered William Marshal's skills. The rebels were defeated by land at Lincoln in May 1217 and by sea at Sandwich two months later. A grand council was called at Westminster, where the regency wisely chose to re-issue Magna Carta to advertise the new regime's commitment to avoiding the mistakes of the old. The only serious edition made was the removal of the contentious clause that insisted subjects had the right to rebel against their Sovereign, as and when they saw fit.

Under Marshal's watchful eye, Henry III received an excellent education and, as a young man, eyewitnesses noted that he spoke with 'gravity and dignity'.[12] William Marshal died in May 1219 and care of the King passed to a triumvirate of guardians, but the other two were eventually edged out to leave Hugh de Burgh, Earl of Kent, solely in charge. De Burgh helped stabilise the government's finances through a clever policy of requesting further taxes in tandem with the re-issuing of charters and promises made by the Crown in regards its subjects' rights.[†] The central idea expressed in Magna Carta, the link between taxation and representation, the rights of the ruled and the responsibility of the ruler, became a reality reaffirmed in the public's mind with each financial success of de Burgh's regency.

However, French attacks on the beleaguered English empire in Europe continued and Henry III began to chafe at de Burgh's control. Even after the King had undeniably passed into adulthood, de Burgh refused to relinquish power. Henry's younger brother, Richard of Cornwall, was outraged on his brother's behalf and he became the leader of those at court who were either jealous or suspicious of the regent. Matters eventually came to a head over the issue of the King's marriage. Two candidates were proposed: the Duke of Brittany's daughter Yolanda, or the King of Scotland's younger sister, Marjorie.[13] The Scottish match should have pleased de Burgh, had he been thinking clearly, since he had recently married Marjorie's eldest sister Margaret. This could have increased de Burgh's closeness to the royals and helped secure his position as Henry passed into adulthood. Instead, all de Burgh seemed to see was the short-term. After a royal marriage, it would no longer be possible to pretend that Henry III was still too inexperienced to rule in his own name. If he was head of his own household, surely he should also now become head of his inheritance? Panicked, de Burgh betrayed his monarch by spreading the wholly untrue rumour that the King was physically malformed and, as a result, impotent. Perhaps needless to say, few people had seen the King's genitals, much less in a state of arousal, to challenge de Burgh's medical report on the royal nether regions, but some unfortunate credibility was leant to the tale by a minor physical fault that was visible to onlookers. Henry, standing at about five foot

† In the course of twelve years, de Burgh tripled the royal household's income, but it was still only two thirds of what it had been under Richard I.

six in adulthood, had a drooping eyelid that partially covered his pupil in one eye. De Burgh's story that there were far more serious abnormalities lurking beneath the King's clothes thus did not seem quite so incredible.

Frustrated and trapped, Henry III's feelings boiled over in a council meeting when he flung himself at de Burgh, brandishing a sword. From a peaceful man with little interest in violence or martial combat, it was a vivid indicator of how unhappy he was. After a final quarrel, de Burgh was arrested and tried for corruption. Henry, always dependent on strong surrogate father figures, replaced him with his childhood tutor Peter des Roches, Bishop of Winchester, but he proved no more popular. Des Roches's links to King John did not endear him to the aristocracy and he was perceived as a living reminder of the excesses associated with Henry's father. After only two years as favourite, des Roches was the subject of a blistering public condemnation from the Archbishop-Elect of Canterbury. The King, who was devout, felt compelled to push des Roches to one side and, at long last, to rule in his own right. But by freeing himself of de Burgh only to subjugate himself to des Roches, Henry III left the impression of a King who was willing, even eager, to be dominated. Two years later, he married Eleanor of Provence, a young lady still in her early teens. At the beginning of their marriage, Henry treated her with great kindness and managed her finances for her. The two soon discovered a shared love for luxury and the arts, with huge sums being spent on the complete renovation of the royal palaces and construction of elaborate European-style gardens, a particular passion of the Queen's. Her youth and inexperience made her seem like a political non-entity until she provided the kingdom with an heir, christened Edward in honour of her husband's favourite saint. After that, Eleanor of Provence had enough leverage to make herself a force to be reckoned with, a fact she lost little time in advertising.

Eleanor's father, Raymond. ruled over the province of Provence in what is now south-eastern France. Her mother, Beatrice, was related to the House of Savoy, an ambitious clan who eventually became the first royal family of a united Italy in the nineteenth century and who in the Middle Ages were noted for their wealth, power and influence in southern France, the Alpine passes and northern Italy. Like many members of her family, Eleanor of Provence's mother was clever, ambitious and full of loyalty to her kin. These traits she passed on to her four daughters, of which Eleanor was the second. She also passed on her beauty. The youngest of the Provençal sisters, another Beatrice, was said to be so beautiful that she could set most men's hearts a-thumping, while physical descriptions of Eleanor mention her lovely eyes and gorgeous dark hair. Even the family's many critics compared Beatrice of Savoy's appearance to that of the great beauties of Greek myth. (Rather pointedly, the English monk Matthew Paris compared her to Niobe, a woman whose overweening pride in her children brought about the ruin of a kingdom, which rather took the edge off his compliment.) The Savoy connection placed Henry III's Queen at the centre of a vast family network that spanned most of western Europe, with power equal to its ambition and costs proportional to both.

Eleanor's generosity to her relatives was lavish, sustained and notorious. She arranged a marriage between her sister Sanchia and Henry's unmarried brother Richard, Earl of Cornwall. She promoted the candidacy of her uncle Boniface to become the new Archbishop of Canterbury, and she secured enormous grants of land for Boniface's brother Peter, her favourite uncle, as well as funding the family's politicking in Italy. She arranged the marriage of five young English and Irish aristocrats to her Savoyard cousins. She insisted on royal favour being shown to her cousin Gaston de Béarn, who subsequently and embarrassingly sided with a rebellion against Henry. She secured royal patronage for an incredible one hundred and seventy members of her mother's extended family, and no matter what objections were raised – and there were many – she refused to moderate her behaviour, which produced a widespread feeling that Eleanor of Provence not only wielded undue influence over her pathetic husband, but that she used it solely for her own benefit. Why had the King's brother not been married to a princess from another royal line? What possible need was there to reaffirm the alliance with the Savoyards? The Queen had evidently secured her brother-in-law's marriage to suit her family's ambitions and, having achieved that, she and Sanchia had orchestrated a chillingly expensive plan to push Richard onto the vacant German throne and thus give Sanchia a crown of her own – just like the rest

of her sisters.† Later, Queen Eleanor also spent a fortune trying to win
the crown of Sicily for one of her younger sons, Edmund. Matthew
Paris wrote, 'The whole community of England, taking it ill, began to
fear that the whole business of the kingdom would be disposed of at
the will of the Queen and her sister.'[14] Priests who disagreed with her
referred to her as the King's 'nicticorax', his 'night bird'.[15]

Eleanor's ceaseless and highly unpopular promotion of her own
relatives was not simply a result of insatiable greed, as her critics
claimed. A large part of her motivation stemmed from the family
obligation inculcated on her mother's knee, but another part of it was
self-preserving pragmatism. Henry III's sense of family was no less
vital than Eleanor's and, as he grew older, he began to promote his
tribe of half-siblings, the products of his mother's second marriage
to Hugh de Lusignan. Henry III's desire to be generous to the
siblings he had not grown up with struck many, his wife included, as
excessive. Hugh and Isabelle had produced nine children together –
Hugh, Aymer, Agnes, Alice, Guy, Geoffrey, Isabelle, Guillaume and
Marguerite – and five of them became semi-permanent residents at
their half-brother's court. Queen Eleanor did not like it, or them, one
little bit. A child of dynastic politics, the Queen did not care if her
policy annihilated her popularity with the common people as long
as by promoting her relations she was creating a faction of her own
that counter-balanced the Lusignan siblings. For Eleanor of Provence,
what happened within the palace walls would always matter far more
than what happened beyond.

The rivalry between the King's relatives and the Queen's turned
the court into a viper's nest of one-upmanship, which weakened
the government and the King's attempts to present a strong, quasi-
absolutist front to the nation. A quarrel between Eleanor's uncle
Boniface and Henry's half-brother Aymer over whether a man loyal to
Boniface or Aymer should be appointed prior of the monastic hospital
of Saint Thomas in London rapidly spiralled from legal disputes into
retaliatory arson and kidnapping by the two men's household staff.
The Queen backed her uncle to the hilt and Henry lost his temper,
reduced his wife's income and temporarily banished her uncle Peter

† During a family reunion in Paris in 1259, Marguerite, the eldest sister, who had married
  King Louis IX of France, caused a row (and nearly an international incident) by refusing
  to let their youngest sister Beatrice sit at the family table during a banquet, on the grounds
  that she was not a queen like the rest of the girls. Beatrice was deeply offended, but she had
  the last laugh when her husband Charles later took the throne of Sicily.

from court. The Lusignans viewed the matter as a personal victory, but both sides should have been aware to how badly this incident of violent and greedy foreigners pillaging England for their own profit appeared to the outside world.

It was this unlovely and self-serving factional infighting at the court that eventually caused the great rebellions that shook the latter half of Henry III's long reign and in the process gave birth to parliamentary democracy in the British Isles. Magna Carta may have unleashed the theory of a monarchy checked and balanced by its subjects, but it was the Second Barons' War under Henry III which turned it into a reality that persists to the present day.

Simon de Montfort, Earl of Leicester, was a national hero due to his religious piety and his father's savage suppression of the Cathars during the Albigensian Crusade in the previous generation. The Cathars, a bizarre and rather sinister pseudo-Christian sect, are usually presented in modern accounts as free-thinking radicals, who eschewed the dogmatic restrictions of organised religion in an attempt to get back to a purer and more sexually liberated form of Christianity. In fact, what little we know of Catharism suggests that it was a cold and morbidly self-righteous cult, although the ferocity with which the Roman Catholic Church attacked it over the first three decades of the thirteenth century still has the power to shock. Young de Montfort had inherited his father's politics – something was either entirely right or entirely wrong, to be championed or crushed. His valour in the field and his impressive masculine self-confidence meant that even Henry III initially stood in awe of him and his fawning hero-worship of the handsome Earl can be seen from the King's actions in 1238, when he allowed de Montfort to marry his widowed sister, yet another Eleanor. Eventually de Montfort's greed and his use of the King's name to borrow huge sums of money turned the monarch against him and the Queen, who had liked and trusted him, began to grow cold.

De Montfort resented this demotion and his enormous ego could never quite reconcile itself to the loss of royal favour. In time, his conscience conveniently transformed his personal quarrel with Henry III into a belief that the clique-riddled royal court was preventing proper governance of the realm. By the time de Montfort had reached this conclusion, many of his peers firmly agreed with him and they were looking for a leader to strike at Henry and the Queen. The plotters got to work with industrious efficiency.

Despite the King's suspicions of de Montfort, he and the Queen were unprepared for the impending drama. They were certainly distracted. In 1257, their youngest child Katherine died at the age of three. She had been described as a beautiful infant, but she was apparently deaf and may also have suffered from mental difficulties. The monk Matthew Paris cruelly described her as 'beautiful, but dumb and useless'.[16] In contrast to the stereotype of medieval parents anaesthetised to the pain of a child's death by high levels of infant mortality, Henry and Eleanor were grief-stricken when Katherine passed away. The child was given a stately funeral in Westminster Abbey, with a sepulchre near the shrine of her father's beloved Edward the Confessor, surmounted by a solid silver sculpture showing the young princess in the guise of her patron saint, Catherine of Alexandria. Shortly after the funeral, the rebels struck. Their timing was fortuitous. Not only was the King distracted by the death of his daughter, but a prolonged spell of terrible weather had ruined the harvests, ensuring food shortages and thus a disaffected and suffering populace. The King was caught by surprise by this aristocratic coup and, with his tendency to panic under pressure particularly when it came to personal confrontation, he signed the Provisions of Oxford, which went further than Magna Carta by creating institutions that would actually implement checks on the power of the Crown, rather than simply allowing for it in theory and then trying to legitimise rebellion in the case of errant Sovereigns. A council of twenty-four barons, twelve appointed by the King and twelve the chosen representatives of the nobility, would meet to rule the realm in the King's name. To widen support for the new system, a parliament was to meet three times a year to monitor the council's performance. The last vestiges of the absolute monarchy created by the Anglo-Norman kings had been swept away

Royal shock at what had happened soon gave way to incredulity and then fury. Within months of the Provisions being signed, the Queen was siphoning funds to her cousin, Isabella de Fiennes, to begin hiring a mercenary force from Flanders that would provide the King with the muscle he needed to destroy de Montfort. Suspecting much but able to prove nothing, in 1259 the anti-royalists tried to tighten their grip on the King and his wife. The Provisions of

Westminster reinforced the political set-up established at Oxford, but they also specifically sought to limit the Queen's access to money. Eleanor solemnly swore to uphold the humiliating Provisions, and the fact that she was forced to make the promise independently of her husband indicates how powerful she was.

In the spring of the following year, her family's network came to her rescue. At the request of Eleanor's uncles, the Pope absolved the King and Queen of England from the oaths they had sworn regarding both Provisions. Eleanor was blamed, only half-fairly, for enticing her husband back to absolutism and one monastic chronicler described her as 'the root, the formentor and disseminator of all the discord which was soon between her husband King Henry and the barons of his kingdom'.[17] Attacks on those loyal to the Queen escalated throughout the summer and while she was crossing London Bridge with her eldest son, a crowd pelted her with rubbish and abuse. Centuries later, beleaguered royals beset on all sides recalled the advice of Catherine the Great: 'Kings ought to go their own way without worrying about the cries of the people, as the moon goes on its course without being stopped by the cries of dogs.'[18] Eleanor of Provence was made of slightly more flamboyant stuff and she began hurling the refuse back at the crowds, along with a few choice insults of her own. Even she could not hope to defeat an entire mob single-handedly and the royal party had to retreat to sanctuary at the home of the Bishop of London. Eleanor's French in-laws were horrified at this civic *lèse-majesté* and after visiting them in Paris she announced that she was not going back to England.

The Queen's flight meant that battle-lines were clearly drawn and in 1263 the country degenerated into a civil war subsequently known as the Second Barons' War.[19] In 1264, at the Battle of Lewes, Simon de Montfort's forces emerged victorious and in the aftermath the King and his eldest son were captured at Lewes Priory. The building was assaulted with flaming arrows until it surrendered, Henry was forced to swear to uphold the Provisions once again and his twenty-five-year-old son was taken into custody as a guarantor of his father's good behaviour. In France, Eleanor's mother and eldest sister lent the royalists huge sums of money to facilitate retaliation. Her uncle Peter secured loans from the Papacy, she herself negotiated a further loan from Prince Enrique of Castile and pawned her own jewellery, a move loyally imitated by her daughter-in-law, who used the funds generated to pay for a company of mercenary archers. However, their fundraising was essentially pointless so long as the King and the heir remained in de Montfort's custody.

De Montfort knew that reducing kings to little more than a figurehead and placing them under de facto house arrest seemed unnatural to many of his contemporaries. To bolster support for his regime, he hit upon the ingenious idea of broadening participation in the new parliamentary system: representatives of England's counties, major cities and the gentry, rather than simply the aristocracy, were invited to attend. For the first time in English history, they were not just being asked to acquiesce to taxation but also to participate in deciding how that money was spent. On a far less positive note, de Montfort also incited his followers to murderous attacks on the Anglo-Jewish community. Since they were not Christian, the Jews had no rights and English law held that they were protected from harm solely by the patronage of the royal family. De Montfort's attack on them was partly inspired by his own Christian fanaticism, but also to advertise how denuded royal authority had become. Parliaments and pogroms – a chequered legacy.

In a cycle repeated throughout history, the liberators soon became the oppressors and the self-serving avarice of de Montfort's allies, coupled with unease at how the royal family had been treated, meant that within a year of his victory at Lewes, Simon de Montfort's rule was under threat. Some of his earlier allies had bristled when he widened participation in the political process and, on 28 May 1265, Prince Edward escaped from captivity with the help of Lady Maud de Mortimer. A staunch royalist, Maud arranged horses, supplies and shelter for the prince. Six weeks later, at the Battle of Evesham, the royalists crushed the rebel army. Among the thousands dead was Simon de Montfort, whose body was hacked to pieces. Queen Eleanor sent his head and testicles to Maud de Mortimer as thanks for her loyalty.

At first it appeared as if the royalists had learned almost nothing and forgiven even less. Henry III was freed, the Provisions were scrapped and Eleanor of Provence returned from Paris with a Papal Legate at her side to negotiate peace. The Legate was Ottobuono di Fieschi, another one of her uncles. Many of those who had sided with de Montfort were either executed or reduced to ruin. Even de Montfort's widow, the King's sister, chose exile at a convent in

Europe. Queen Eleanor continued to use her unpopular international connections and resorted to unusual or unpopular methods to supplement her income.[20] Money continued to pour into the King's expansion of Westminster Abbey – the artistically spectacular result was unveiled in a ceremony at the end of his reign in which the King and his sons processed before a glittering court and clergy to prostrate the dynasty's efforts, and give thanks for its salvation, before the shrine of Saint Edward the Confessor. However, the ideas that Simon de Montfort had unleashed, almost despite himself, were too powerful to be eradicated. The institution of Parliament was one that the monarchy could not do away with no matter how hard it tried, and for the moment the best that could be done was to assert beyond doubt that the monarchy was the dominant power in the land.

Henry III died at the Palace of Westminster on 16 November 1272. He was sixty-five years old and had reigned for fifty-six of those years. His heir, the new King Edward, was still travelling home from the Holy Land and the Crusade he had embarked upon in the years after de Montfort's defeat. Power passed, uncontested, to him and Eleanor of Provence retired to a convent in the Wiltshire countryside, where she professed a desire to take the veil as a nun. She never quite got round to taking her vows, although she did spend the rest of her life at Amesbury. True to form, a small fortune was spent on making the convent suitable for her, including the planting of an avenue of oak trees to provide the Queen Mother with a view she approved of. Her husband was buried in one of the most sumptuous tombs in British history, immortalised in gold. Little niches dot the sepulchre, as if to house holy relics, leaving the observer with the impression that Eleanor of Provence oversaw the construction of a tomb that she hoped would one day become a shrine and that Henry III would follow in the footsteps of his hero, becoming both king and saint.

KNOW, SIRE, THAT LLYWELYN AP GRUFFUDD IS DEAD

WHEN EDWARD Longshanks was a boy, part of the roof in his chambers caved in and nearly killed him. A large stone gave way and landed on the chair where, minutes earlier, the young prince had been playing chess. Pondering his next move, Edward stood up to stretch his legs and, in the process, saved his own life. This kind of luck followed him throughout his life. On a visit to Gascony, he escaped with nothing more serious than a broken collarbone when the floor of the top-most room in a tower collapsed beneath him, dropping him eighty feet and killing three knights. Edward did not see any of this as coincidence. As a child, he attributed his escape at the chess game to the intercession of Our Lady of Walsingham, a miraculous vision of the Virgin Mary who had appeared in Norfolk in the reign of Edward the Confessor, and the collapsing Gascon tower fell on Easter Sunday. All his life, Edward I believed that God was watching over him, saving him for a higher purpose. His piety and his self-assurance were inextricably linked.

As his sobriquet suggests, he was tall. An examination of his remains in the eighteenth century established that he stood at six feet and two inches.[21] One of his eyelids drooped slightly, but not as obviously as his father's. Apart from that, Edward was considered very handsome – tall, blond, well-built and broad-chested like his Norman ancestors. He enjoyed hunting, riding and fighting, but it would be wrong to dismiss him as a philistine. Although he dressed simply, avoiding the ostentatious frippery of his parents' court, he had a great interest in history and architecture, and his first wife was shared his interests.

Eleanor of Castile was two years her husband's junior and the daughter of King Ferdinand III of Castile.[22] Like Edward's mother, she came from an exceptionally religious family. Four hundred years after his death, Eleanor's father was canonised by Pope Clement X and today the city of San Fernando and 'the Valley' in California are named in his honour. Ferdinand III died when Eleanor was ten or eleven years old and her half-brother became King Alfonso X. The Iberian Peninsula had a relatively cosmopolitan atmosphere in comparison to the rest of Europe, thanks to the large Jewish and

Islamic communities that still lived there in the thirteenth century, and Eleanor was to carry some of this attitude with her by proving to be far less anti-Semitic than her husband or her mother-in-law.[23] The couple were married at the convent of Santa María la Real de Las Huelgas in Eleanor's native Castile in the autumn of 1254, when Eleanor was in her early teens and Edward was fifteen. When she first arrived in England, there was a frantic scramble to decorate the apartments in the style she had been accustomed to in Castile, which included lining the walls with decorative tapestries and carpeting the floors, a near-unheard of luxury in England at the time.[24] It was here that Eleanor got to know her domineering mother-in-law and, for the first sixteen years of her married life, the younger Eleanor remained very much in the shadow of the elder, particularly when it came to money.

Whatever else anyone may have thought of them, Edward I and Eleanor of Castile loved each other very much. There is no record of Edward ever taking a mistress and unlike most medieval kings, he took his wife with him wherever he could.[25] Eleanor's pregnancies indicate how close they were and how widely they travelled – there were royal births between 1264 and 1290 in England, Wales, Paris, Gascony (part of what remained of the Aquitaine) and on pilgrimage to the Holy Land. Infant mortality carried off many of the royal children. Seven of Edward and Eleanor's daughters died as babies or toddlers. Their two eldest boys, John and Henry, both died at about five or six; Alfonso, referred to as 'the hope of us all' by the Archbishop of Canterbury, died at the age of ten.[26]

Despite this large family and the tragedies that beset them, Edward and Eleanor have not traditionally been depicted as loving parents. Long separations from their children and even non-attendance at some of their funerals suggested a couple more involved with each other than with their offspring. Compared to Henry III and Eleanor of Provence's grief at the death of their three-year-old daughter Katherine in 1257, it does appear that Edward and Eleanor's seeming indifference to their children was the product of personality rather than cultural context. It has recently been suggested that this charge of parental neglect is unfair. Although Eleanor did not, or could not, attend the funeral of her son Alfonso in 1284, she had his heart preserved so that it could one day be buried with her own. She also quarrelled with her mother-in-law over the upbringing of her daughter Mary, and a list of her expenses show that even when she was far away from them, gifts for her children were a significant part of her spending. Perhaps the safest conclusion is that while they were certainly less preoccupied by family than Edward's parents had been, that does not mean they were as cold or even cruel to their children as has been suggested.[27]

The couple were in Sicily, returning from the Holy Land, when they received the news that Henry III was dead. Edward I's coronation was held in Westminster Abbey, the first since his father's renovation of it. Everything was done according to the ancient rite until the end when Edward, with his usual flair for public gestures, apparently removed the crown from his head and announced that 'he would never take it up again until he had recovered the lands given away by his father to the earls, barons and knights of England, and to aliens'.[28] Like so much of medieval politics, the gesture was theatrical but telling. Edward I came to the throne determined to undo the damage inflicted in his father's reign and, although he could not eradicate the institution of Parliament, he meant to take back everything else that had been given away: land, money and prestige. It was therefore particularly worrying that one of the few magnates who refused to attend his coronation was Llywelyn, the fifty-year-old Prince of Wales who had once leant support to Simon de Montfort and exploited the Second Barons' War to secure the Treaty of Montgomery, whereby England's historical lordship over Wales was reduced and the homage of other Welsh lords was to be paid to Llywelyn, not to Henry III or his heirs.

The resurgence of so-called 'Celtic nationalism' in the twentieth century and the inescapable romance of a lost cause saw Llywelyn ap Gruffudd cast as the heroic leader of a lost golden age, but this *Gone with the Wind*-esque rehabilitation of Llywelyn has more to do with Edward's vices than Llywelyn's virtues. By the time Edward I came to the throne in 1272, Llywelyn's rule in Wales was detested. His military skills and long run of good luck when it came to the internecine incompetence of the neighbouring government in England meant that he was begrudgingly respected, but his attempts to modernise the Welsh economy and his bullying demands for money from his subjects did not make him popular. Wales was, and is, one of the most beautiful countries in the world. However, Llywelyn was sufficiently astute to realise that its stunning hills and mountains made agriculture difficult – in a moment of admirable honesty from any country's leader, he compared the 'fertile and abundant land' of Edward's kingdom with the 'barren and uncultivated land' of Wales.[29] This agricultural shortfall meant that the entire principality relied on a few pockets of arable land for its subsistence, namely the island of Anglesey. The economy and trade networks, drastically underdeveloped in comparison to England's, were the focus of much of Llywelyn's reforming zeal, and an indicator of the disparity between the two countries can be gauged by comparing the revenue generated by customs for Llywelyn, estimated at about £17 per annum, against roughly £10,000 for the King of England.[30] The assessment of one modern historian, that despite its internal difficulties England remained 'a thirteenth-century superpower', particularly in relation to its neighbours, is fair.[31]

In the centuries after the Norman conquest, English domination over Wales had increased greatly. Nowhere was this more obvious than with the Marcher Lords, English aristocrats who held sway in the disputed borderlands between the two countries. Llywelyn quarrelled with them often and it was their most recent spat that provided him with the excuse he needed to decline his invitation to Edward's coronation. He must have been desperate to find a reason, because had he gone Edward would almost certainly have kept him there until he could bully him into undoing the Treaty of Montgomery.

Tensions boiled over when Llywelyn's devious and stupid youngest brother, Dafydd, fled to England after a family quarrel. Edward granted him sanctuary, much to Llywelyn's anger since it violated the spirit, if not the letter, of previous Anglo-Welsh agreements about political refugees from the two countries. When Edward reiterated his demand for Llywelyn to perform homage before him for his power in Wales, Llywelyn refused. Relations took a further tumble when Edward's navy intercepted a ship just off the Isles of Scilly carrying Simon de Montfort's daughter back from exile in France. Llywelyn had proposed marriage to her and she was travelling to Wales to accept. The captured de Montfort girl was taken to Windsor where she was kept in close, if comfortable, confinement for the next three years and Edward informed the Marcher Lords that their antagonism towards Llywelyn would no longer be checked by the English government. Realising, too late, what he had done or perhaps simply accepting that he had been caught, Llywelyn tried desperately to convince the world that he wanted peace. Letters to the Pope and Robert Kilwardby, the Archbishop of Canterbury, attest to Llywelyn's apparently genuine wishes to avoid conflict with his powerful neighbour. His epistles to Edward cried for peace, but only on condition of partial homage – Llywelyn still had terms and conditions and Edward would not accept them. He did not negotiate, he commanded.

A large English army marshalled on the Welsh borders. At its height, it had fifteen thousand infantry men in its rank, eight hundred cavalry and nearly three hundred men carrying the crossbow, the most technologically advanced and lethal individual weapon of the era. Many of the earls called on to serve provided more men than their feudal dues required of them, so anxious were they to participate in Longshanks' already-famous military endeavours. The King went on pilgrimage to the shrine of Our Lady of Walsingham as the initial onslaught began. His friend, Roger de Mortimer, whose wife Maud had helped organise Edward's escape from custody under de Montfort, led a force that struck directly at the Welsh heartlands with the intention of capturing and sacking Prince Llywelyn's new castle at Dolforwyn; another English force, commanded by the Earl of Warwick, swept in from the north with Llywelyn's brother in its ranks, and a third contingent moved in from the south, where local dissatisfaction with Llywelyn's rule assured an English victory. The haste with which so many in southern and central Wales abandoned their Prince and pledged fealty to Edward proved how unpopular he had become, but fighting in the more loyal north-west was protracted and vicious. Edward arrived to spearhead the attack on the island of Anglesey, the bread basket of the principality, known in Welsh as *mam Cymru* ('mother of Wales'). The King had a group of 360 English soldiers sent over to the island to reap the harvest for themselves and Llywelyn, facing starvation, had to surrender.

He was brought to Rhuddlan Castle, one of many built by the English as they marched through Wales, and from there to the Palace of Westminster for a Christmas Day ceremony in 1277 where, in front of English and Welsh magnates, Llywelyn knelt before Edward, placed his hands in the King's and swore to be his good, faithful and obedient servant. No conditions, simply total obedience. In return, the King waived some of the money Llywelyn still owed England and allowed him to proceed with his marriage to Eleanor de Montfort. With a supreme lack of subtlety, the wedding took place in an English cathedral, at the cathedral church of Christ and the Blessed Virgin Mary of Worcester, on the feast day of King Edward's patron saint, and the bride was given away by his younger brother, Edmund, who bore the title snatched from the ruined de Montfort family, Earl of Leicester. It could not have been made any more obvious who had triumphed or that England no longer saw any danger in allowing the Welsh Prince to unite with a de Montfort. They were both broken.

Victors often incinerate their own victories. English domination became so insufferable that many in Wales began to pine for life under Llywelyn. More castles sprang up to protect the colonies Edward created for English settlers. A particular gripe was the attempts to replace Welsh law with England's and the ways in which Edward's sheriffs and bailiffs exploited this to their own advantage. The most important defector from Edward's side was Llywelyn ap Gruffudd's brother, Dafydd. As he watched the trampling of his country, Dafydd discovered, perhaps to his own surprise and certainly to everybody else's, that he had a spine.[†] In an argument with the King, he bravely remarked, 'Let the laws of Wales be unchanged, like the laws of other nations.'[32] Before the invasion, the question of whether or not Wales was actually a separate nation to England or simply a semi-autonomous region had never quite been settled. Now, in the minds of many Welsh people, it had, thanks to Edward's idiotic forcefulness. On Palm Sunday 1282, Dafydd led a night-time raid on the English-controlled castle of Hawarden. It was captured, burned to the ground and the King's friend and constable, Roger Clifford, was kidnapped. Emboldened by the fall of Hawarden, rebellions broke out across the principality. Llywelyn recovered his old fighting spirit and, after some hesitation, sided with the brother who had once betrayed him. In a moment of superb, if not entirely accurate, rhetoric, he would later justify his uprising against Edward by saying, 'The people of Snowdonia do not wish to do homage to a stranger, of whose language, manners and laws they are entirely ignorant.'[33]

Edward received the news on the Feast of the Annunciation (25 March), the day set aside by the Church to commemorate the visit of the angel Gabriel to the Virgin Mary in the New Testament.[34] Prior

† Dafydd had actually been unhappy even during the initial invasion. The Earl of Warwick, who commanded the segment of the English army Dafydd was serving in, had written to the King to warn him of Dafydd's growing dissatisfaction. At that time it was assumed, perhaps correctly, that he was simply worried that he would not get a big enough share in the spoils once his brother was defeated.

to 1752, the festival was also used to mark the start of the English new year.[†] Since all years were dated from the year 0, taken to be the most likely year for the birth of Christ, the question arose of whether or not to date each new year from the pagan date of 1 January or from a more Christian starting point. Initially, there had been those who favoured starting it on 25 December. It is not true that medieval Christians believed that this was actually the anniversary of Christ's birth. Like most modern Christians, they understood it to be a date selected by the Church centuries later to replace a pre-existing pagan festival with a Christian equivalent and to provide Christians with a date on which to commemorate an important event. However, since the year 0 was taken to be the first of what Christians dubbed 'the years of Grace' or *Anno Domini*, 'the year of Our Lord', 25 March was eventually settled upon in England as the point when the Incarnation of Christ had occurred.[35] Those who wanted to see increased devotion to the Virgin Mary championed the Annunciation as the logical start of the new year, giving it its colloquial name of Lady Day. At this stage, 31 December and 1 January were still part of the Christmas festive season that ended with the Feast of the Epiphany on 6 January.

Edward's reaction when the Annunciation celebrations were interrupted by word of Llywelyn and Dafydd's treachery – and there can be no doubt that he viewed it as such, not as a war – was predictable but frightening. The King dispatched a force to Wales, where it met with disaster when hit by an incoming tide during a surprise attack on Llywelyn's residence near Bangor. Cheered by this pharaoh-in-Exodus sounding defeat for the English, there were fresh Welsh protests even in the previously quiet south. Llywelyn moved his army to meet the English in open combat. It is possible that someone in Llywelyn's entourage betrayed him or had long been secretly working for the English, but it was equally possible that his defeat and death at the Battle of Orewin Bridge were simply the result of bad luck or poor leadership. In the heat of battle, nobody realised that he had been killed. It was only afterwards, when the bodies were being identified, that an exultant messenger was able to kneel before Edward with the words, 'Know, Sire, that Llywelyn ap Gruffudd is dead, his army broken, and the flower of his men killed.'[36] To prove the point, Llywelyn's severed head was then dropped at Edward's feet. Edward had it sent on a tour of the English garrison at Anglesey

---

[†] This is why British tax returns are still required by April, the beginning of the 'tax year', shortly after what was once the actual new year.

before parading it through the streets of London to be displayed on a pike outside the Tower.

Edward and Eleanor of Castile, pregnant as usual, took up residence in Llywelyn's former home at the Conwy River, while their troops squatted in a nearby Cistercian abbey where many of the late Prince's ancestors were buried. As Dafydd ap Gruffudd tried to avoid capture, property, land and goods were seized from those who had supported him, while Edward granted pardons to some of those who peacefully resubmitted. The Welsh caught Dafydd themselves, hiding on Mount Snowdon, and turned him over to the English. He was put on trial for treason in Shrewsbury. It was an important moment in English jurisprudence. Never before had treason been applied to a rebellion. Plotting a king's death or betraying him had always constituted treason, but rebellion had never legally been classed as the same thing, even if there were many who regarded it as such. Now Edward I was using the triumphalism at the fall of Wales to re-categorise rebellion as a state axiomatic with treason. It was no longer lawful to rebel against one's monarch, no matter what the cause or provocation. The legacy of Magna Carta and the Provisions of Oxford and Westminster were dealt a serious blow and the grandsons and sons of the men who had authored them were there, cheering it along.

A punishment should fit the crime and since Dafydd's treason was new, so too was his manner of death. The method chosen was to be repeated down the centuries as a uniquely English and grotesque form of capital punishment. For his treason, he was dragged through the streets behind a horse. For the murders he was responsible for in attacking Hawarden Castle at the start of the rebellion, he was hanged, but cut down while still alive. The attack on Hawarden at taken place on Palm Sunday, and so for his violation of Holy Week, he had his entrails ripped out and burned in front of him. Finally, for having plotted to murder the King – the least convincing of the charges against him – Dafydd's body was cut into four parts and those parts were then sent to be displayed in the four parts of the country most affected by his rebellion. Dafydd ap Gruffudd thus became the first man in British history to be hanged, drawn and quartered.

Five months later, on 25 April 1284, Eleanor of Castile gave birth to a son amidst the building site of Caernarfon Castle in north-western Wales, the region once most loyal to Llywelyn. The castle was enormous, a looming testimony to Edward's power in the region, and it was modelled on the walls of Constantinople, the great Christian citadel in the East. The child Eleanor gave birth to was christened Edward after his father and the choice of where the Queen spent her pregnancy was deliberate. The child was born in the same land that had once birthed Llywelyn, and so he was given the title that had once been Llywelyn's – Prince of Wales. A later legend said that Edward I promised the Welsh lords a new prince of their own who spoke no English, before presenting his baby son to them atop a shield. Unfortunately, there is no contemporary evidence for this pretty anecdote, although the baby's first wet-nurse was a Welsh woman called Mariota Maunsel. Perhaps Edward I was planning to make his second son prince of an independent or semi-independent Wales or, more likely by far, governor of the province sweetened by the old title of prince. At the time of little Edward's birth, his elder brother Alfonso was still heir-apparent to the throne, but three months after the birth, news reached Edward and Eleanor that Alfonso had died at Windsor Castle. With so much to occupy them in Wales, they did not return for their son's funeral at Westminster Abbey. The infant Prince of Wales was now heir to the throne of England and the custom that the heir should bear that title, which persists down to the present day, was birthed by the unexpected death of a ten year-old at Windsor.

THE JEWISH DIASPORA

BETWEEN 1290 and 1656 there were no Jews in England. Or at least none who could admit to it. In November 1290, Edward I had the entire community expelled from England in an event known as the Diaspora. Jews had no civil rights in thirteenth-century England, only Christians had rights vis-á-vis their ruler. As a result, Anglo-Jewry existed as a unique legal class that was offered protection by the Sovereign. The rub was that they were expected to pay for that protection and after Magna Carta they were the only group in England that the royals could continue to target for money whenever they felt like it. Some members of the Jewish community were very wealthy and at one point an English Jew called Aaron of Lincoln was said to be the richest man in the kingdom.[37] The stereotype of Jewish links to money-lending arose in the Middle Ages, when two Christian teachings forced many Jewish families into it. The first was that Jews were barred from an increasing number of alternative occupations by a Church anxious to limit contact between Christians and non-believers. The second was that Christians were forbidden from charging interest on a loan. The Church preached that interest of any kind, known as usury, was an exploitation of the vulnerable. Since Christians were forbidden from profiting from usury, very few had any incentive to do it and, with the Jews prevented from participating in so many other jobs, this presented an opening for Jews to make a living that they were then criticised for by the Church, who claimed that usury was a uniquely Jewish vice.

Royal protection was not always efficacious. Anti-Semitic riots had erupted during the festivities for Richard the Lionheart's coronation in 1189 and the King was severely criticised by the clergy for allowing Jews who had been forced to convert to Christianity during the violence to return to their old religion. When Richard went on Crusade, the absence of their protector left the Jews particularly vulnerable and massacres of local Jewish communities occurred at Stamford, Bury St Edmunds and Lynn. The Jewish community in Lincoln were granted sanctuary in the royal castle, but during the celebrations for Passover their co-religionists in York were not so lucky. They were surrounded in Clifford's Tower by a baying mob, who demanded that they either convert to Christianity or perish.

Imitating the actions of the Jewish martyrs at the fortress of Masada in the first century AD, the Jews of York chose mass suicide over falling into the hands of their enemies. Those few who did not were butchered within minutes of leaving their place of shelter.

There were some Christians who objected to the persecution of the Jews. The Bishop of Lincoln had criticised Simon de Montfort's cruelty towards them by reminding him that the Jews 'are a wandering people [...] they are fugitives from their proper home, that is Jerusalem, they wander through uncertain stopping places and flee from fear of death'.[38] But the majority of Christians believed sympathy to be wasted on the non-believer. In 1234, Pope Gregory IX argued that there was strong theological justification for discriminating against the Jews, because the Gospel according to Saint John made it quite clear that the Jews were forever stained with the blood of Christ.[39] The clergy's concern over the potential heretical impact of Judaism resulted in them more clearly defining the lines of segregation. Christian conversion to Judaism was miniscule in numerical terms, but that did not stop scandalous Christian stories of seductive Jewesses enticing Christian priests away from the true faith or of converts slandering the Virgin Mary in language so foul that no Christian pen could repeat it. Clerical concern was still mirrored by popular prejudice; despite the fact that the Jewish community made up less than a quarter of a percent of the overall English population in the thirteenth century, anti-Semitism was widespread, as were stories of Jews participating in human sacrifice or the kidnapping and murder of Christian martyr-children. Christians, so it was claimed, were the real victims and their way of life was being threatened.

In contrast to this consensus of clerical and popular paranoia, the royal family struggled to define their policy towards the Jews on both a personal and political level. On the one hand the royal family's contact with their Jewish subjects was far greater than that of most of the general population's. Queens were likely to be particularly familiar with high-ranking English Jews due to a levy known as the queens-gold. It had originally been created by Henry I to supplement the income of his second wife, Adeliza of Louvain; it meant that an extra ten percent was added to any fine owed to the Crown by a Christian over the value of ten marks, as well as on any tax paid by the Jews. Kings too needed Jewish money and Henry III had been particularly open about his need for it as all other avenues were closed to him by the machinations of Simon de Montfort.

However, considerable popularity could be won by any Sovereign who took a firm stand against the Jews and there were also signs that the monarchy's overzealous taxation of the community may have killed the proverbial goose that laid the golden egg. In 1244, it had taken the Jewish community nearly six years to collectively pay off a fine of sixty thousand marks levied by Henry III, a sum so exorbitant that it prompted Elias le Evesque, the Jewish Archpresbyter (English Judaism's highest-ranking priest or official), to faint in the presence of the King's younger brother.

Shortly after his coronation, Edward I decreed that all Jews should be removed from any estates that had been granted to the Queen Mother in her widowhood. Eleanor of Provence had apparently made this request herself, since she did not want any contact with sin imperilling the salvation of her soul. This led to the eviction of Jewish communities in Marlborough, Gloucester, Worcester, Andover, Bath, Guildford and Cambridge.[40] Later in the same year, Edward implemented that Statute of the Jewry, which outlawed usury, forbade Christians to live near Jews, implemented a special new tax on every Jew above the age of twelve, restricted where Jews were allowed to live and, amongst other provisions, declared that when in public every Jew over the age of seven had to wear a yellow badge, known as the tabula, measuring six inches by three. The urban areas where the Jews were allowed to live were known as the archæ, after the archa they contained, a strongbox of documents pertaining to this well-documented and well-watched community.

Like his mother, Edward I had a pious abhorrence of Jewish money because he believed it had been obtained through usury and the corresponding exploitation of Christians. His wife had no such qualms. Eleanor of Castile came to the throne with a neurotic fear of poverty. She was also entrusted with the task of helping to replenish and stabilise the monarchy's assets after the financial freefall of the last few years. This meant that when it came to the payment of the queens-gold tax, Eleanor was quite prepared to accept payment of it in the form of the transfer of Jewish debt. Since Jews were no longer allowed to profit directly from usury themselves, thanks to the Statute of the Jewry, but were still expected to contribute payment to the Queen's household, many chose to do this by transferring the debt owed to them by Christians over to Eleanor and her stewards. This in turn enabled Eleanor to expand both her income and her property portfolio, since many Christians in debt to the Jews were landowners who could only liquidate this debt by handing over land or selling their estates at reduced prices.

That accepting the transfer of Jewish debt was a lucrative and even sensible strategy on Queen Eleanor's part was borne out by the speed with which she was able to financially stabilise her coffers after the damage inflicted by her mother-in-law and a century of financial mismanagement before her. Christian debt owed to the Jews and transferred to the Queen brought her the manors of Burgh in Suffolk, Quendon, Fobbing and Shenfield, all in Essex, Westcliffe and Longele in Kent, Torpeyl and Upton in Northamptonshire, Nocton in Lincolnshire on a fourteen-year lease, and her beloved Leeds Castle, which she spent a small fortune renovating.

Eleanor of Castile was not a popular Queen, partly because she was accused of enriching herself at the expense of her husband's Christian subjects. In 1283, the Archbishop of Canterbury wrote to her, reminding her that, 'when you receive a land or manor acquired through the usury of the Jews, take heed that usury is a mortal sin to those who take the usury and those who support it [...] you must return the things thus acquired to the Christians who have lost them [...] My Lady, know that I am telling you the lawful truth and if anyone who gives you to understand anything else he is a heretic.'[41]

The Queen's interactions with the Jews increased even as her husband tightened the noose around an unpopular minority who had been bled dry, and thus useless, by the Crown's exploitation of them. In 1287 all Jews were expelled from English territory in Gascony and on 18 July 1290, the policy was extended. In the midst of the wedding celebrations for his daughter Mary, who was marrying the Duke of Brabant, Edward issued a decree banishing all the Jews from England. They were given just over three months to pack up their lives and leave in time for the Feast of All Saints, which fell on the first day of November. The reasons for Edward's decision are still a subject of debate. The most charitable conclusion is simply that, 'In his anti-Semitism, as in other aspects of his bigotry, Edward marched in step with his subjects.'[42] Whether he did it to court popularity, appease the aristocracy and knights, many of whom were in debt to Jewish moneylenders, curry favour with the Church or because his conscience told him that it was the right thing to do, is unknowable. It may very well have been a combination of factors. In any case, it was loudly applauded. The knights of England were so thrilled at the Diaspora that in their gratitude they voted the King one-fifteenth of all their goods, a tax return so enormous that it constituted the biggest single tax collected in the British Isles for the entire medieval period. The Church followed suit and gave the King a generous financial gift.[43]

Some of those in the elite who had maintained relatively friendly relations with the Jews, like the King's younger brother Edmund, Queen Eleanor and the Archbishop of York, tried their best to secure safe passage out of England for their former associates. Desperate to prevent a jubilatory pogrom against the émigrés, Archbishop John le Romeyn of York threatened any Christian caught in his diocese molesting or harming the Jews as they left with excommunication. Prince Edmund managed to obtain a special license for a Jewish gentleman called Aaron fil Vives to sell his houses and rents in London, Canterbury and Oxford to Christians and Queen Eleanor begged Edward to grant Hagin fil Deulecresse, the Jewish Archpresbyter, a similar permit. He did so on the grounds that Hagin was 'the Jew of his dearest consort Eleanor'.[44]

The majority of English Jews were not so lucky. We know that violence carried out against the Jewish community as they left and le Romeyn's threat of excommunication only applied to those of his diocese. As one ship carrying the exiles sailed up the Thames, the captain claimed that his ship had run aground on a sandbank. To lighten the load as the vessel was refloated, the Jewish passengers were allowed off to stretch their legs on the bank. Once they had disembarked, the captain and crew sailed away, leaving them to drown in the incoming tide. Those who survived the Diaspora of 1290 were scattered to the wind and Anglo-Jewish settlers were found in Amiens, Paris, Spain, northern Italy, Germany and even as far afield as Cairo. Under Edward's ancestors, the Jews of England had 'been to a certain extent left alone; they had been loyal and industrious subjects, and had ministered much to the prosperity of the country of their adoption; they worshipped in their synagogues in peace, bought land and amassed riches; their lives had fallen in pleasant places and they concluded that the future would be as the past had been.'[45] As they were expelled in 1290, a London scribe reflected that they had become 'a fugitive people exiled from England for all time, always a wretched people to wander anywhere in the world'.[46]

Edward did not have much time to bask in the self-righteous glow produced by the Diaspora. Twenty-seven days after it was completed, his wife died. A few years earlier, during a visit to Gascony, she had contracted malaria and her health never recovered. In that weakened state, matters cannot have been helped by her fifteenth and sixteenth pregnancies. In the week immediately preceding the Diaspora, one of her servants was sent to procure better medicine, but nothing helped and a pilgrimage was planned to the shrine of Saint Hugh of Lincoln. En route, the Queen's health rapidly deteriorated and her servants commandeered the house of a local justice, Richard de Weston. It was there, in the village of Harby, a few miles from Lincoln, that she died on 28 November. Edward was devastated and in a letter written a few months later, he referred to her as a love 'we dearly cherished, and whom in death we cannot cease to love'.[47]

Such sentiment was not shared by the wider population who remembered the late Queen as a grasping manipulative thief. It was only the elaborate pageantry of her funeral, particularly the famous Eleanor Crosses, beautiful monuments constructed at Lincoln, Grantham, Stamford, Northampton, Sony Stratford, Woburn, Dunstable, St Albans, Waltham, Westcheap and Charing (hence Charing Cross) to mark the spots where her body rested on its final journey back to London, which helped soften the hostility towards her while she lived. By the time the Victorians came to write about 'fair and faithful Eleanora', the romantic legend of Edward's perfect and loving Queen who must have deserved such a funeral had replaced contemporary criticism of her closeness to Jewish money.[48]

Reflecting on the importance of History is easy, but its applicability is an altogether more fraught concept. The expulsion of the Jews in 1290, with all the cruelty it showcased and the misery it entailed, certainly has an even more sinister appearance in light of the Holocaust of the twentieth century. That the Holocaust had nothing to do with Christian teaching should be obvious to all but the most zealous and disingenuous of Christianity's critics. What happened in the 1940s was the result of a totalitarian political ideology and a perverted interpretation of evolutionary science. However, simply because Christianity's fundamental teachings are the antithesis of the horrors found in Auschwitz does not mean that it is automatically innocent of nurturing the long-term European anti-Semitism that helped make Auschwitz or its sister camps possible.

For centuries, the Christian faith taught that Jews were not only inferior to Christians but also harmful, a tumour in the body politic. This was not a view unique to Catholicism. The diatribes of Martin Luther and the pogroms carried out by Russian peasants show that Protestantism and the Orthodox churches were just as capable of whipping-up hatred of God's Chosen People. Jews were treated badly under the Roman Empire and their religion was mocked, but so too were many other peoples of the empire. Anti-Semitism as we know it was encouraged and hideously magnified by medieval Christianity and it is impossible to escape reaching that conclusion when examining the fate of the Jewish community in thirteenth-century England.

Every piece of prejudice and every act of discrimination can eventually be traced back to that society's interpretation of the Bible. To cut off the right hand that offends thee, to pluck out the errant eye and flee from sin, these were all Biblical teachings that, when set alongside limits placed on Jewish employment and contemporary financial concerns, conspired to produce the terrible events of 1290. Even the few members of the royal family and episcopacy who did their best to help individual Jews leave the country safely did not, or could not, plead for Anglo-Jewry as a whole.

Medieval Christianity was an extraordinarily beautiful thing. It moulded some of the noblest minds in European history. Its capacity to move the faithful towards acts of courage, charity and compassion, the haunting beauty of its music, its art, the brilliant and subtle complexities of its theology, the men and women who sacrificed everything to live by its teachings, its cathedrals, built by thousands of hands over the course of generations, are proof of the devotion it inspired and the wonders it was capable of. In a violent age, it tried to promote values like chivalry, mercy and honour. It preached strongly against rape and canonised dozens of young women who had been its victims. And yet, it condoned and even celebrated the persecution of the Jews. In 1943, even as the Nazi Holocaust gathered its dread momentum, the historian Joshua Trachtenburg wrote that 'the most vivid impression to be gained from a reading of medieval allusions to the Jews is of a hatred so vast and abysmal, so intense that it leaves one gasping for comprehension'.[49] Perhaps, in the end, the Diaspora's greatest lesson is not just of what was wrong with the thirteenth century or medieval religion, but a reminder, if ever one was needed, of man's inhumanity to man, how readily he can justify it and the tragedies of the past.

UNTIL A KING IS PROVIDED

IT SAYS much for the skewing of history to fit contemporary prejudices that Edward Longshanks is today vilified not so much for how he treated the Jews, but for how he dealt with Scotland. The commercial success of the 1995 movie *Braveheart* about Scotland's struggle against English domination presented Edward, played by Patrick McGoohan, as a border-line psychopath. In one scene, he is shown throwing his pathetic son's gay lover out of a window while his regime in Scotland condones the infamous *droit du seigneur*, a wholly fictitious custom by which lords were permitted to deflower their female serfs or tenants.[†] There is no evidence to support the idea that the *droit du seigneur* ever existed and it seems to have been propagated in polemical histories in the febrile atmosphere preceding the French Revolution, when painting the nobility as an inherently corrupt and licentious group obviously had a certain political motivation. *Braveheart* too was accused of polemic and of reducing the complex relations between Scotland and England to nothing more than a morality tale of a freedom-loving people against a tyrannical oppressor. With its beautiful cinematography and music, however, *Braveheart* weathered the criticism and its success helped enshrine a villainous Longshanks in the public's mind.

The events that led to Edward's involvement in Scotland were a vivid demonstration of the truth in Alexis de Tocqueville's reflection on how much history owes to luck, happenstance and the improbable. Prior to this, relations between the two countries had been fairly civil and certainly far less antagonistic than England's tortured relationship with France. The two countries even shared a fairly similar political and civic culture. The process by which they began to closely resemble one another began shortly after the Norman conquest, when Edgar the Ætheling's mother and sisters had sought sanctuary in Scotland. Margaret of Wessex's subsequent marriage to King Malcolm III, who had himself spent part of his youth at the court of Edward the Confessor, saw the introduction of many European customs and forms of etiquette at the Scottish court, and this process was widened to the whole kingdom under his son, King David I, who possessed huge estates in England thanks to his sister Matilda's marriage to King Henry I. By a natural process,

† Sometimes known as the *prima nocta* or *droit du jambage*.

English eventually replaced Gaelic as the dominant language in the south-east of Scotland and, by the time Alexander III succeeded to the throne in 1249, the population had been further diversified by the migration and promotion of Anglo-Norman aristocratic families like the Bruces and an influx of immigrants from England, Flanders and France into Scotland's eastern towns and villages, a movement encouraged by Scottish kings keen to bolster their economy. The links between Scotland and England were occasionally tense, as any countries sharing a land border in the Middle Ages were bound to be, but by and large they were co-operative. Alexander III sent aid to the English royals during the Second Barons' War and in 1251 he married Longshanks' younger sister, Princess Margaret.

However, Scotland was not Wales and despite England's attempts to prove otherwise, Scotland's monarchy had never submitted itself to the idea that English kingship was the highest authority in the Isles. Scottish kings had a mythic ancestry that rivalled England's claims to be descendants of Rome and King Arthur. The Caledonian royal line allegedly descended from the pharaohs of ancient Egypt and a princess called Scota who founded Scotland by wresting it from the control of the ancient Britons. Such a claim, and certainly the Egyptian princess's far-too-convenient name, seems patently absurd to a twenty-first century observer and how anyone could ever have believed it fuels the modern notion that the people of the Middle Ages were gullible morons crippled by their collective credulity. Much like the erroneous assertion that medieval people believed the world to be flat before the adventures of Columbus (they did not – the ancient Egyptians, the Greeks, the Bible and the Qu'ran all mentioned that the world is round), the image of Alexander III and his courtiers listening to a genealogy that traced his family back to the pharaohs seems laughable. However, that is to miss the point of these genealogies. In much the same way as a modern audience watching an historically-based movie might 'know' that it will not be completely accurate, they might still unconsciously absorb it as conveying a general truth, such as an individual's status as hero or villain, or the role a particular country played in history, medieval audiences may have suspected that the exact details of the royal family's ancestry were unlikely to be wholly accurate, but they nonetheless believed that it validated a wider symbolic point. In this case, that Scotland's crown sprang from its own ancient sources and that it was not, and never had been, subservient to England's.

At the same time as Henry III was struggling with his aristocracy in England, Alexander III was succeeding against his in Scotland. Under Alexander, royal authority was solidified at the expense of the nobility. His reign also saw the expansion of Scotland's territory, as the Western Isles, previously under the rule of Norway, were incorporated into the kingdom. However, in February 1275 the first in a catalogue of dynastic disasters beset the Scottish royal family. Alexander's wife and Edward's sister, Queen Margaret, died at Cupar Castle. She left behind three children. Six years later, the youngest, David, died at the age of nine. Two years later, news arrived from Tønsberg that Alexander's daughter, the Queen consort of Norway, had died giving birth to a daughter and then in 1284, the last of the royal offspring, Prince Alexander, died four days before his twentieth birthday, leaving a childless widow and a devastated father.

Like Henry I of England in the previous century, Alexander III had to remarry quickly to produce a replacement heir. He had no brothers, no uncles and, now, no children to succeed him. His daughter's child still lived in Norway with her father, King Eric II, and until he fathered another child, Alexander had her proclaimed heiress-presumptive. No one relished the prospect of a fragile foreign-born baby girl inheriting the crown and so in 1285 Alexander married Yolande de Dreux, a French aristocrat twenty-two years his junior. A year later, the young Queen was stuck at Kinghorn during a ferocious storm. She was already pregnant and in a rush of protective love Alexander wanted to be at her side. He set off from Edinburgh Castle and in the course of the journey, his horse lost its footing and stumbled down a steep embankment. It was not until sunrise the next day that the King's body, neck broken, was found by his attendants. Scotland had lost a great and powerful monarch and everything now rested on the child in Queen Yolande's womb. Six guardians, four nobles and two bishops, were to oversee the government until she delivered, but the Queen's pregnancy ended in a miscarriage, rebellion against the guardians spread in the south of Scotland and communications were exchanged with Norway encouraging Eric II to send his daughter, nicknamed 'the Maid of Norway', over to claim her inheritance. As Alexander III's granddaughter, she was now the only member of the royal family left.

Little Margaret's journey from Norway was marred by bad weather and delays. The child-Queen suffered terribly, as did her entourage and the crew. The food began to rot and the ship put into the Orkney Islands, off the northern coast of Scotland. There, already weakened, the Maid of Norway died at the age of seven, probably after eating some of the ship's infected food. Like most royal children who died in isolated locations, a pretender subsequently arose claiming to be Margaret. Clearly a fraud, she was executed by the Norwegian government.

As the remains of the real Queen Margaret were taken back to Norway to rest alongside her mother's, Scotland descended into panic. In the space of a decade, three generations of the royal family had been wiped out due to an improbable series of tragic accidents. The question of who should succeed the Maid was a vexatious one and, like most vexatious questions in medieval politics, it had the potential to turn ugly, quickly. To find the next in line, one had to go back to the family of the little Maid's great-great-great grandfather to determine which of his descendants now had the right to rule. Perhaps needless to say, there was more than one claimant and the Bishop of St Andrews, one of the guardians of the realm, wrote to King Edward in England asking him to adjudicate as a supposedly impartial third party. Edward agreed and readily consented to the Scots' conditions that he should act as 'chief lord and guardian of the kingdom, until a king is provided'.[50] They trusted in him to act as a chivalric monarch, but despite his public protestations of good faith, Edward had already apparently boasted in private that he planned to 'reduce the king and kingdom of Scotland to his rule, as he had recently subjected Wales to his authority'.[51]

Whether Edward intended to go to war with Scotland or to set up the same kind of colonial government established in Wales at this stage is doubtful, but he certainly planned to use the succession crisis to his own advantage by holding control of the Scottish government for as long as he could and then pick a candidate dependent on England. Once that happened, Edward would coerce the English-appointed King into publicly pledging homage to England as his country's overlord.

There were two candidates who had the best blood claim to the Scottish throne. Both men were descendants of a younger brother of King William the Lion, Alexander III's grandfather. The first, John Balliol, was the son of an English lord who founded the Oxford college that bears his name, and a Scottish noblewoman, Dervorguilla of Galloway, the daughter of King William the Lion's eldest niece. Against him was the elderly but fearsome Robert Bruce, Lord of Annandale on the Anglo-Scottish border. Balliol's claim to the Scottish throne rested on the fact that he was the senior living descendant of the eldest of King William the Lion's nieces, but Robert Bruce argued that such a claim only settled the matter when it came to the inheritance of aristocratic estates, and that monarchies and aristocracies were two very different institutions. Primogeniture was primary in aristocratic inheritances, but not in successions to a throne. In the latter case, so Bruce argued, it was a combination of nearness in blood and the appropriateness of the candidate that mattered. Bruce was the son of the second-born of William the Lion's nieces, which meant that under primogeniture the senior line rested with Balliol (the descendant of the eldest sister), but under the criteria Bruce wished to be judged by, he was nearer in blood to the royal line because he was born in the previous generation to John Balliol.

The succession of Longshanks' disastrous grandfather, King John, in 1199 supported Robert Bruce's argument. John had been challenged by his nephew, the son of John's elder brother, but other considerations carried the day and now Bruce was asking for the same thing to happen in Scotland. However, the thirteenth century had seen primogeniture rise to pre-eminence and although it had not quite acquired the near-sacrosanct status that subsequent generations of royalists would endow it with, Longshanks was nonetheless loath to move against it. He also guessed that with an English father and an English upbringing, John Balliol would prove the more malleable of the two men.

With the benefit of hindsight, many reached the conclusion that Edward I had probably decided to favour Balliol before the process even began, but even a puppet king was a poor substitute for ruling in one's own right. It was in Longshanks' best interest to draw the process out for as long as was humanly possible. Rather than simply deliberate between the two main candidates, Edward declared that for justice's sake he must hear the petitions of all the claimants to the Scottish crown. This widened the field to fourteen and an awful lot of time-wasting. A revealing example of the game Edward was playing came through his treatment of Count Floris of Holland, the great-great grandson of William the Lion's younger sister, Ada. Both Balliol and Bruce claimed descent from William's brother and nobody in their right mind believed that the descendants of William's sister could possibly trump those of the brother, but Floris claimed that he had an obscure piece of documentation that proved that Ada's line had been given seniority. Edward pretended to believe him and adjourned the court for ten months to give Floris time to find the necessary paperwork. The paperwork was never found. It is quite probable that it never existed and more than possible that Floris was put up to the charade by Edward, who needed some kind of excuse to prorogue the hearings for nearly a year, during which time he could carry on ruling Scotland himself.

Eventually, Edward settled the matter in John Balliol's favour and the coronation took place at Scone Abbey, the traditional crowning site of Scotland's kings, on the Feast of Saint Andrew the Apostle, the country's patron saint. A far more important ceremony took place twenty-eight days later at Newcastle in England. King John Balliol visited Edward I's Christmas court and knelt before him, pledging allegiance and performing homage to his overlord. Documentation swiftly followed to confirm that Edward was Balliol's overlord. Within a week of Balliol's coronation, even before he arrived in Newcastle, Edward I had already started to undermine his underling by responding to petitions from civic leaders who, unhappy at a decision reached by Balliol's government, simply went over his head and appealed to Edward, who settled the matter in their favour.

The Scottish aristocracy were faced with a King who was undoing centuries of independence. Everything in the Middle Ages was based on precedent and Balliol was handing the English enough evidence to claim for years to come that the Scottish government was a vassal of England's. Borrowing from the example of Simon de Montfort, they tried in vain to impose limits on Balliol's power and in 1295 they negotiated an anti-English alliance with the French. This alliance became the cornerstone of Scottish foreign policy until the sixteenth century and its longevity earned it the nickname of 'the Auld Alliance'. That one of the longest-running anti-English alliances in history was born under Edward I is a tribute to his detestable and divisive policies. As their actions after Margaret of Norway's death in 1290 had shown, the Scots had regarded him as their friend. Now he, and England, were their enemy.

Realising that Scotland and Balliol were slipping from his grasp, Edward mobilised yet another enormous army and headed north. He crossed the border and his army took and ransacked the town of Berwick. Shortly before its capture and many of their deaths, the townsfolk had remained defiant by taking to the town walls to bare their buttocks at Edward and his men. Utterly miserable with the crown he had been given, John Balliol offered to step aside. He dreamed of being allowed to live out his life peacefully in England, 'to dwell there in the ways that used to be his, and would hunt in his parks, and do what he wished for his solace and his pleasure'.[52] Edward accepted his offer to quit Scotland, but instead of the aristocratic sunset he pined for, Balliol was incarcerated in the Tower of London. With its King imprisoned, Edward swept to Scone to take away the Stone, the ancient rock upon which Scottish kings were traditionally crowned. It was removed to Westminster Abbey and kept beneath the English coronation chair until 1996, when Queen Elizabeth II decided that it should henceforth be kept in Scotland except for during future coronations.[53] The Stone was returned there on Saint Andrew's Day.

In his victory, Edward decided to install a system like that which had been inflicted upon Wales, with English officials put in charge of Scottish towns and institutions. Edward's uncle by marriage, John de Warenne, Earl of Surrey, was appointed governor of Scotland in the King's absence.† Revealing his true feelings about the country he had betrayed and invaded, Edward joked as he handed the reins of government over to Surrey, 'A man does good business, when he rids himself of a turd.'[54] The King returned south to prepare for a forthcoming war against France while Surrey, his reluctant deputy, spent as much time as he could on the English side of the Scottish border.

The Scots unsurprisingly loathed the English administration, particularly Edward's constant demands for more money from them to fund his war against their French allies. Two Scotsmen emerged to lead opposition to him – William Wallace, the son of a minor landowner, and Robert Bruce, grandson of Balliol's one-time opponent and thus a man with a claim to the empty Scottish throne. Not much is known of Wallace, except that he was patriotic and charismatic. He led the army that scored a major victory against the English at the Battle of Stirling Bridge in 1297. Surrey rode south with the news,

---

† Surrey was married to Alice de Lusignan, one of Henry III's half-siblings.

but the King failed to appreciate the seriousness of the situation. He was too preoccupied with war against France and, as he focused on Gascony, Wallace's army rode into the north of England, laying waste to most of Northumbria and Cumbria.

Belatedly acknowledging the threat, Edward returned to Scotland with a force that may have numbered up to thirty thousand. No longer young, the King lived in the same Spartan conditions he demanded of his men, sleeping 'with their shields as pillows, and their armour as bedclothes'.[55] It was said later that the only wound Edward received on the campaign was when his horse, which he slept next to in case of a surprise attack, accidentally trod on him. Edward won a costly victory at Falkirk. William Wallace escaped the battlefield, but his credibility as a leader was badly damaged by the defeat. With Scotland seemingly cowed, Longshanks returned home to negotiate peace with France. Hoping to drive a wedge between the two former allies, the widowed Edward offered himself as a husband for the French King's youngest daughter, Marguerite. Not yet twenty, the princess was over forty years Edward's junior, but that did not seem to worry anyone. If it bothered Marguerite, she gave no sign of it and after their wedding at Canterbury, her new husband presented her with two new crowns, including a magnificent piece from the goldsmith Thomas de Frowick.[56]

The last eight years of Edward's life were spent preoccupied with Scotland. William Wallace was captured in 1302 and subjected to the same hideous death as Dafydd ap Gruffudd. Not long after, Robert Bruce murdered one of Edward's few Scottish supporters, John Comyn, Lord of Badenoch, and with the help of the Bishop of St Andrews, he made a dash to Scone Abbey to proclaim himself King Robert I. In doing so, he proclaimed Scotland a Sovereign and independent kingdom once more. It was said that when the news was brought to Longshanks 'he went nearly out of his mind' with fury.[57] As he marched northwards once again, he made threats of laying Scotland to waste from coast to coast, his moods were unstable and his temper terrifying. During a row with his eldest son, the King lost his temper and flew at the young man screaming, 'You bastard son of a bitch!'[58] He began beating him and tearing out the young man's hair, only stopping when he ran out of energy.

The end came as the army moved along the Cumbrian coast on the Feast of Saint Thomas the Apostle. Edward had been ailing for some time but he had refused to turn back from the march on Scotland. As his servants tried to raise him from his sickbed to feed him, he slipped quietly away. It was ironic that a man who had been so full of certainty in his lifetime should die on the feast day of a saint remembered for his capacity to doubt.

The news of Edward I's passing was kept secret for nearly two weeks. The only three people who were told immediately were his widow Queen Marguerite, the new King, and Longshanks' old friend, Henry de Lacy, Earl of Pembroke, who had been left in charge of the government in London while the King was campaigning in the north. When the news was officially announced, the public reaction to Edward's death was almost hysterical and unexpected. However enthusiastic they had been for his earlier victories, many English aristocrats had long ago wearied of his constant campaigns and the expense they brought with them. Edward's reputation, once golden, had long ago been soiled internationally by his duplicity after the Maid of Norway's death. His one-time friend, Pope Boniface VIII, had begged Edward to cease his attacks on Scotland 'out of reverence of God, the Apostolic See and ourselves', but Edward had refused.[59] Yet when the Pope heard that Edward was dead, he apparently fell to the floor in grief and many of Edward's subjects reacted similarly. The procession of the old King's body back to London was slowed by crowds gathering to grieve as it passed by and surviving testimonies from 1307 indicate that Edward's death was sincerely mourned by many of his subjects. Comparisons were made to Alexander the Great and the same sobriquet was suggested for Longshanks. In much the same way as he had dressed simply in comparison to his decadent parents, his tomb is stark in comparison to theirs. Edward is buried in Westminster Abbey in a plain sepulchre made entirely of black Purbeck marble. The words EDWARDUS PRIMUS SCOTTORUM MALLEUS HIC EST – 'Edward the First, Hammer of the Scots, is here' – are still visible in faded lettering.

Edward Longshanks took a monarchy that had been humiliated and degraded for the best part of a century and turned it into the most powerful force in Europe. That he achieved this by crushing his neighbours is unsurprising when viewed in the context of medieval warfare, in which right nearly always favoured might. His treatment of the Jewish community was appalling, cruel and extortionate, but it was undoubtedly one of the most popular decisions he ever took. His suppression of Wales solidified his reputation as a powerful monarch and at least initially, it met with the support of many segments of the Welsh population. As Papal and ecclesiastical unease with his actions in Scotland show, the great obsession of Edward's final years divided his contemporaries more than anything else he did, even if the cost and the trouble brought by interfering in Scotland was something his subjects ceased to blame Edward for once he was dead. Edward I involved his empire in more wars than any of his immediate ancestors, but while they were vilified, he was lauded. His subjects' love for him, as evinced at his funeral in 1307, showed that many of them did not want a good king in the way that we might now conceive of goodness. What they wanted was a great king and, on the surface at least, that was what Longshanks gave them.

But the cost of Edward's greatness was crippling and the signs of the damage it was inflicting began to appear in his lifetime. Ireland and England both suffered greatly through the cost of his wars. The great irony in the career of the King associated with trying to unite the British Isles under English rule is that he damned royal rule in Ireland to centuries of instability. Ireland was forced to send over huge amounts of food to feed the English army, first in Wales, then in Scotland and then in France. Even as Ireland slipped into famine, Edward refused to lessen his demands on it for supplies. In return for service in the wars against Scotland, Edward allowed troublesome Irish lords to get away with murder, sometimes quite literally. The Earl of Ulster's debts to the Irish Exchequer, standing at the astronomical figure of £11,000, were simply written off in return for supporting Edward against Robert Bruce. As more and more of the Anglo-Irish settlers were called to fight in the Scottish Wars of Independence, law and order in the English colonies collapsed, unrest erupted in Ulster and Leinster, and in 1297 the Irish had to summon their own parliament in Dublin to take emergency action to restore peace on the island. Crown control contracted to the area around the capital, known as the Pale, and Edward did absolutely nothing to stop it. Before the wars with Scotland, Ireland was an English success story – wealthy, loyal and peaceful. At that time, a visitor had been able to say that Ireland was 'so pacified these days that in no part of the land is there anyone at war, or wishing to go to war, as is known for sure'.[60]

In England, urban crime rose greatly in the second half of Edward's reign and he left his son with a war that could not be won, a former friend turned into a fervent enemy on the northern borders and a country that expected a king to achieve greatness through force of arms.

ENEMIES FOREIGN
AND DOMESTIC

THE FOURTEENTH-CENTURY
MONARCHY

'All live to die, and rise to fall.'

Christopher Marlowe, *Edward II*, Act IV,
scene vii

THE WILTON Diptych is a superb piece of Christian and
monarchist art. A portable religious icon that moved with the
court from one palace to another, the left panel shows Richard II,
King of England at the end of the fourteenth century, gorgeously
robed and prostrate in prayer, flanked by the pontificating figures of
Saint John the Baptist, Saint Edmund the Martyr and, of course,
Saint Edward the Confessor, while the beautiful right panel shows the
Virgin Mary, garbed in blue, holding forth the Christ Child, who in
His turn proffers the English flag to a kneeling King Richard. A court
of blue-clad angels watch on, all wearing badges that show the King's
heraldic crest. Never was the theory behind the Divine Right of
Kings, the sacred contract between God and royalty, more hauntingly

or vividly expressed. Not even *The Apotheosis of King James I* on the ceilings of Whitehall captured it so perfectly. Yet the art, like so much of the gorgeous ceremonial of Richard II's court, belied an ugly reality. Richard was the second fourteenth-century English King to be deposed. The century after his deposition witnessed five more. The kings of England were not so much being handed the flag by Christ as snatching it from His hands. Within a century of Richard's disappearance, the French had taken to joking that the English bore the mark of Cain for the frequency of their regicides.[1]

OUR FRIENDS DO FAIL US ALL

IN 1325, King Edward II, Longshanks' son, spent four days in a row with a sailor called Adam Cogg. While it is highly unlikely that they spent all that time playing Chess, we will never know for certain what went on between them. At the time, his courtiers seemed to find it more upsetting that the King enjoyed the company of the low-born, as opposed to the fact that he might be sleeping with some of them. What went on between the sheets was one thing, but socialising with sailors, barge-masters, carpenters and fishermen was another thing entirely. His kindness to those far beneath him in the hierarchy contrasted painfully to his contempt for many of the aristocrats who thronged his court. One afternoon in 1326, while Edward was helping a group of workmen dig a ditch in Wiltshire, he noticed the poor state of one of the men's shoes, so he turned to a member of his entourage to borrow twelve pence for the chap to buy new footwear.[2] The King later reimbursed the twelve pence and there are numerous examples of similar behaviour.

In the propaganda that justified his downfall after 1327, sly allusions were made about Edward's attraction to his own gender and a grim story even claimed that he had been murdered by having a red-hot poker inserted into his rectum, in a macabre parody of anal sex. This version of the man who ruled England for twenty years has lasted down to the present day, with one modern account of royal adulteries imagining how difficult it must have been for his wife to have 'known only the smooth girlish hands of Edward upon her'.[3] That quote tells us far more about entrenched and unwarranted stereotypes than it does about Edward II. As his courtiers would no doubt have despairingly pointed out, the King's passion for rowing, swimming, thatching roofs, shoeing horses, working in a smith's and digging ditches were likely to have produced hands that were anything other than smooth or 'girlish'.

Alongside suggestions of his effeminate appearance, ludicrous stories about Edward's private life proliferate. Strangely, many of them seem to have appeared in the last two centuries rather than closer to the time, like suggestions he indulged in wife-swapping, allowed one of his male favourites to sexually assault his Queen, or that he handed all of her jewellery over to his lover, Piers Gaveston.

None of these charges have much foundation, yet they all contribute to a pervasive but misleading view that Edward II was dragged off his throne because of the 'perverted sexual dominance' he allowed other men to exert over him.[4]

Like his father, Edward II was tall and robust. The *Vita Edwardi Secundi*, which was an account of the King's life written by a clerk who lived at Edward's court and who recorded his experiences at the time, observed that the King was 'a fine figure of a handsome man', while Sir Thomas Grey, whose father fought in Edward's army, wrote that 'physically he was one of the strongest men in the realm'.[5] Another thought Edward moved well despite his size: 'elegant, of outstanding strength'.[6] None of the eyewitness descriptions of Edward's contradicts one chronicler's description of him as 'fair of body and great of strength'.[7] There are no surviving accounts that mention his eye colour, but illustrations and his effigy all show wavy blond hair that fell either to his chin or his shoulders. Later in life, he grew a beard.

He had a ribald sense of humour. In a letter to a French prince, the Comte d'Évreux, he joked about the sexual prowess of the Welsh, or the 'plenty of wild men' in 'our land of Wales', as he put it.[8] Growing up, he saw little of his parents and was only six when his mother, Eleanor of Castile, died, but he was close to his stepmother Marguerite and he took an interest in helping former servants of Eleanor. Queen Marguerite came to Edward's aid in 1307 when Piers Gaveston, the prince's favourite, was exiled on the old King's orders. The exact nature of Edward's relationship with Gaveston has perplexed scholars, with some cautioning against 'anachronistic and futile' attempts to impose modern concepts of sexuality on the medieval period.[9] However, the contemporary accounts leave little room for reasonable doubt that it was a romantic relationship and while it will always be impossible to verify how far they went sexually or how often, what mattered was that it was a love affair, the great love affair of Edward II's life.[10]

Piers Gaveston was the son of a Gascon knight, born a year or two before Edward II in 1284.[11] His father, Arnaud, had served Edward I in the wars in Gascony, Wales and Scotland, although it was through his mother, Claramonde, that the family acquired most of their wealth. Piers was barely a teenager when he joined his father in combat, where he apparently impressed the King with his manners and skills as a soldier. Shortly after that, Edward I appointed him as one of ten young men to attend on the Prince of Wales to provide him with some suitable company. Gaveston seems to have been the oldest of the ten and that, coupled with his good looks – one contemporary wrote that Gaveston was 'graceful and agile in body, sharp witted, refined in manners [...] well versed in military matters' – his prowess as a jouster and the fact that he had already experienced the battlefield, perhaps explain young Edward's initial infatuation with him.[12]

Infatuation quickly turned into obsession. A clerk in Edward's service wrote, 'I do not remember to have heard that one man so loved another. Jonathan cherished David, Achilles loved Patroclus.'†[13] Another chronicle wrote that after a short separation, Edward ran over to Piers 'giving him kisses and repeated embraces; he was adored with a special familiarity'.[14] In an age when embracing and kissing, even on the lips, was an accepted form of greeting within the upper classes, it was not so much Edward's actions that caused offence as the effusiveness with which they were bestowed. During the last years of the old man's life, Longshanks grew so concerned about the two men's intimacy that he sent Gaveston abroad, still well-provided for but abroad nonetheless, and it was Edward's request to provide Gaveston with an overly generous amount of land that prompted his father to scream, 'You bastard son of a bitch! Now you want to give lands away – you who never gained any? As the Lord lives, were it not for fear of breaking up the kingdom, you would never enjoy your inheritance!' And he began viciously beating him.[15] In a ruthless and mercenary age, the Earl of Pembroke would later remark, 'he perishes on the rocks that loves another man more than himself'.[16] It was a lesson that Edward II never learned.

One of Edward's first acts upon becoming King in 1307 was to summon Gaveston home and at a winter joust held shortly after Edward I's funeral, Gaveston 'very proud and haughty in bearing' carried the day.[17] It was victory at the jousts that apparently helped turn some of the magnates, like the bested Earl of Surrey, against Gaveston. The favour Edward II lavished upon him raised eyebrows and blood pressure. Aristocratic jaws collectively hit the floor when

---

† In the Old Testament, the future King David was the friend of the Israelite prince Jonathan, who ultimately saved his life, while in Greek myth the relationship between Achilles and Patroclus was usually presented as a romance. The ambiguity continues elsewhere in the *Vita*, with the clerk saying that there was no evidence to prove that Edward and Gaveston had ever been 'immoderate' with one another, then going on to say that in this case, Edward seemed incapable of moderation. A platonic example is supplemented by a conclusion with one that suggests romance.

Edward made Gaveston the new Earl of Cornwall, a title that had previously been held by the younger brothers of Henry III and Edward I. Queen Marguerite may have expected the earldom for her eldest son, Thomas, Edward's eight-year-old half-brother. Despite her previous sympathy for the pair, the gentle Dowager Queen had been turned into an enemy and it is possible that the allocation of the Cornwall earldom played a part in that, while the other nobles at Edward's court 'looked down on Piers, because, as a foreigner and formerly a mere man at arms raised to such distinction and eminence, he was unmindful of his former rank'.[18] (Particularly unmindful when he dared to beat them in the tilts, one suspects.) Gaveston was witty and his tongue cut like a scythe. Cocksure, charismatic and eye-wateringly rude, he was clever but he was not wise. He gave scornful nicknames to the earls, the most powerful members of the aristocracy, a closed blue-blooded group of eleven who did not take kindly at having their corpulence mocked, as he did with the rotund Earl of Lincoln, or being publicly referred to by his nicknames for them, including 'the Jew', 'the Actor' or 'the Black Dog'. Piers turned up to the coronation wearing purple, a colour associated with royalty, and he was left in charge of the government when the King visited France in 1308. In a world obsessed with rank and precedence, Gaveston constituted an offensive anomaly. At the coronation banquet, the King's two brothers-in-law, Charles de Valois and Louis d'Évreux, left in protest at the upsetting of etiquette in Gaveston's favour. Further anger came when Edward arranged for Piers to be married to his niece, Margaret de Clare, a more-than advantageous match for the son of a knight.

In 1308, Edward himself was married to his stepmother's niece, Princess Isabella of France. Although she had only just passed the age of consent, it was already clear that Isabella would grow to inherit the good looks of the French royal family. Her father, King Philippe IV, was nicknamed Philippe the Fair, a tribute to his appearance since his personality was that of a ruthless egotist with a predilection for savage cruelty. The girl's mother, Queen Jeanne, was Queen regnant of Navarre. As the daughter of two monarchs, Isabella was a great catch as well as the living seal on the Treaty of Montreuil between her husband and her father. The wedding took place at the Church of Our Lady of Boulogne in January 1308 and Queen Marguerite presented her niece with a solid silver casket, engraved with their respective coats of arms, as a wedding gift. Although aunt and niece were close, Isabella showed no inclination to join the intrigues against Gaveston. However, there is sufficient evidence to support the belief that Marguerite used her influence to help anti-Gaveston nobles pursue their vendetta against him. She secured sizable loans from her brother the King of France for the earls of Lincoln and Pembroke, both of whom were determined to have Gaveston sent into exile for a second time and who were networking behind the scenes to make that happen.[19]

Three months after his marriage, Parliament presented Edward with a declaration asking for Piers Gaveston to be banished and stripped of his title. Faced with united opposition from his peers, Parliament and family, Edward had to acquiesce, but he did so begrudgingly and with minimal sincerity. In return for losing the earldom of Cornwall, Gaveston was appointed Lord Lieutenant of Ireland, a job he executed with great success. The state the island had been left in after Longshanks' dereliction of duty there meant that governing Ireland in the King's name was a thankless task. Gaveston did not succeed in restoring royal authority to the levels it had enjoyed prior to the wars with Scotland. However, he was an effective and honest Lord Lieutenant who oversaw the fortification of vulnerable towns, avoided lining his own pockets, waged successful war in the Wicklow Mountains and, if he did not manage to retake the entire country, he at least solidified English control over the province of Leinster. In the summer of 1309, he was brought back to England and two years later, Edward took him with him on campaign against Scotland. Here Gaveston was far less successful. Edward II is often blamed for losing the Scottish Wars of Independence, but while he was an infinitely less talented general than his father it is unlikely that Longshanks himself would have won even if he had lived longer.

In a climate of military failure and aristocratic unrest, Gaveston was exiled for a third time, but hope triumphed over experience as Edward brought him back two months later. This time, despite their happiness at being reunited, Edward and his favourite were aware of the net tightening around them. In the spring of 1312, they had to vacate Newcastle in a hurry when they were warned that there were forces moving against them. They fatefully chose to briefly separate. The King went to York, while Gaveston made for Scarborough Castle where he was surprised and surrounded by his enemies. He surrendered on condition of safe conduct to York, where he would be allowed to join the King for another round of negotiations. Three of the earls swore a solemn oath that they would answer for his safety and he was placed in the custody of the Earl of Pembroke. Through accident or design, Pembroke was not an effective guardian. The Earl of Warwick managed to kidnap Gaveston from Deddington in Oxfordshire and brought him to Warwick Castle, where he was tried by a panel of his enemies, including the earls of Arundel and Hereford, and the King's cousin, Thomas of Lancaster. Piers was taken to nearby Blacklow Hill, where two Welsh soldiers had been instructed to run him through with their swords before hacking off his head and leaving the body where it fell. A passing group of Dominican friars recovered the corpse and his remains were eventually laid to rest at the priory of Kings Langley, a Dominican house that Edward had founded himself.

Edward II's grief at Piers Gaveston's death can only be imagined and there are signs, not least in the terrible hatred he bore towards his killers, that he never fully recovered from it. For a year after the murder, every Augustinian abbey in England and Ireland was ordered to say a daily Mass for the repose of Gaveston's soul. His funeral at Kings Langley saw the embalmed body dressed in three hundred pounds' worth of cloth of gold. His grave, lost during the iconoclasm of the Reformation, was originally decorated with cloth imported from Byzantium. Even in the last year of his life, fourteen years after Gaveston's, Edward was still conscientious about making arrangements for requiems and prayers for his soul.

Public sympathy was, at least initially, firmly on the King's side. What the earls had done was astonishing and repulsive. Gaveston's death looked more like a lynching than a lawful execution. Even some of the dead man's former enemies, like the Earl of Surrey, were unhappy with what had occurred and Queen Isabella sided completely with her husband. But how to account for the extraordinary venom Piers Gaveston provoked in the other earls while he lived? The most obvious answer is what we would now call homophobia. That was the interpretation taken by Derek Jarman when he directed the 1991 movie Edward II, with Steven Waddington and Andrew Tiernan playing the couple opposite Tilda Swinton as Edward's malicious wife, who allies herself with the worst elements of the puritanical Far Right in order to gain power. The film dramatised Christopher Marlowe's play of the same name and, in order to make the modern parallel work, the nobles surrounding Edward II were shown to be disgusted by his sexuality. As a director, Jarman was less interested in historical accuracy and more in the applicability of the story to Thatcherite Britain, dedicating the film to the repeal of the country's anti-gay laws, which were then so pernicious that they prohibited the discussion of homosexuality in schools even if a child's mental health was at risk.[20] The idea that Gaveston died because he was Edward II's lover is a popular one and it enjoys some support academically.[21] However, medieval attitudes to sexuality were not as simplistic as is commonly supposed and a case could be made for arguing that the problem was the background and prominence, rather than the gender, of the royal favourite.[22]

Gaveston also had the bad luck to be the favourite of a King who inherited a tainted throne from an awe-inspiring father. Surrounded by military failure, economic problems and diplomatic stalemate, the barons and earls vented their frustration on the most convenient scapegoat, the King's right-hand man. Jealousy too must have played a part in what happened, for royal largesse always brings out the green-eyed monster in those excluded from it. That is why the most successful monarchs try to balance their favour between different factions, but Edward II, as the contemporary Vita attests, was incapable of moderation. There were many men and women in history who paid for royal friendship with their lives – Robert Cochrane, favourite of King James III of Scotland, was frog-marched to his own hanging by a group of earls much like Gaveston had been; Philibert Le Vayer, confidante of the future King Henri III of France, was found murdered in an alleyway near the Louvre, possibly with the connivance of the fretful Queen Mother; Mary, Queen of Scots' faithful secretary, David Riccio, was dragged screaming from her presence and stabbed to death by her husband and his aristocratic allies.[23] There was also Concino Concini, a favourite of Marie de Medici, the Duke of Buckingham under Charles I, Dr Johann Streunsee in eighteenth-century Denmark, Marie-Antoinette's beloved Princesse de Lamballe and, of course, Grigori Rasputin, hounded to his death in the last days of Imperial Russia. Gaveston may be one of many royal intimates who was undone not because of what he did, but because he had access to something others wanted.

Finally, personal blame cannot be discounted. The victim's actions may not make the crime excusable, but they may help render it explicable and in Gaveston's case, his arrogance and his insensitivity to others may have helped hasten his end. A palace clerk who witnessed his rise and fall wrote later, 'I therefore believe and firmly maintain that if Piers had from the outset borne himself prudently and humbly towards the magnates of the land, none of them would have opposed him'.[24] Today, a private dining club at the University of Oxford still bears his name but his daughter died young and by the time the earldom of Cornwall was revived, it was once again given to a member of the royal house. The Duchy of Cornwall is now part of the traditional inheritance given to the heir to the throne, an unintentional merging of the titles once held by Edward II and Piers Gaveston.

Edward II did his duty by fathering four children with Queen Isabella who, as she grew older and became a mother, was given more of a say in her husband's government. The birth of an heir, another Edward, at Windsor Castle on 13 November 1312, five months after Gaveston's death, was a personal triumph for the King.[†] The child was followed by a younger brother, John, four years later and two sisters, Eleanor and Joan, in 1318 and 1321. The King briefly attempted to repair his relations with the nobility by resuming the war with Scotland, in the hopes that victory would paper-over the cracks shown by Gaveston's demise. On 24 June 1314, near Stirling, he was surprised to see the opposing Scottish soldiers kneel before his army and joyfully exclaimed that they were prostrating themselves to ask for mercy. A Scotsman in Edward's entourage jolted the King from his naiveté – 'they ask for mercy but not from you. To God they pray, for them it's victory or death.'[25] If that was the Scottish prayer, God answered with the former.

The English failed to break King Robert's front rank and were forced to retreat. Despite possessing a larger army, English losses may have been up to ten or eleven times higher than the Scots' and Edward had to quit the battlefield, providing his critics with the

---

† There is no truth in the oft-repeated historical canard that Edward III was illegitimate or that Edward II could not have been the father of Isabella's children because he had also taken male lovers. Candidates for Edward III's 'real' father include William Wallace, of *Braveheart* fame, who was executed seven years before Edward III was born, when Isabella was under the age of ten and still living in France; Edward I, incredibly, has also been suggested, despite the fact that he died five years before his future daughter-in-law's pregnancy, as has Roger Mortimer, Earl of March, who was living in Ireland. Given Edward II's later fury at Isabella's alleged adultery, if there had been any suspicion against their children's legitimacy, it is not credible that he would have allowed it to pass unpunished.

chance to claim he fled like a coward while his men were slaughtered, although in fact while the fighting continued, he soldiered bravely in the thick of the violence 'like a lioness deprived of her cubs'.[26] The Battle of Bannockburn, which put an end to any serious hope of England re-establishing its influence over an independent Scotland, was later immortalised in the Scottish anthem *Flower of Scotland* and it annihilated Edward II's political credibility.

With Gaveston dead and his army vanquished, it was not until he found a new favourite, Hugh Despenser the Younger, that Edward began to dream of reasserting his own independence. Whether Despenser was Edward's lover or not is unclear, despite Queen Isabella's heavy hints that he was, but in every other way he was like the second coming of Piers Gaveston, with one crucial extra difference. Gaveston may have been cocky and unpopular, but he was never corrupt or violent. Despenser and his father, who became the King's most trusted advisers, were. They were rapacious, domineering and mendacious, replenishing the monarchy's depleted coffers while also enriching themselves and infuriating the aristocracy, who could be forgiven for looking back on the slaughtered Gaveston with something akin to nostalgia.

Galvanised by the Despensers, Edward shook off the restraints placed on him after Bannockburn and ruled with an absolutism that had not been seen in England since the days before Magna Carta. The settling of old scores was his chief priority. His cousin, Thomas of Lancaster, one of the earls who had condemned Piers Gaveston to death, was captured and executed – denied any chance to defend himself at a fair trial, just as Gaveston had been ten years earlier. Of this period in Edward's life, one writer ruled, 'it would not be too much of an exaggeration to say that, between them, Edward and Despenser subjected the country to a reign of terror.'[27] That assessment does go too far, however, and by a long way, particularly when the governments of the French Revolution, Soviet Union, Third Reich, Maoist China and the Khmer Rouge taught and practised what government-by-terror authentically was. Edward II's actions do not even compare unfavourably to some of the things habitually carried out under William the Conqueror or his own father. It was, however, a tyranny in that it was an unaccountable regime that placed self-interest before the national good and it was deeply resented. It also began to place a strain on the previously relatively successful royal marriage.

In March 1325, Edward sent his twenty-nine-year-old wife to Paris to negotiate a treaty with her brother, King Charles IV. One palace servant mused, 'she will not (so many think) return until Hugh Despenser is wholly removed from the king's side'.[28] Isabella asked for her eldest son to join her in Paris for the ceremonies to mark the end of the talks. Since the King could not go himself, he agreed. Isabella now had the heir at her side, her most valuable bargaining chip and, as predicted, she refused to return. In December, some of her servants quit her service in disgust and returned to England, bringing with them news that Isabella had taken a lover in the form of the thirty-six-year-old Roger Mortimer, a 'vigorous man', a former ward of Piers Gaveston's and the man who had eventually succeeded him as Lord Lieutenant of Ireland.[29] In Ireland, Mortimer had acquired a reputation for great military skill, driving an invading Scottish force back into the sea at Carrickfergus and suppressing threats to English control from the western province of Connacht. He subsequently turned his talents to attacking the Despensers' estates in Wales, for which Edward had him arrested and thrown in the Tower of London. The resourceful Mortimer drugged his gaolers by lacing their wine with a sedative, stole the keys and escaped across the Channel to France, where he joined, and seduced, the Queen.

Dubbed a she-wolf by eighteenth-century historians, Isabella has enjoyed a kinder press in the twentieth and twenty-first, but it is perhaps going too far to describe her as 'a dutiful and highly religious woman [...] a woman of conscience'.[30] Although she was not responsible for mass bloodshed, her actions between 1325 and 1330 show that she was every inch her father's daughter – ruthless, clever and often selfish. Perhaps the best modern assessment of her comes from one of her son's biographers, Bryan Bevan, when he described her as 'a woman of beauty and charm and some intelligence, but she was passionate, querulous and a cunning dissembler'.[31] All of these traits were on display in 1325 and 1326, when she and Mortimer raised an army to invade England with the ostensible aim of forcing the King to part with the Despensers. However, by keeping her son at her side Isabella made it clear that her ultimate goal must have been the hitherto-unthinkable task of replacing an anointed Sovereign. Publicly she maintained that her quarrel was solely with Despenser the

Younger, but Edward II did not believe her and his surviving letters to his son in Paris reveal his fury at the Queen's conduct. 'Edward, fair son,' he wrote, 'you are of tender age, take our commandments tenderly to heart, and so rule your conduct with humility, as you would escape our grief and indignation and advance your own interest and honour. Believe no counsel that is contrary to the will of your father'. In another letter, he raged against Isabella's 'devious pretences' and left the young prince in little doubt about the state of his mother's private life, writing that Isabella 'openly, notoriously and knowing it to be contrary to her duty and against the welfare of our crown, has attached to herself and retains in her company the Mortimer, our traitor and mortal foe and worse than this can be, in allowing you to consort with our said enemy and you openly to herd and associate with him in the sight of all the world, doing so great a villainy and dishonour both to yourself and us, to the prejudice of our Crown and of the laws and customs of our realm, which you are supremely bound to hold, preserve and maintain'.[32] Prince Edward's misery at the situation he found himself in only became clear much later. At the time, he was powerless to prevent his mother launching an invasion of England in his name in September 1326.

Edward II and the Despensers were so unpopular that Isabella had no difficulty in raising the country against them. Everywhere she went she was greeted with cries of acclamation, with the exception of Wales, which remained relatively loyal to Edward, 'their' prince, born at Caernarfon. With Edward swiftly routed, his wife had to figure out how to retrospectively justify the deposition of a King. She hit upon the Articles of Accusation, which listed all the faults committed by Edward II during his time as monarch and cited them as the reason why his wife and magnates had betrayed him. Having gone so far, however, even Isabella and her supporters could not quite bring themselves to be the reason why Edward II was replaced with Edward III. Perhaps she knew what long-term damage she was inflicting to solve a short-term problem and wanted to avoid establishing the precedent whereby kings could simply be removed when they ceased to be popular. The final decision must come from Edward II himself. It had to be, or rather it had to look, voluntary and pressure was duly applied to persuade him of the merits of abdication. It is said that he sobbed at the humiliation of having the Articles of Accusation read aloud in his presence, but in January 1327 he stepped aside in favour of his eldest child. Nobody was blinded by the word abdication and a cartoon drawn shortly afterwards showed a queen standing at the centre of Fortune's wheel, turning it to install new kings and depose old ones.

Nine months after his abdication Edward II vanished. The new regency government, headed by Mortimer and Isabella, claimed that Edward had died of a grief-related illness on 21 September, the feast day of Saint Matthew the Evangelist. The news reached the adolescent King at Lincoln three days later, who told his cousin 'my father has been commanded to God'.[33] But few believed the Queen regent and her lover. The lawyer Adam Murimuth, who had once worked for the former King, wrote later that Edward had been dead for over a week by the time the official announcement was made and 'it was commonly said that [...] he was craftily killed.'[34] It has already been mentioned that the story claiming he was murdered by having a red-hot poker inserted into his anus is untrue. More recently, Kathryn Warner has put forward the idea that he may have been drugged and then smothered.[35] Mortimer had a working knowledge of sedatives and given Edward II's physical strength, his murderers would have needed to quieten him before attacking. One chronicle claimed that he had been fed terrible food for weeks beforehand, in the hope of weakening him.[36] The rationale for committing the terrible sin of regicide, spilling the quasi-sacred blood which justified Isabella's place in society as much as her husband's, sprang from panic when Edward briefly escaped his captivity. The regency needed to ensure that did not happen again. Edward's body was taken to Gloucester Cathedral, where stories of his lonely death soon obliterated criticism of him and brought pilgrims to pray at the grave of their martyr-King.

But was he really there? Ian Mortimer, a biographer of both Edward III and Roger Mortimer, has recently resurrected the idea that Edward II was not murdered on 27 September 1327 but that he was in fact smuggled abroad, via Ireland, received sanctuary at the Papal court and lived in obscurity, probably dying some time around 1341.[37] This version of events is not nearly so absurd at it sounds. An extraordinary letter written by Manuel Fieschi, the future Bishop of Vercelli, relates this version of Edward II's life after September 1327 and so far no historian has been able to satisfactorily prove how Fieschi came by his information.[38] From about 1327 until 1343, Fieschi worked as a notary to the Papal court where, according to his own narrative, Edward II had been granted asylum. The problem with Fieschi's intriguing account is that there is no other evidence that firmly corroborates it and the image of Edward II wandering around western Europe disguised as a pilgrim perhaps stretches credulity beyond its limits. Yet the theory that Edward II did not die on 27 September 1327 in his cell at Berkeley Castle cannot lightly be dismissed. In 1330, his younger brother Edmund, Earl of Kent, attempted to lead a rebellion against Roger Mortimer and Queen Isabella on the grounds that Edward II was still alive. This was a belief apparently shared by William Melton, Archbishop of York. That two men so close to the throne both believed Edward II was still living in 1329 or 1330, and going so far as to specify that he had been moved to captivity at Corfe Castle in Dorset, lends credence to the theory that he was not killed in 1327 and, at that juncture, Isabella had still recoiled from the idea of shedding royal blood. If Edward II had been left alive after 1327, it is possible that his brother's attempts to overthrow Isabella prompted her to take decisive action and that Edward II therefore died circa 1330. This would explain why both the Earl of Kent and the Archbishop of York believed Edward II was still alive and it would explain some, but not all, of the inconsistencies in the official version of events.

Obviously, none of this conclusively proves that Edward II survived the year of his abdication and a healthy scepticism should always be maintained. It is possible to square some of the circles in the story, while still adhering to the traditional date of Edward II's death. The murder was carried out at Berkeley Castle in September 1327 and the news reached his son three days later, a suspiciously short time to travel the distance between Berkeley and Lincoln, not because it was a lie but because it was pre-arranged by his killers. Or, as Adam Murimuth believed, perhaps Edward had actually already been dead for several days before the twenty-seventh. Later, as Roger Mortimer became more unpopular, other members of the royal family, like the Earl of Kent, began to plot against him. Hoping to push his enemies into committing an open act of treason against the new regime, Mortimer deliberately orchestrated a campaign of misinformation which tricked them into believing that Edward II was alive at Corfe.

Whatever happened to Edward II, and the riddle may never satisfactorily be resolved unless his tomb at Gloucester Cathedral is broken open, a habit that the current Sovereign is loath to condone lest it lead to the mass-desecration of royal resting places, Mortimer and Isabella did not waste much time in making themselves every inch as unpopular as the government they had replaced. Like Simon de Montfort in the previous century, their selfishness, their dishonesty and their greed cost them the goodwill that had given them power in the first place. Isabella did not help her reputation by attending the brutal execution of Hugh Despenser in 1326, which involved him being hanged, drawn, castrated and quartered before her and a large crowd, while she and her ladies enjoyed a picnic in the viewing gallery. Despenser had tried to starve himself in gaol to avoid the indignity of a public death and his stoicism lasted until he began to be hacked to pieces, at which point an inhuman cry was said to have escaped his lips.

Mortimer, now Earl of March for his pains, has not enjoyed a good historical press namely because any defence would be hopeless. His success as Lord Lieutenant of Ireland was the high point of his career, which otherwise seems to have existed solely to further his insatiable ambition. Writing of him in 2004, R. R. Davies hit the proverbial nail on the head when he concluded that nearly all of Mortimer's actions show 'that he was, ultimately, a man without political principle or political judgement.'[39] His rule was corrupt, decadent and detested. He dominated and bullied the young King he had installed on the throne. Queen Isabella appeared to be nothing more than the greedy dupe of her rapacious lover. Edward III wrote coded letters to the Holy See complaining of his lack of power at Mortimer's hands. The latter tried to separate Edward III from the gallant young bloods he was friends with, who dreamed of saving and serving their King as the brotherhood of the Round Table had once served and saved King Arthur. As one of this bunch, William Montagu, was dragged away by Mortimer's men, he managed to whisper some advice to the King: 'It is better to eat the dog than be eaten by the dog.'[40]

Montagu euthanized the dog when he and his companions snuck into Nottingham Castle one night through a secret passageway, known only to a few loyal servants, who had deliberately unbolted the door earlier that evening. The young knights killed a steward who tried to raise the alarm, and took Mortimer as he rushed to defend himself. He was taken away to the sound of Isabella's screams echoing through the castle's corridors as she begged her son, feigning sleep nearby, to show mercy to Mortimer. He did not. The fallen Earl was tied to a horse and dragged to face trial and subsequent execution for treason. Isabella was packed off to the countryside for a few years of rural rustication before she was accepted back into the bosom of the royal family, who maintained that she had been Mortimer's unwilling victim. Despite what she had done, her children evidently adored her and relationships are often a good deal more complicated and surprising than outsiders may appreciate. Before she died in 1358, Isabella certainly proved this by requesting to be buried with the embalmed heart of the husband she had deposed and who it is often claimed she found repulsive, with her corpse clothed in 'the tunic and mantle of red silk lined with grey cindon in which she had been married'.[41] Or, to use the modern equivalent, her wedding dress.

THE GLORY OF THE ENGLISH

PIERS GAVESTON, Thomas, Earl of Lancaster, Hugh Despenser and his father, King Edward II, Edmund, Earl of Kent and Roger Mortimer, Earl of March, had all perished in the tit-for-tat vindictiveness between Crown and nobility in the early fourteenth century. Edward III came to the throne determined to put an end to that dolorous trend by wedding the nobility closer to the throne than it had been at any point since the conquest of 1066. The sword that gleamed for Edward III, even more so than any for any of his Arthur-dazzled ancestors, was Excalibur, symbol of that potent myth endlessly repeated in the chivalric romances devoured by the young men and women of the upper classes, of Camelot, knights, great quests, bold deeds and the fraternity of the Round Table. Edward would bind his nobles to him as Arthur had done. His charisma had already been sufficient to persuade a small group of friends to risk life and limb for him by attacking Roger Mortimer. They would be his brothers-in-arms who won victories on the battlefield and pursued glory together, rather than petty self-aggrandisement. What made the policy so successful was that it does not seem to have been a cynical ploy on Edward III's behalf. He genuinely believed it.

The Most Noble Order of the Garter was founded by Edward III to foster this self-perpetuating culture of noblesse oblige. Its headquarters were at Windsor Castle, which was rebuilt and expanded by Edward at enormous cost – one estimate stated that the renovations carried out by Edward III at Windsor exceeded the amount spent by Edward I on four of his castles in Wales.[42] Every year, on the feast day of Saint George, all twenty-four members of the Order are supposed to meet at Windsor to attend a service in Saint George's Chapel and since its foundation under Edward, the Order has remained the highest honour that can be bestowed upon a subject of the British Crown. As a gift, membership remains part of the Sovereign's prerogative and the Order retains the insignia and motto of Edward's day, *Honi soit qui mal y pense*, Middle French for 'Shamed be he who thinks badly of it'. The legend of how the motto was chosen, alongside the Order's unusual name, told that one night Edward was dancing with a young countess, whose garter fell from under her dress during a particularly energetic move. Rather than have the lady's reputation besmirched by those who suggested her garter must be lose for some other reason, Edward gallantly picked up the garter and proclaimed '*Honi soit qui mal y pense*'. It was a chivalrous gesture and one cannot help but hope that it is true.[43] The creation of the Order of the Garter, with its overtones of Camelot and the Round Table, prompted a wave of copycat chivalric orders in other Christian monarchies.

At Edward's court, frequent jousting tournaments kept his knights in shape and allowed them to hone their martial skill, while adhering to the intricate codes of social etiquette created by the cult of chivalry. Music, poetry, architecture and arts flourished at court and, in his bid to re-ennoble the nobility, Edward introduced the title of duke. It is still the highest rank available to a member of the British aristocracies. In the fourteenth century, it had existed for the nobles of France, but not of England.[†] Prior to that, earl and its female equivalent, countess, had been the top rank. The new title was bestowed on all five of Edward III's surviving sons – Edward, Lionel, John, Edmund and Thomas. However, lest the old guard of the nobility be offended by the new rung, it was also given to some of Edward's closest comrades in arms, who were elevated from their previous rank of earl.

Edward's wars were excoriated by later historians, particularly those of the Whig tradition in the nineteenth century, who characterised him as an egomaniacal warmonger who put pursuit of glory before the good of his people, but that is to completely misread the mood of the mid-fourteenth century. When Edward and his men scored victories against the Scots at the battles of Dupplin Moor and Halidon Hill, the general feeling was that he had removed the stain of Bannockburn. Four years after victory at Halidon Hill, Edward III launched his kingdom into the longest-running war in human history and it is that in particular which caused nineteenth-century liberals to paint him in such a negative light. At the time, no one could have predicted that the war would last on-and-off for one hundred and sixteen years. Furthermore, few in England questioned that their

† In decreasing order, the titles today are duke, marquess, earl, viscount (introduced in 1440) and baron; or duchess, marchioness, countess, viscountess and baroness. The introduction of the rank of marquess, from the French *marquis*, was more problematic. One of Edward III's grandsons, Richard II, briefly introduced it by bestowing the title of Marquess of Dublin on the de Vere family in 1385, but another, Henry IV, discontinued the practice on the grounds that the title was an alien one to the English nobility. The half-French King Henry VI restored its use in 1442 and Henry VIII's French-educated wife, Anne Boleyn, enjoyed the rank in her own right after a ceremony at Windsor Castle in September 1532.

King was justified in taking up arms to pursue his claim to the French crown.

It was that claim, via his mother Isabella, which made Edward III's wars with France so different to those fought by his ancestors. Edward was not fighting to secure English control in Normandy, now long gone, or Gascony and the Aquitaine. He was not invading France in the hope of expanding English influence in the region. He was invading it because he believed that he should possess the country itself. He wanted to rule over France in the same way he ruled over England and he believed, emphatically, that he had every right to do so. The fact that England's monarchs kept calling themselves the rightful kings and queens of France until the French Revolution persuaded George III that it was no longer necessary makes the claim seem an exercise in ego and royal imagination not too dissimilar to Philip II of Spain's claim to be the rightful King of Jerusalem in the sixteenth century. However, in 1337, there were many who believed that Edward III should and could become the next King of France.

Twenty-three years earlier, Edward's grandfather, Philippe the Fair, had died to be followed by his son and Edward's uncle, King Louis X. Louis had set in motion the abolition of serfdom in his country and allowed the readmission of Jews to the kingdom, but he lasted less than two years on the throne before he died, leaving behind a pregnant widow, Queen Clementia. Unlike poor Yolanda of Scotland in the previous century, Clementia produced a living son, dubbed King Jean the Posthumous. But the child lived for less than a week and he was succeeded by his uncle, King Philippe V, who died leaving four daughters and no sons, to be followed by his younger brother, King Charles IV. He reigned for six years before also dying in his thirties and leaving a pregnant widow. This pregnancy resulted in the birth of a princess, which led technically to a change of dynasty as the dead King's cousin, Philippe de Valois, took the throne as King Philippe VI. This run of dynastic ill-fortune stoked a rumour that a curse had been placed upon the Capetian line, the French ruling house, by the last Grand Master of the Knights Templar, a crusading order of monks who had been framed on charges of heresy, robbed of their wealth, persecuted, tortured and executed by Philippe the Fair. Apparently, as he burned to death in front of Philippe's eyes, Grand Master Jacques de Molay proclaimed that God would avenge his wrongful death. Philippe the Fair passed away within the year and all his sons died without sons of their own, bringing to an end the direct line of the Capetian kings.

Edward III's mother had been a Capetian princess and, although the French had recently reaffirmed Salic Law, by which only men could inherit the crown, there was still some disagreement over whether Salic Law also invalidated inheritance through the female line. Edward argued that it did not. Therefore, although his mother could not rule in her own right, she could pass her claim on to her children. In the Anglo-Irish monarchy and nobility, one's maternal ancestry was held to be of equal importance to the paternal, as the accession of Henry II had shown in 1154. As far as they were concerned, the death of all four of Queen Isabella's brothers and her infant nephew meant that her son Edward should succeed before a cousin, like Philippe de Valois.† Edward and his armies landed in France where they won one of the most impressive military victories of the century at the Battle of Crécy, despite being outnumbered. King Philippe VI was wounded and his ally, King Jan of Bohemia, was killed. Apparently, as he was facing death, Jan cried out, 'With God's help, it will never be that a Bohemian king will run from a fight!' Edward appreciated the courage of his enemies.

Back in England, church services praying for further victories and a Parliament regularly consulted about taxation to fund the King's wars created a political culture invested in supporting everything that Edward did. Support for the King, the war and the nation were symbiotic. On the back of his triumphs, trade increased, the economy expanded and the population grew.

But in 1348, the Black Death struck Europe. Plague epidemics were a hazard of life in medieval Europe and they occurred with varying degrees of severity at frequent intervals, but nothing ever approached the scale of the Black Death. Tumours appeared on the groin or the armpits to spread across the body, turning black and oozing puss, what Boccaccio called 'the infallible token of approaching death'. At a conservative estimate, in the course of two years, one third of the population of Western Europe perished. Graveyards could not cope with the number of bodies, so mass burial pits had to be dug across the continent. An Italian survivor recalled that, 'great pits were dug and piled with the multitude of the dead. And they died by the hundreds, both day and night, and all were thrown in those ditches and covered

† Ironically, by this criteria, Charles II, King of Navarre, a grandson of King Louis X through the female line, arguably had a stronger claim to the throne than Edward III.

with earth. And as soon as those ditches were filled, more were dug. And I, Agnolo di Tura, buried my five children with my own hands.'[44] Within eighteen months of reaching the kingdom, it had wiped out between one third and a half of the English population. Among the most famous of the early victims was Edward III's fifteen-year-old daughter Joan, who died in the city of Bayonne on her way to marry Pedro, the future King of Castile.

In the aftermath of the Black Death, the collective mood was hysterical. At its peak, there were many who believed that the horror was so widespread that it marked the opening stage of the Apocalypse. On the continent, over two hundred Jewish settlements were attacked in pogroms that blamed them for bringing the misfortune to Christians. Gypsies, lepers and even those who suffered from psoriasis were not exempt from the climate of recrimination and persecution. Among those who survived the plague, hedonism or morbid piety were common. The experience of Christianity itself began to change. The growth in the number of chantries, institutions set up solely to pray for the souls of the Dead, reflected the shattered psyche of the nation. The cult of the Virgin Mary as Our Lady of Sorrows, the Mater Dolorosa, her heart pierced by seven swords symbolising the grieves she endured at the martyrdom of her Son, as per Simeon's prophecy in Saint Luke's gospel, became a phenomenon, with devotion to it mushrooming throughout the traumatised parishes of Western Christendom.[45] Alongside it there appeared increasingly graphic crucifixes, Christ in His death throes, His agony making Him eternally at-one with His suffering people, as well as carvings of the danse macabre, intertwined putrefying grinning corpses, supplemented by homilies and manuals that stressed the inevitable nature of death and the reality of the pains of Purgatory far more so than at any previous point in the Middle Ages.

In the terrestrial world, the holocaust shattered the social status quo. Before the pandemic, labourers had been plentiful and as a result labour was cheap. Afterwards, the aristocracy and gentry found it impossible to maintain serfdom; there were now so few skilled labourers and farmhands that they began to leave the aristocratic demesnes to search for better jobs and higher wages. Edward's government introduced laws that fixed labourers' wages at the levels set prior to the Black Death, citing as justification 'because a great part of the people, and especially the workmen and servants, late died of the pestilence, many seeing the [...] great scarcity of servants, will not serve unless they may receive excessive wages'.[46] Regardless, social mobility increased and one landowner complained of seeing dozens of people dressing like the class above them had done before the plague or, as he put it, 'asses now took it upon themselves to enjoy jewelled saddles'.[47] Sumptuary Laws were passed to reinforce social distinctions. Female servants and their daughters were banned from wearing any veil that cost more than twelve pence, the wives of skilled craftsmen or yeomen were not allowed to wear veils made from silk, fur was allowed for members of a knight's family if they had an annual rental income over two hundred marks, but the same class were forbidden to wear velvet, labourers' wives could not garnish any of their clothes with silver, and purple silk and cloth of gold were preserved solely for members of the royal family. An outward sign of collective neuroses, the Sumptuary Laws reflected a society in flux, as the rigidity of the pre-plague hierarchy fell apart.

The glory of the first half of Edward III's reign thus gave way to the long malaise of his second. The death of his Queen in 1369 made the rot more evident, as without her watchful influence, standards began to slip at Edward's once-perfect court. The second daughter of the Count of Hainault and Holland, Philippa of Hainault had been at Edward's side for over forty years and they had a dozen children together. A dignified and religious lady, she had been the perfect consort for someone like Edward. She died in her apartments at Windsor Castle on the Feast of the Assumption, with the King and their youngest son, Thomas, at her side. She held her husband's hand as she slipped away and the King, 'very sorrowful at heart', granted her three final requests – that he should settle any debts she might owe, make bequests on her behalf to her servants and churches, and that they would one day be buried together at Westminster. Later, she made the sign of the cross and, according to one account, 'gave up her spirit, which I firmly believe was caught by the Holy Angels and carried to glory in Heaven for she had never done anything by thought or deed which could endanger her losing it.'[48]

Although Edward had affairs during his wife's lifetime, he respected her and their shared vision of a glorious monarchy too much to flaunt them. With Philippa gone and his own prowess failing as he grew older, Edward fell under the influence of a new mistress called Alice Perrers. Alice's ego was of equal size to her greed, which is to say enormous. Her acquisition of land, manors, jewels and pensions made the King look like feeble putty in her hands. Her endless pretensions, such as referring to herself as 'the Lady of the Sun', embarrassed where they did not enrage. The King's eldest daughter-in-law, Joan of Kent, called 'the Fair Maid of Kent' for her beauty, took particular umbrage at the fact that her own position as first lady of the court was being usurped by the vulgar and curiously unattractive Perrers. Tacky and unlikable, as the French wars resumed, Alice became a liability. With or without her, Edward III would have struggled to fight Time itself, but her presence at his side gave the appearance of a doddering old King neglecting his duty to pursue a greedy arriviste who was fleecing him for all he was worth. Parliament once again became the hotbed of unrest and factionalism it had been in years gone by, with the Parliament of 1367 moving to impeach some of the King's advisers and launching bitter criticisms of Edward's mistress.

Edward III made it to one last ceremony for the Order of the Garter on Saint George's Day 1377. During an earlier audience with representatives of the city of London, the only way the King could make it through was to be swathed in cloth of gold and muslin, a kind of adult swaddling clothes, and quite literally nailed onto his throne, with nails piercing his robes to keep him upright. The King's mind slipped from lucidity to dementia and back again. In a secret audience, he urged civic leaders from London to construct an enormous candle bearing the crest of the King's eldest surviving son, the Duke of Lancaster, process it through the streets of the city to burn before a statue of the Mother of God. He was at Sheen Palace on 21 June 1377 when he suffered a stroke and lost the power of speech. It is said that as he lay dying, Alice Perrers removed the rings from his fingers and kept them for herself.[49] At the very end, she too left and the King was alone, save for the company of a priest, who soothed his final moments with talk of God's mercy, repentance and the life to come.

Death can wipe away many of the ambiguities of life and Edward III's was no exception. Gone were the uncertainties and troubles of the last decade along with the memory of the half-dead statue nailed into his throne. It was the victorious warrior and the founder of the Garter who was celebrated and mourned in 1377. By the standards of his own generation, Edward III was one of, if not the, greatest kings in the Middle Ages. The splendour and lustre he brought to the English Crown were all the more remarkable considering the awful circumstances in which his reign began. Undiluted praise was heaped upon the dead man as his grandson succeeded to the throne as Richard II and on his grave at Westminster, these words are inscribed:

> Here lies the glory of the English, the flower of kings past, the pattern for kings to come, a merciful king, a bringer of peace to his people, Edward III, who attained his jubilee. The undefeated warrior, a second Maccabeus, who prospered while he lived, revived sound rule, and reigned valiantly; now may he attain his heavenly crown.[50]

SHAMELESS FIRE WAS THUS MIXED WITH SACRED FLAME

GEOFFREY CHAUCER, the son of a London-based merchant, began his career in royal service as a messenger boy for Elizabeth de Burgh, Countess of Ulster, who subsequently married Edward III's son Lionel, Duke of Clarence. From there the adventurous young man, whose time in the Duke's service saw him briefly taken hostage during the French wars, moved deeper into the royal family's orbit, using his literary skills to eulogise the King and Queen's lovely daughter-in-law Blanche after her death in 1368. Proximity to the royals was solidified when his wife's sister, Katherine Swynford, became the mistress of Blanche's widower John of Gaunt, Duke of Lancaster. Katherine bore the prince several bastards before the couple married and retrospectively legitimised their offspring.

Chaucer was still an upwardly mobile successful courtier, with writing a passion on the side, when he began to pen poetry in honour of England's new Queen, Anne of Bohemia. After evening garden parties at the Queen's favourite residences at Eltham and Sheen, Chaucer wrote of a princess weaving her way through the guests wearing a crown shaped to resemble a garland of flowers, its decorative daisies crafted from pearls and gold. The eldest of the six children from Emperor Charles IV's marriage to his fourth wife, Elisabeth of Pomerania, Anne's father ruled over most of central Europe and roughly half of the continent's population as Holy Roman Emperor. Her childhood, which began in Prague, had left her with an indelibly imperial interpretation of kingship. She helped bring that attitude to England where she and her husband, King Richard II, presided over a court that glittered with sumptuous ceremonial. Etiquette was turned into an art form, an elaborate and complicated political dance with the King and Queen in the starring roles. Deportment was compulsory, manners strict and pageantry, even when surrounding seemingly trivial everyday moments such as the royal family's mealtimes, was constant. Bejewelled cutlery was introduced alongside gastronomic delights boasting the latest spices and recipes, as silent courtiers, decked out in ruinously expensive finery, watched their masters eat. Fashion at Richard II's court was dedicated to showing off the male physique – tights accentuated muscles well-toned from hunting or jousting, high-necked robes complemented broad shoulders, while the arrival of the codpiece obviously drew attention to the most prized attribute. Queen Anne and her European entourage also pioneered riding side-saddles for ladies, as well as modish continental conceits like shoes for men that were so long and pointed they required golden chains buckled to the knees to hold their curls upright. Anne, shimmering from head to toe, was doted upon by her husband, who built her a bathhouse, a painted audience chamber and a new ballroom in her favourite home, along with a private lavatory decorated with two thousand painted tiles.

Richard II, fair-haired and softly handsome, and Anne of Bohemia, by no means a great beauty but with a regal presence and a 'gentle and pretty' face, gazed down at their courtiers from the remote plinths on which they had installed themselves as icons of absolutism, the venerated custodians of the Plantagenet legacy.[51] Yet Richard II's reign had begun in trauma when the nine-year-old prince inherited the throne on his grandfather's death in 1377. His own father, Edward, Prince of Wales, had predeceased him and the regency was passed to his uncle, John of Gaunt.

The after-effects of the Black Death and the government's attempts to shore-up the faltering social hierarchy had produced resentful fear in the upper classes and simmering fury in their lower. The war with France stumbled on, feeding on most of the kingdom's revenue, with victories like Crécy a faint-remembered dream, replaced by the reality of, at best, stalemate punctuated by the occasional defeat that left the southern coastal counties open to intermittent raids by French-backed pirates and the northern shires watchful for invasion by France's Scottish ally. Social unrest was compounded by spiritual turmoil as the Church leadership spat venom at challenges to its authority in the form of Lollardy and Wycliffitism, schools of thought that emerged from the debates of theologians at Oxford and flowed outward, demanding an end to clerical corruption, the secularisation of Church estates and a simpler form of worship. Unsurprisingly, the cash-strapped John of Gaunt cast covetous eyes on the Church's wealth but his household's flirtation with Lollardy (who could forget Chaucer's memorably foul Pardoner, an avaricious con-artist peddling false relics and redemption-for-a-price pardons, in *The Canterbury Tales*?) came to a swift end when the movement began to question core Catholic doctrines, such as the miracle of Transubstantiation, the moment at Mass when the elevated Host (bread and wine) became the literal spiritual embodiment of the body and blood of Jesus Christ.

Nor did the regent's personal unpopularity help quiet stormy seas. From his enormous London home, the Savoy Palace, John of Gaunt was perceived as a bullying megalomaniac pursuing the war for reasons of personal aggrandisement and mismanaging everything he turned to. The House of Commons detested him as, in the words of one contemporary, 'their most hated enemy of all mortal men'.[52] While contemporary criticism of the Duke does seem to have been too harsh with the benefit of hindsight, there can be no doubt that he was dealt a bad hand that he proceeded to play poorly. The financial demands of the war prompted several attempts to introduce one of the recurring eruption points of English history – a poll tax. The tax, which played no small part in bringing down the premiership of Margaret Thatcher as recently as 1989 and 1990, levies a fixed charge equally against everyone in the country, regardless of their economic situation or, as Parliament put it under Richard II, a payment 'to be given from each person of the realm [...] both male and female and of whatsoever estate or condition, who have reached the age of fifteen'.[53]

The poll taxes provided a spark to the fuse and by the spring of 1381, the country was on fire with a revolt that had spread from Yorkshire to Kent. Wat Tyler, of whom little is known prior to the uprising, emerged as its most prominent leader, while the radical priest, John Ball, preached sermons that attacked both the Church and the upper classes as the chief architects of national misery. Social hierarchy itself was denounced as fundamentally unjust, a perversion of Christian principles, a view best captured in the rebels' cry of, 'When Adam delf and Eve span / Who was then a gentleman?'[54]

Despite these ideological undercurrents, the Peasants' Revolt was an explosion not a movement, but what an explosion it proved to be. On the Feast of Corpus Christi in June, a festival that usually saw street theatre and civic celebrations around a procession in honour of the Eucharist, the rebellion breached the capital, where they launched an attack on the regent's palace at the Savoy, burning it to the ground along with anything else they came into contact with, including churches. The streets ran red with blood as the rebels broke into religious institutions to drag foreign merchants who had sought sanctuary there into the streets to hack them to pieces for taking English jobs and making money in England when they themselves had not. John Gower, a landowner from Kent, wrote, 'it was Thursday, the Festival of Corpus Christi, when madness hemmed in every side of the city. [Tyler was] supported by his many men, he crushed the city, put the citizens to the sword, and burned down the houses. He did not sing out alone, but drew many thousands along with him, and involved them in his nefarious doings. His voice gathered the madmen together, and with cruel eagerness for slaughter he shouted in the ears of the rabble, 'Burn! Kill!' [...] Holy buildings burned in wicked fire, and shameless flame was thus mixed with sacred flame. The astonished priests wept with trembling heart and fear [...]'[55]

From her rooms, the King's widowed mother could hear the screams of those dying in the streets and when the uprising broke through into the Tower of London, one of Joan's ladies-in-waiting was raped while royal councillors, including Simon Sudbury, Archbishop of Canterbury, were dragged from the fortress to be publicly executed on Tower Hill. The prelate had dashed into the sombre cool of the Tower's chapel of Saint John the Evangelist, which dated from the reign of the Conqueror, where he began intoning the opening cry of the Prayers for the Dead. The chapel was breached and 'those limbs of Satan laid their impious hands on him', as one outraged chronicler recalled.[56] Apparently, the last words the Archbishop managed to utter were 'Omnes sancti orate pro nobis...' ('All the saints, pray for us...') On Tower Hill, it took eight blows of the axe to hack through the Archbishop's neck. Back inside, John of Gaunt's fourteen-year-old son Henry was only saved from being lynched when a loyal guardsman hid him from the crowds.

London's elite were thrown into blind panic by the horrors unfolding in front of them. Most of the nobility and the gentry seemed to regard the self-organisation of peasants into a political movement as a development only marginally less shocking than if French invaders had sailed up the Thames on the backs of choreographed dancing whales. The fourteen-year-old King took matters into his own hands by visiting the shrine of Saint Edward the Confessor at Westminster Abbey, where the traumatised priests and monks, still reeling from the Archbishop's execution, watched as pious, receptive tears poured down the young monarch's face while he prayed. He then went into the abbey's gardens where he consulted with an anchorite, who heard his confession and blessed him before he rode with a large entourage through the smoking destruction in London to Smithfield, just across

London Bridge, to parlay with the rebels. Those who accompanied the King, including London's mayor William Walworth, donned body armour beneath their robes, despite the sweltering heat. As they moved towards Smithfield, soldiers were deployed along the city walls in case the King lost the day and Tyler ordered a second attack on the capital.

The rebels on one side of the field faced the sceptical royalists on the other as Tyler's horse trotted forward. Tyler enraged the spectators by taking the King's arm, the era's equivalent of a handshake, a suggestion of equality that stiffened the spine of everyone behind the young King. He too ignored the suffocating temperature by refusing to remove his thick woollen hat, lest it be interpreted as a sign of deference to the courtiers. Richard held his nerve, even as his questions about what Tyler wanted angered the older man, who began to swear and rage as he articulated a list of fantastic impossibilities that essentially demanded a return to the political structure that had existed (or been imagined to exist) under Alfred the Great, as well as the total abolition of the Catholic Church's hierarchy in England. In the words of one history of the Peasants' Revolt, 'What could Richard reply? This was not a negotiating position. It was the fantasy of a madman.'[57]

Tyler took a drink of a water and spat some of it out, a gesture some interpreted as spitting in the King's presence. When Richard refused to give him everything he asked for, Tyler threatened to burn London to the ground. As he turned to ride away, a valet from the royal household shouted after him that he was nothing more than a common thief. This wounded Tyler's pride and he swung back to defend himself, striking his sword against Walworth's clothes. The blow struck off the mayor's concealed armour, who retaliated by drawing his own dagger, which he stabbed through Tyler's neck. Another frenzied servant rushed forward and ran Tyler through. Bleeding profusely, he tried to make it back to his followers on the far side of the field but collapsed off his horse into unconsciousness before he reached them. Richard II spurred his own mount forward and invited the rebels to join him in another location where he would listen to their grievances. Tyler was taken to the nearby hospital priory of Saint Bartholomew, where he was later dragged from his sickbed on the mayor's orders and murdered.

The government reacted savagely in the aftermath of the Peasants' Revolt. Royal Commissions to the countryside instructed that order was to be restored 'either according to the law of our kingdom or', and this was surely the most chilling part, 'by other ways and methods'.[58] Richard II's promises of clemency and reform were replaced by repression. The Westminster Chronicle recorded that 'the populace shuddered at the spectacle of so many gibbeted bodies exposed to the light of day [...] the severity of the royal displeasure seemed to be in no way mitigated but rather to be directed with increased harshness [...] It was widely thought that the King's generous nature ought to exercise leniency rather than vindictiveness.'[59]

Richard II looked upon the old nobility who tried to dominate him in the years after the Peasants' Revolt with contempt. Indeed, he began to look on everyone that way. As he saw it, at the age of fourteen he had provided decisive leadership which had saved London from total ruin when everyone around him had descended into feeble-minded fear. He may have referred to Tyler and his cohorts as 'wretches', but he did not think much more highly of his courtiers in the long-run, either.[60] Richard entered adulthood determined to rule with no input from anyone unless he specifically requested it. There was to be no more camaraderie in arms as in the days of his grandfather Edward III, but rather a system in which the monarch was removed from everyday life, a being far above the common herd who had to be as obeyed and venerated by earls and barons as he was by merchants and farmers. Richard II was sophisticated, devout and there has never been a monarch in English history who made court life so unrelentingly stunning to behold. Indeed, in European history, he might only have been eclipsed by Louis XIV of France or, as things unravelled, perhaps the fairer comparison is to Ludwig II of Bavaria. Sadly, he was also capricious, manipulative and egotistical. As his reign progressed, comparisons were made more frequently between the King and his great-grandfather, Edward II. Richard's detested cabal of favourites were likened to Piers Gaveston and probably untrue allegations that he had gone to bed with some of them, including Robert de Vere, Earl of Oxford, and Michael de la Pole, Earl of Suffolk, heightened speculation that the reign might end in the same way as Edward's.

In 1394, a childless Queen Anne died at the age of twenty-eight at Sheen Manor during another outbreak of the plague. She had never

been particularly popular in England, not least because of her failure
to conceive, which was considered enough of a black mark against
her to outweigh her frequent interventions to reconcile her husband
with those who opposed him. Only one chronicler noted that she
had, 'contributed to the glory and wealth of the realm, as far as she
was able. Noble and common people suffered greatly at her death.'[61]
Richard was demented with sorrow, so much so that a legend persists
that he had Sheen, where she died, burned to the ground. He did
not, but he did not return there and the house fell to ruin. Without
Anne's moderating presence, Richard II succumbed to the worst
elements of his personality. As his feckless taunting of his courtiers,
his indifference to their needs, his paranoia and reliance on unpopular
intimates grew, there were those at court who paid only lip service to
his kingship and began to look to his cousin Henry of Bolingbroke,
Duke of Hereford, the prince saved by a guardsman from death
during the Peasants' Revolt, as a man who might rescue them from
the man in the golden robes on his far-removed throne.

SPILLED BLOOD
DOES NOT SLEEP

THE WARS OF THE ROSES

'For God's sake, let us sit upon the ground
And tell sad stories of the death of kings;
How some have been deposed; some slain in war,
Some haunted by the ghosts they have deposed.
Some poison'd by their wives, some sleeping kill'd;
All murder'd – for within the hollow crown
That rounds the mortal temples of a king,
Keeps Death his court...'

William Shakespeare, *Richard II*, Act III, scene ii

IN TOTAL, William Shakespeare is believed to have written eight plays inspired by the dynastic conflicts that shaped the fifteenth century, beginning with his interpretation of Richard II and ending with his famous but controversial depiction of Richard III. The plays recount an epic of glory amid duplicity and hubris. In his two plays inspired by the life of King Henry IV, Shakespeare presented a reign stricken by Divine judgement because it, and the cursed century that followed, commenced with the deposition of an anointed Sovereign.

Shakespeare's posthumous popularity and the haunting brilliance of his pen prompted one of Henry's recent biographers to observe, 'Shakespeare has a lot to answer for [...] because of Shakespeare, we believe that the English royal family after 1397 was a crucible of glory and terror'.[1] And yet in one respect Shakespeare had it right when he depicted Henry IV as a King plagued by fear of God's retribution. At the end of his life in 1413, Henry gave the appearance of a man who believed he had brought down the wrath of Heaven by usurping the throne from his unstable cousin. Tempering this image of soulful regret, there is a maxim he quoted in a letter from 1403, the shiver-inducing 'Necessitas non habet legem', which translates roughly into English as 'Necessity knows no law'. It was these two world views, one of spiritual self-reproach and the other of unapologetic pragmatism, that defined not only the course of Henry IV's life but also the strange and brutal journey of the monarchy in the decades after him – a story of war, fratricide, love, illicit marriages, betrayal and treason.

NECESSITAS NON HABET LEGEM

BORN AT Bolingbroke Castle in Leicestershire in the spring of 1367, Henry IV was the fourth son of John of Gaunt and his first wife, Blanche of Lancaster.[2] All contemporary accounts of Henry's mother agree that she was young, lively and very pretty. By the time Henry was born, Blanche had already given birth to six other children. Three of her sons died as infants, but Henry lived to maturity along with his two elder sisters, Philippa and Elizabeth. Blanche died at the age of twenty-three, possibly during another outbreak of the plague. Her death was immortalised by court poets and chroniclers, most famously in the aforementioned *The Book of the Duchess* by young Geoffrey Chaucer, who left lengthy descriptions of Blanche's blonde hair, wide eyes, kindness, pleasing voice, tactfulness and grace. Her infant son was raised in the care of an Irish nurse, Mary Taaf, and two years later her widower married the Infanta of Castile.

Despite this early bereavement, the future King's childhood seems to have been relatively happy and active. He had his father's physical strength, ambition and intelligence, and his mother's eloquence and charm. He remained close to the servants who helped raise and educate him, and he was fond of the siblings born to his father's second marriage. His curriculum stressed the importance of religion and throughout his life his personal sense of faith was sincere and conservative. He carried the sword at his cousin Richard's coronation in 1377 and three years later, not long after passing the age of consent, he was married to Lady Mary de Bohun, the vivacious co-heiress of the deceased Earl of Hereford and Essex. Since the bride and bridegroom were so young, Henry's father intended that they wait a few years before consummating their marriage but Henry and Mary defied him. Their first child, a son christened Edward who lived for only a few days, was born less than a year after their wedding. After that, there was evidently a more effective intervention because Mary was not pregnant for three years. Their second child, Henry, was strong and healthy; he was followed by three more brothers and two younger sisters. In total, Mary de Bohun was pregnant every calendar year between 1385 and 1394. The final pregnancy killed her in her early twenties; the child, a daughter, survived. It was the same year as Queen Anne's death at Sheen and Henry went into mourning for twelve months.[3]

By the time of their respective wives' deaths, Henry's relationship with his cousin King Richard had reached breaking point. They were almost exactly the same age, both were grandsons of Edward III and both possessed great wealth to fund their respective political ambitions. But while the King's many political mistakes eroded his popularity, Henry was in the enviable position enjoyed by political alternatives – the heir-apparent, the president-to-be. All the hopes and expectations of the discontented could be projected onto him because he had no power with which to disappoint them, yet. He travelled widely across Europe, participating in many wars, cultivating a reputation as a man of honour and skill. In contrast, Richard II looked unhinged, remote and increasingly pathetic. By the time Queen Anne and Mary de Bohun died in 1394, Henry had already seen action with the Teutonic Knights in Lithuania, as well as travelling to Frankfurt, Prague, Vienna, Paris, Venice, Milan, Corfu, Rhodes, Cyprus and the holy of holies, Jerusalem. As he went, he was wined and dined by local royalty, building up a valuable network by impressing most of them with his intelligence, looks and lovely manners.

Back home, his royal cousin found him decidedly less delightful and the feeling was mutual. Henry participated in intrigues and even skirmishes designed at ending Richard's closeness with the Earl of Oxford. Perhaps mindful of Piers Gaveston long before him, Oxford fled abroad before he could be captured. Parliament, which was in the pocket of the King's enemies, sentenced him to death in absentia, but he cheated them, after a fashion, and died in Louvain of natural causes at the age of twenty-nine or thirty. It seems that even at this stage there was whispered talk of deposing Richard himself and the plan failed not because of his own merits, but rather because the cabal against him, known as the Lords Appellant, could not agree on whether to replace him with his cousin Henry or their mutual uncle, Thomas, Duke of Gloucester.

Passing over Henry's own father, the former regent John of Gaunt, who was still alive and vitally so, was a reflection of the fact that father and son did not agree politically. Whatever his difficulties with Richard II, John of Gaunt was too much a son of Edward III, too heavily influenced by a childhood education spent venerating the throne, to contemplate rebelling against his lawful Sovereign. He even dutifully co-operated in Richard's attempts to limit Henry's career by forbidding Henry to join any further military campaigns in Europe. Perhaps chastened by this slow suffocation of his talents, Henry temporarily reconciled himself with the regime and, if one version of events is to be believed, was actually instrumental in saving it two years before he destroyed it by alerting the King of another aristocratic plot against him.

Richard II struck at the conspirators with terrifying efficiency and at the subsequent trial Henry sat near the King as his former allies were degraded and sentenced. The fabulously wealthy Lord Arundel was beheaded on 21 September 1397 for his part in the conspiracy. The more contrite Lord de Beauchamp was stripped of his titles and incomes, sentenced to life imprisonment and, after a stint on the Isle of Man, eventually housed in the tower within the Tower of London which still bears his name. The most high profile victim was Henry and Richard's uncle Thomas, Duke of Gloucester, Edward III's youngest surviving son. Like Isabella with Edward II, Richard hesitated at shedding royal blood, at least in public. His uncle was dispatched to Calais, where he was murdered by a gang of men in the pay of the Duke of Norfolk.

The murder of the Duke of Gloucester aggravated public opinion in England and lost Richard much of the sympathy he could have harvested by exposing his uncle's plots against him. The Duke of Norfolk, who had also helped identify the plotters, was now the regime's most obedient Rottweiler, but Henry, created Duke of Hereford for tipping-off the government, was less convinced about Norfolk's loyalty and soon accused him of harbouring treasonous thoughts as well. The men quarrelled and Richard declared that the dispute should be settled through trial by combat, a slightly Roman solution to the problem but one that tickled the Arthurian sensibilities of the era. At the last minute, the King revealed that it had been a ruse right from the start. Since he could not decide whether Norfolk or Henry were telling the truth, he decided to punish them both. Henry was sent to exile for the next decade, Norfolk was banished for life. Ever the faithful royalist, John of Gaunt ensured his son followed the King's orders and Henry, admittedly very well-provided for, settled down to exile as a guest of the French royal family at the Hôtel Clisson in Paris. They could be trusted to watch him. Relations between England and France were going through one of their rare rosy patches. After three years without a wife, Richard had finally consented to his courtiers' advice that he marry again. He chose the French King's eldest surviving daughter Isabelle, who had yet to reach her seventh birthday when she was carted off to England and presented to the strange man who had apparently become her husband. She was installed in her own nursery to enjoy what remained of her childhood, given her own household and treated with every kindness.

In February 1399, John of Gaunt died and Richard II made the mistake of his life by changing Henry's sentence of exile to one of perpetual banishment and robbing him of his inheritance by declaring that all of John of Gaunt's possessions would revert to the Crown. The King's tyrannical actions forced Henry to retaliate and united most of the landowning classes behind him. None of them could afford to stand by while the King tampered so arbitrarily with the laws of inheritance. In May, while Richard visited Ireland, Henry returned to England with a small force of two or three hundred men. The size did not matter because his invasion quickly became a triumphal progress. By the time he reached Pontefract Castle, the great families of the northern aristocracy had flocked to his side, their banners fluttering in the wind as testaments to how heartily sick they were of Richard II's rule. Another of the King and Henry's shared uncles, Edmund, Duke of York, who had been left in control of England while Richard was in Ireland, threw his support behind Henry meaning that the kingdom was effectively lost to the former King. When he returned from Ireland, he was arrested and imprisoned, while Parliament was asked to strip him of his title to make way for Henry.

From the outset, Henry IV was plagued by allegations of illegitimacy. Parliament put forward a frustratingly vague justification of the coup, alluding to multiple tenuous arguments but never settling on one as the primary reason for Henry's seizure of the throne. At his coronation in October 1399, held on the feast day of Saint Edward the Confessor to suggest a link between the new King and the most revered of the old, there were stories of evil omens – such as the King losing his shoe or his crown falling off during the coronation banquet. Plots aimed at restoring Richard II were foiled, but they frightened Henry into ordering his cousin's death. How he died is unclear, but four months after Henry's coronation Richard's body was publicly displayed to quash any possibility of future pretenders. The weight of evidence suggests that the horror of regicide was technically avoided by inflicting an even more terrible death on the ex-monarch: he was simply denied adequate food and starved to death. Thus, and this is hair-splitting at its finest and most grotesque, Richard II was not technically murdered on Henry IV's orders. Instead, he died as a result of natural causes.

Richard II's death only strangled one threat to Henry IV's reign. In the same year as the royal corpse was displayed, a revolt began in Wales led by Owen Glendower (sometimes given in Welsh as Owain Glyn Dŵr), a wealthy landowner with distant ancestral ties to the pre-conquest Welsh princes. He hoped to capitalise on uncertainty about the legality of Henry's rule and thanks to Glendower's charisma and talent, as well as Henry IV's instability, the uprising enjoyed significant early successes. It sought, and secured, assistance from France, who was only too happy to benefit from England's problems, especially after Henry dispatched Richard's child-widow Queen Isabelle back home but refused to part with her dowry. French aid to the Welsh rebellion was supplemented three years later when the north of England rose against Henry, led by Sir Henry Percy, heir to the earldom of Northumberland, nicknamed 'Henry Hotspur' for his skills on the battlefield. An alliance between the Welsh and the northerners was sealed by a marriage between Owen Glendower's daughter Catrin and Hotspur's brother-in-law Edmund. Caught up in the excitement, the Archbishop of York, the second highest-ranking churchman in England, denounced Henry IV for perjury, regicide and extortionately high taxation. Henry had him executed for treason. It was a scandal, but there was no outcry comparable to that which greeted the news that Becket had been slain three hundred years earlier. By then, people seemed to be adapting to the idea that necessity knew no law.

Henry IV held onto his throne. Hotspur was killed at the Battle of Shrewsbury, his father was eventually caught and killed in a skirmish by the Sheriff of Yorkshire and in 1409, Harlech Castle, one of the Welsh revolt's strongholds, was starved into submission. The support of the Church was bought with the introduction of harsh new heresy laws that mandated death by flame for religious dissent for the first time in English history and the Bible in English was banned, lest it encourage fresh false interpretations. The bodies of well-known former heretics, like John Wycliffe, were dug out of their graves for ceremonial torching. Their ashes were then tossed into a river.

The illnesses that plagued Henry IV for the rest of his life were probably a result of stress, but at the time they fuelled the popular belief that he was accursed. In 1405, shortly after the execution of the Archbishop of York, Henry was left temporarily paralysed. For most of 1408 and 1409, he was unwell to the extent that his life was feared for and some political responsibilities began to be delegated to his talented but impatient heir. Court whispers, almost certainly vicious fabrications, accused the prince of plotting to depose his father.

Henry IV died in 1413, probably as a result of complications arising from diabetes, which speculation claimed was leprosy sent from God on High. As King, he had taken Joanna of Navarre as his second wife, the sumptuously glamorous widow of the Duke of Brittany.[4] She had a penchant for rather mean-spirited practical jokes, which she liked to play on her ladies-in-waiting and her children from her first marriage, but she was an efficient and elegant Queen consort, whom Henry esteemed and trusted. He was generous to her in his will, as her first husband had been, with the result that the Dowager Queen Joanna was one of the wealthiest women in Christendom. In 1413 all eyes were on her stepson, the hard-drinking and womanising Prince Henry, who put his wild days behind him to embrace, with total commitment, his vocation as King.

THIS STORY SHALL THE GOOD
MAN TEACH HIS SON

HENRY V CAME to the throne determined to heal the divisions made by the previous generations. Those who had been loyal to Richard II, like the earls of March, Huntingdon and Oxford, were rehabilitated into royal favour and Richard's body was exhumed from where it had rested at Kings Langley to be given a grand reburial at Westminster Abbey.[5] It was quite literally laying the past to rest amid a grand reassertion of the sacred nature of kingship. By organising and attending Richard II's funeral, Henry V cleverly posited himself as the heir to Richard's legacy as well as Henry IV's. If he felt any bitterness at having been briefly imprisoned at Trim Castle in Ireland on Richard's orders in 1399, he was wise enough to hide it.

No one could fairly doubt the new monarch's intellectual acumen or his bravery. At the age of fifteen, he had helped defeat the rebellions against his father. He was wounded in the face by an arrow in one skirmish, but kept fighting until a royalist victory was secured. He had been instrumental in weakening Owen Glendower's influence in Wales and at nineteen had successfully besieged Aberystwyth. The list of books he read suggests that he, along with his younger brother Humphrey, was interested in promoting the English language, carrying on the work of Chaucer's generation, which sought to make it, rather than the French brought by the Normans and embraced by their descendants, an acceptable medium for literature.[6] Later in the reign he began to write and sign more often in English, leading the way for many of his peers. Like Alfred the Great and Elizabeth I, one of Henry V's talents was his skill in selecting good advisers. His surviving letters reveal that he was obsessively hardworking, with an eye for detail and a single-minded determination to get what he wanted, no matter how much effort it cost him or his subordinates. He was an inspirational military leader, fated to die young. Few kings were better suited to be moulded into a legend as Henry V was by posterity and William Shakespeare.

The seeds of the legend grew in the soil of his battlefields. The conflict with France had not abated since Isabelle de Valois, child, virgin, Queen and widow, had been unceremoniously shipped back home after her husband was deposed in 1399. A savvy manipulation of internal French disputes eventually gave Henry V the upper hand and in 1415, the House of Commons voted him a subsidy to pursue an invasion. What Henry aimed for was sure to titillate national sensibilities. Before he went, he made it clear that he intended to reclaim the entirety of the old Plantagenet empire as well as pursue Edward III's dream of conquering France itself. His experience of fighting against the Welsh rebellion in his father's time had shown Henry V how difficult a cash-strapped war effort could be and he was determined that similar problems would not bedevil his attack on the French. This zeal for money to fund the invasion, notwithstanding the grant from Parliament, caused one of the more unappealing acts in Henry V's career: his attack on his widowed stepmother who, barring her occasionally cruel sense of mischief, does not seem to have done anything to warrant how he treated her. She was accused of witchcraft and separated from her fortune, which passed conveniently into the King's hands.

The English army crossed to France on 11 August 1415, departing from Southampton and arriving in Normandy in time to celebrate the Feast of the Assumption, when the Church marked the anniversary of the Virgin Mary's ascent into Heaven. [7] Henry V's veneration of the Virgin was particularly strong and in keeping with the spiritual cries of his generation. Marianism gripped the nation, with the country patriotically referring to itself as 'Our Lady's Dowry', and Henry dedicated his kingdom to her patronage and intercession. Harfleur fell to the English on 22 September, despite the fact that most of the army had been fighting while weakened with dysentery. As they headed back to the English-controlled port of Calais, they were blocked near the Somme River at Agincourt by a French army outnumbering them nearly six to one.[8] The subsequent battle enshrined Henry's name in the rose-tinted view of patriotic posterity. He lost less than four hundred men, while the French casualties hovered around six thousand. The scale of the English victory meant that the number of prisoners actually outnumbered the captors, prompting Henry to order their deaths. When some of his men refused to carry out the order, he had two hundred of his archers do it. This horror was in contravention to the accepted laws of chivalric conduct, but it is interesting that not even the French chronicles criticised Henry for the executions, which raises the possibility that the prisoners had attempted to overpower the English soldiers after surrender. Either way, it exhibited a ruthless strain in Henry V that had first been on display in his treatment of the Dowager Queen Joanna.

After Agincourt Henry's campaign became a juggernaut. The mood back home was exultant and even the financial cost of the reconquest of Normandy did not seem to dent the public's enthusiasm for the war. In January 1419 Rouen, the ancient capital of the dukes of Normandy, was taken. By spring of that year, Normandy itself was once again under English control. Powerful allies flocked to help – Richard II's one-time brother-in-law, Emperor Sigismund, signed an alliance with England and when the Duke of Burgundy was murdered by friends of the French Dauphin, his successor went over to Henry.[†] With so many tactical setbacks and her husband steaming through the industrial heartlands of insanity, France's Queen, Isabeau of Bavaria, felt she had no choice but to capitulate. For this she earned the opprobrium of generations of nationalist historians who generally wrote about her with a bile that was only surpassed when it came to Catherine de Medici and Marie-Antoinette.

Isabeau of Bavaria lacked Marie-Antoinette's sweetness, but the two women had comparable amounts of bad luck. Married into the French royal family in her early teens, she and her husband Charles VI had eight surviving children together. One of those children, Isabelle, had briefly been married to Richard II, before being sent home to France where she married the Duke of Orléans to die in childbirth at the age of nineteen. Charles VI suffered his first spell of psychosis seven years into the marriage and these progressed in severity and longevity. He frequently could not recognise Isabeau or their children. Extra walls had to be erected in the royal apartments to prevent the King going on a rampage that endangered his physical well-being. For half a year he refused to bathe or change his clothes. At another point, he became convinced that he was made of glass and suffered panic attacks at the thought of breaking.

With an incapacitated husband and a country on the verge of conquest, Isabeau signed the Treaty of Troyes with England in May 1420. Showing that he had learned from his father's mistakes when it came to deposing kings, Henry did not intend to rob Charles the Mad of his throne. The treaty allowed for the latter to keep the crown for the duration of his life, with Henry nominated as his heir. Isabeau was sharply criticised, then and later, for effectively disinheriting her

---

† Dauphin was the traditional title for heirs to the French throne.

own son in order to buy peace with the English. However, her son's irresponsible feud with the late Duke of Burgundy had helped speed along English victory and the nomination of Henry as heir-apparent was contingent on his marriage to one of Isabeau's daughters, Princess Catherine. That way at least the family's position would be safeguarded once the two countries were united in the next generation. Isabeau was scraping some victory from the ashes of terrible defeat.

Luckily, given that they were to marry no matter what, Henry seemed quite taken with Catherine de Valois when they first met.[9] Their wedding took place in Troyes on 2 June and in December they made their formal entry into Paris. The quest of his ancestors had been fulfilled; Paris had fallen to the English. By February of the next year, the King and Queen were back in England for Catherine's coronation, which was followed by a triumphant tour of the country, during which Catherine conceived. On 6 December 1421, the 'bride of peace' gave birth to a baby boy at Windsor Castle, christened in his father's honour.

Like flies frozen in amber, thus spared the first signs of decay, those who die young and at the height of their fame leave their legends intact for future generations. As it was with Eva Perón, James Dean, Marilyn Monroe, John Fitzgerald Kennedy and Princess Diana in the twentieth century, so it was with Henry V in 1422. His achievements were colossal. He had secured a dynasty hounded by allegations of illegitimacy, he had reconciled those who felt excluded by the divisions of his two predecessors' reigns, he had turned the dreams of Edward III into a reality by uniting France's monarchy with England's, he had retained the love of his people despite the costs and length of his wars, and he had married a princess who provided him with a healthy son. When he returned to France in 1422 to crush those who remained loyal to Catherine's brother, he was already beginning to flag. It may have been dysentery or some other chronic intestinal condition, but 1422 was a hot summer and the water, wine and ale the King was given to drink on campaign would not have sufficiently compensated for the loss of fluid and nutrients he endured as he weakened. He was thirty-five, but knew that he was dying. He spent a great deal of time going over the details of the regency council for his infant son, with Henry's younger brother Humphrey, Duke of Gloucester, given power in England and England's ally, the Duke of Burgundy, granted authority over France until the baby prince reached maturity.

He made meticulous arrangements for his funeral and insisted that Masses in honour of the Holy Trinity and the Virgin Mary should be given special prominence. He died at the Château de Vincennes near Paris on 31 August 1422 and requiem Masses were conducted at the nearby basilica of St Denis, the traditional burial ground of the kings and queens of France. Over the course of two months, his coffin with a lifelike effigy that rested atop it processed through France, stopping for more Masses, surrounded by hundreds of attendants. Queen Catherine, swathed in black, arrived to escort the body for burial at Westminster. The final stretch of Henry V's internment saw the procession joined by representatives of the guilds of the city of London, garbed in white and carrying over two hundred torches, as it moved over London Bridge through flickering light, clouds of incense curling forth into the air from the swinging censers of the clergy, and choirs singing the hymn *Venite*, the ninety-fourth Psalm and one traditionally associated with triumph. Even in death, Henry V wanted to return victorious. The coffin, covered in black velvet with a white satin cross upon it, was flanked by four knights carrying a canopy as it was greeted at the doors of Westminster Abbey by a large group of 'bishops and other worthy lords', and it was there on Saturday 7 November, two months after his death, that Henry V was 'buried with great solemnity'.[10]

THE LORDS IN ENGLAND KILL
THEIR ENEMIES

HENRY VI CAME to the throne at the age of nine months, the youngest Sovereign in English history.[11] A month later, he became King of France when his grandfather Charles VI ended his sad and tortured life in Paris. Henry was crowned King of England at Westminster in July 1429, when he was seven years old, and King of France at Notre Dame two years later.[12] Suspicious of her ancestry and her links to France, the council established to take care of the child-King gradually isolated him from the company of his mother, Queen Catherine. Lonely and still in her prime, the Queen Mother looked for romance and eventually gravitated towards one of her servants, a Welsh gentleman called Owen Tudor.

He joined Catherine de Valois's household around 1427, five years after her first husband's death.[13] There are two stories of how he attracted his employer's attention. All available descriptions of Owen Tudor agree that he was 'adorned with wonderful gifts of body'.[14] Some claim that Catherine was unable to forget him after accidentally spying him swimming naked one afternoon. Another story, judged probable in a recent history of the family, is that she first noticed him at a party in her rooms when the energetic Owen performed a dance move that unfortunately did not finish as competently as it commenced.[15] He tripped and fell into the Queen Mother's lap. They were smitten and although she never could follow what her new in-laws were saying since she neither spoke nor understood Welsh, and Owen was the only member of his family to speak English, the couple loved each other enough to face down the tidal wave of disapproval that crashed over them once their marriage became public knowledge.[16] Servants reported that when the couple made love, Queen Catherine could be heard screaming with pleasure, a dynamic to their relationship that presumably made disregarding the critics an awful lot easier.[17]

Henry VI, who knew nothing of his mother's other family, was only fifteen years old when she died of an unknown illness that had long troubled her and that may have been exacerbated by her final pregnancy. As far as the King knew, his mother was still a widow and she was buried as such in Westminster Abbey. For reasons that were probably a cocktail of prudery, snobbery and shame, his advisers had never told him about his mother's remarriage, incredibly managing to shield him from the fierce public debate over Catherine's actions. It was only with Catherine prematurely in her grave that they felt they had to enlighten him. Owen Tudor, understandably, feared the worse. Those who resented the late Queen's choice of husband were not slow in having him imprisoned in Newgate prison.

As muscular on his feet as he was between the sheets, apparently, he overpowered his gaoler and went on the run. He was captured and re-incarcerated, this time at Windsor. Here, the young King's influence prevailed, because Owen was released shortly afterward and the King grew fond of his handsome, impetuous and athletic stepfather. Henry VI was also generous to his Tudor half-brothers, Edmund and Jasper, whom he created earls of Richmond and Pembroke respectively. The eldest of the boys, Edmund, made an advantageous marriage with the adolescent Lady Margaret Beaufort, a great-granddaughter of John of Gaunt and niece of the Duke of Somerset. Their child, baptised Henry in the King's honour, was born in Wales in January 1457 and he carried the blood of the kings of France from his grandmother Catherine de Valois and the blood of the kings of England from his mother, Margaret. Unwittingly, Catherine de Valois had helped found a new dynasty, but with Henry VI on the throne and a large number of Plantagenet cousins in line to succeed him if he should die without an heir, to describe the Tudors' prospects of ever taking the throne as slim would have been kind.

Shortly before Owen Tudor fell at the feet of the Queen Mother, Saint Catherine, Saint Margaret and Saint Michael the Archangel appeared in a miraculous vision to a twelve-year-old girl called Jeanne in the town of Donrémy in a part of France that remained loyal to Catherine de Valois's disinherited brother. Jeanne, or Joan as the English called her, received instructions to drive the English out of France and to bring the Dauphin to Rheims for his coronation as the rightful King. When she was sixteen, she revealed her mission to the French royal court in exile and after extensive investigations to establish that she was not a heretic, the Dauphin – Charles VII to his followers – threw his lot in with Joan. Her eyes aglow with devout zeal, she arrived at the siege of Orléans to inspire, and some say lead, the Dauphinist armies to victory.

Joan of Arc's effect on morale among those who did not want a royal union with England was enormous and there is no greater proof of that than in observing how deeply the English came to detest her. Even two hundred years later, when Shakespeare portrayed her as a sexually disreputable megalomaniac, they had not forgiven her. They were determined to prove that not all visions came from Heaven and when she was captured during a French retreat in 1430, they brought Joan to Normandy to stand trial for heresy. She continued to dress like a man, claiming that male attire was her only protection from assault by the prison guards. She defended herself bravely, but the outcome was never in doubt. The nineteen-year-old was burned at the stake before a large crowd and her remains were tossed into the Seine. The public executioner expressed a fear that he would be damned for his role in lighting the flames beneath her and in 1456 Pope Callixtus III overturned the guilty verdict. In 1920, by then an icon of French resistance against foreign invasion, Joan was canonised.

The flames that consumed Joan at Rouen turned her from leader into martyr as English control of France collapsed. The English cause was not helped by the fact that the King's guardians often seemed more preoccupied with outdoing each other than uniting to deal with the problem of Charles VII. In 1449, eighteen years after Joan of Arc's death, Normandy fell to the French and two years later, Gascony was captured when a force led by the Earl of Talbot was cut to pieces at Castillon. After three hundred years, the picturesque territory that had come to England through Eleanor of Aquitaine was lost entirely and the mood in London turned ugly. Somebody had to be held responsible for this national humiliation and public wrath fixed on the King's guardian-cum-favourite, the Duke of Suffolk. He had been instrumental in arranging the King's deeply unpopular marriage with Marguerite of Anjou, the daughter of a down-on-his-luck princeling who claimed to be the rightful King of the Naples. Suffolk was impeached by Parliament and his execution was widely expected until Henry VI arranged for him to escape. Anticipating the King's softness, the Duke's enemies captured the boat as it left England and Suffolk was murdered on the spot. Summary execution was to become a depressingly familiar scene over the next four decades. Two of Suffolk's closest allies, the bishops of Chichester and Salisbury, met similar ends, with Salisbury dragged from the church where he was celebrating Mass to be killed outside on unsanctified ground.

With Suffolk dead, the dominant influence on Henry VI came to be his wife. Marguerite, a tempestuous and determined brunette, had not had an easy time in asserting herself as the most powerful person at Henry's court. The King was a deeply religious young man and when his confessor warned him to avoid having sex with the Queen on the grounds that all sexual intercourse, even within marriage, resulted in impure and sinful thoughts, Henry took that advice to heart. When Marguerite finally managed to overcome his scruples and get him into bed, the resulting pregnancy precipitated some kind of nervous breakdown in the father-to-be. The child, a healthy baby boy called Edward, was dogged by rumours of illegitimacy because Henry's discomfiture at his son's birth suggested that the Queen had taken a lover. Even today, most of the novels dramatising Henry VI's reign cannot resist depicting Marguerite as an adulteress and her son as a bastard. However, if Henry had remained completely faithful to his confessor's teachings, Marguerite would never have been able to pass her son off as Henry's. Put simply, she must have persuaded him to have sex with her at least once.

The King's refusal to have regular sex with his wife and his mental collapse when she became pregnant were the most serious examples of Henry's out-of-control religiosity. His morbid revulsion towards sexual intercourse led to the installation of secret windows so he could spy on his servants 'lest any foolish impertinence of women coming into the house should [...] cause the fall of any of his household'.[18] At one Yuletide party, Henry stormed out of the room when he found the attire of some of the dancers too immodest. In 1440, he founded Eton College, still one of the most prestigious and highest-achieving private schools in Britain, naming it The King's College of Our Lady of Eton besides Windsor, to provide education for seventy poor youngsters and he encouraged the masters never to bring the students to court, lest the young men be corrupted by the plunging décolletages of the court ladies. He also founded King's College, Cambridge, and both institutions continue to mark the anniversary of the King's death by leaving respective bunches of roses and lilies on the site where he perished to show how his memory remains ever-green at the institutions he founded.

Bit by bit, Henry's eccentricities gave birth to the fear that he had inherited the madness of his French grandfather, Charles VI. What exactly ailed Henry VI is never likely to be proven, but based on all the evidence available to us a diagnosis of catatonic schizophrenia seems the most probable. It would explain many of his symptoms, such as the two month period when the King was kept at Clarendon unable to move, speak or recognise anyone. The King's cousin Richard, Duke of York, exploited the uncertainty to establish himself as protector of the realm. Marguerite, smelling a rat, believed that York had ambitions to seize the crown itself.

She was not necessarily wrong, but her implacable hatred of York and inability to choose conciliation over confrontation helped ensure their rivalry spilled out of the palace and onto the battlefield, in a conflict which later generations called the Wars of the Roses.[†] It began with the battle-lines being drawn at court as two factions crystallised around the figure of the Queen on one side and the Duke of York on the other. The Tudor brothers were brought on-board with Edmund Tudor's aforementioned marriage to Margaret Beaufort, niece of the Queen's other ally, the Duke of Somerset; York's most prominent supporter was Richard Neville, Earl of Warwick, a northern magnate with so much land, money and manpower that it was not always clear who the real leader of the Yorkist movement was. Warwick, like York, was a man of infinite ambition who wanted to exploit the crisis created by Henry VI's mental health problems to expand his own power at the royal family's expense. Unlike York, Warwick seems to have nurtured little ambition to take the throne himself. Instead, he was content to work in the shadows, earning the epithet given to him by his contemporaries and used by posterity, the Kingmaker.

When he recovered from yet another period of sickness in 1455, the Queen convinced the King to banish York, who threatened rebellion unless he was reinstated at the same time as the Duke of Somerset was exiled. Henry and Marguerite refused to abandon their friend and a Yorkist regiment attacked their forces at St Albans in Hertfordshire on 22 May 1455. Somerset was killed and the King, who was reluctant to fight at all, was hit in the neck by an arrow. The wound to the King's body was not nearly as deep as the wound to royal authority as Henry meekly accepted York as victor. Later processions had the former courtly adversaries marching hand in hand through

† For some utterly inexplicable reason, a recent trend is to refer to the Wars of the Roses as 'the Cousins' War'. In the first place, this is intellectually presumptuous, since the war has been linked to roses in the reading public's mind since at least the time of Shakespeare and probably earlier than that. Secondly, even if the Wars of the Roses was a name created by a subsequent generation, so too are the names of most conflicts. Finally, the prevalence of monarchies in Europe before 1918 means that nearly ever war in European history between Charlemagne and the fall of the Romanovs could be dubbed 'the Cousins' War'. If one insists upon rebranding a five-hundred-year-old conflict, then '*a* cousins' war' might, just about, make more sense.

the streets of London for a special service of reconciliation at Saint Paul's Cathedral, all encouraged by Henry, who seemed unaware that by arranging the protagonists in this way he was advertising to the general public that there were still two distinct 'sides' at work. Handholding aside, Queen Marguerite neither forgave nor forgot the defeat at St Albans, nor did York help in the quest for peace when he used his victory to inflict further slights on the Queen, such as slashing her income. When a quarrel between two of the great families of the northern aristocracy, the Nevilles and the Percys, gave her an opportunity to re-ignite the blood feud, she took it.

At the Queen's behest, an army marched on the York family's stronghold of Ludlow Castle near the border with Wales. This time, it was the Lancastrians who emerged triumphant. The vanquished Duke fled to Ireland, while his eldest son and the Earl of Warwick escaped across the Channel to Calais, from whence the latter returned with another army that crushed the Queen's forces at the Battle of Northampton. In October, the Duke of York formally submitted his claim to be rightful King of England to Parliament on the grounds that his lineage was the senior surviving line of the Plantagenets, rather than the House of Lancaster, who had illegally seized the throne in 1399.

For purists, the issue of who was the rightful monarch was a difficult one because it boiled down to a forensic dissection of the competing theories on primogeniture and how they applied to the descendants of Edward III (Richard of York and Henry VI's mutual ancestor).[19] For clarity's sake, and with apologies for any repetition, Edward III and Philippa of Hainault had five sons who grew to maturity and fathered children of their own: in order of age, they were Edward, Prince of Wales, Lionel, Duke of Clarence, John of Gaunt, Duke of Lancaster, Edmund, Duke of York and Thomas, Duke of Gloucester. The direct line of the eldest of those boys, the Prince of Wales, died out in 1400 when his only son, Richard II, was murdered. The next of the princes, Lionel, Duke of Clarence, had only fathered a daughter, Philippa, who inherited her mother's title as Countess of Ulster. Henry VI was John, Duke of Lancaster's great-grandson and, on that basis, known as agnatic primogeniture whereby royal and aristocratic descent is determined on a patrilineal basis, the House of Lancaster's claim to the throne was superior.

However, in 1460 the Yorkists began to argue in favour of an inheritance principle known as cognatic primogeniture, which allowed for a female member of the line to inherit if she had no living legitimate male relatives. In this line of argument, it was the Duke of York who was the senior living descendant of Edward III, rather than King Henry VI. The second of Edward III's sons, Lionel, had only produced a daughter, yes, but Philippa of Ulster had grown up to marry the Earl of March and their granddaughter was the Duke of York's mother. Since her brothers and uncles had also died without legitimate heirs, the titles tied to all of these associated families – the earldoms of Ulster, March and Cambridge – had devolved to the Duke of York and by following this extremely convoluted journey through the female line, it could just about be argued that via his maternal great-grandmother, Richard, Duke of York was actually the heir of the Duke of Clarence, the second of Edward III's sons, whereas the King was only the heir of the Duke of Lancaster, the third of the five.

To describe the Yorkist claim to the throne as one of clutching at the proverbial straws is perhaps ungenerous, but only just. Had Henry VI not been so unsuited to the vocation of kingship, it is unlikely that Richard of York would ever have gone rooting back into the family tree to prove that he should replace him. One person who was as unconvinced as she was unsurprised by the Duke's claim was Queen Marguerite, who rode north with her son to reappear with an army. At the Battle of Wakefield, held in the biting cold five days after Christmas, the Duke of York was slain and the Lancastrians had his head hacked from his shoulders and sent back to the city of York to be displayed above the city gates wearing a paper crown. It was, so the Lancastrians joked, the only crown he would ever wear. Maybe it does not seem quite so funny now, but as political points memorably expressed go, it certainly got the message across.

The Yorkist mantle passed to the dead Duke's nineteen-year-old son, Edward. He was a formidable opponent. Over six feet tall, with a flair for bonhomie, natural star quality and a proven valour on the battlefield, he was also very handsome, which always helps in the shallow world of political popularity. The virile, attractive and extroverted soldier, Camelot in tighter pantaloons, certainly looked a lot more like a king than the mentally tortured Henry VI, now entering middle age, disconnected from reality and perceived as being under the thumb of his unpopular wife. A Lancastrian force, led by the King's stepfather Owen Tudor and his younger son Jasper, Earl of Pembroke, caught up with the new Yorkist leader on the day a parhelion appeared in the morning sky. A parhelion is a trick of the light, sometimes known as the sun dog, when light shines through ice crystals in the atmosphere, creating unusual images and extra spots of light in the sky. On the morning of the Battle of Mortimer's Cross, the parhelion made it look as if there were three suns in the sky, a divine omen that Edward of York proclaimed a sign that God the Father, God the Son and God the Holy Ghost were blessing the Yorkist armies. The Lancastrians were defeated and although Jasper Tudor managed to escape, his father was not so lucky. Edward of York ordered Owen's summary execution and the old man went out with the quip, 'The head that shall lie on the stock was wont to like on Queen Catherine's lap.'[20] His head was displayed in a nearby public market, where an anonymous woman caused a scene by washing away the blood and lighting a hundred small candles around it.[21]

As Queen Marguerite and her son marched back to London, the citizens, panicked by (perhaps exaggerated) stories of her soldiers' bloodthirstiness, closed the gates against her. Seizing the advantage, Edward of York galloped south, where he was welcomed and crowned King Edward IV at Westminster. Despite the fact that it was March, spring had not yet arrived and the countryside lay under a blanket of frost and snow. In that inhospitable weather, Marguerite, Henry VI and their son retreated north; Edward caught up with them on Palm Sunday near the tiny village of Towton, where their armies clashed in what was probably the bloodiest battle ever fought on English soil. Nearly thirty thousand men lost their lives as a blizzard raged around them, with the Yorkists pursuing the Lancastrians even as they fled the battlefield. The deposed King and Queen sought asylum in Scotland, and Edward returned to the capital in triumph.

THE SUN IN SPLENDOUR

EDWARD IV KNEW that without Warwick's support, the Yorkist assault on the throne might never have succeeded. He was therefore extremely generous to him and to the wider Neville family, at least initially. Richard Neville, 16th Earl of Warwick, the Kingmaker, expected to call the political shots, while the handsome King was left to indulge his passion for all things physical. During the war that had been on the battlefield, now that victory seemed secure, it was in the bedroom. As the Nevilles targeted pockets of Lancastrian resistance, Edward indulged his passion for the ladies, usually ones a little bit older than himself, although he was not overly discerning. Dominic Mancini, a visitor to England during Edward's reign, wrote that the King went after married women and virgins, highborn and commoners, without discrimination. He never took any by force, Mancini claimed, although other evidence suggests that he tried it at least once. Mancini heard that Edward showered his love interests with gifts and honey-worded promises to get them into bed and, once sated, he quickly lost interest. He even glibly promised marriage to one Eleanor Talbot before bedding her, a ruse that would later take on a grim political significance.

In May 1464, while Warwick was negotiating a betrothal between the King and one of the daughters of King Louis XI of France, Edward fell head over heels in love with a beautiful widow called Elizabeth Grey. Her husband Sir John Grey had died fighting for the Lancastrians at the Battle of St Albans and his death left Elizabeth with two young sons to care for. She was not exactly destitute, but even so her future did not look promising with a Yorkist on the throne. Not only had her husband died fighting for the Lancastrians, but her mother Jacquetta was Henry VI's aunt by marriage. A daughter of the European noble House of Luxembourg, Jacquetta had arrived in English territory at the age of seventeen to marry the Duke of Bedford, one of Henry V's younger brothers. When he died, his childless widow fell in love with a dashing English squire in her service, Richard Woodville, and in an echo of her sister-in-law and Owen Tudor, they eloped. As with Catherine and Owen, no one could fault Jacquetta's taste in picking Richard Woodville on a physical level, because he was 'beautiful and well-formed in his person'.[22] After paying a fine, Jacquetta was forgiven her mésalliance and received back at court. The Woodvilles had fourteen children together of which the gorgeous Elizabeth, with her ivory skin and long blonde hair, was the eldest.

With the family's political fortunes wrecked upon the fall of Henry VI, Elizabeth decided to petition King Edward to restore some of her confiscated lands. She was resourceful; she artfully positioned herself with her little boys at her side beneath an oak tree that she knew Edward IV would ride past while hunting near the Woodvilles' manor house at Grafton. This tableau sounds almost too good to be true, on a par with Robert the Bruce's resilient spider or Walter Raleigh's puddle-defeating cloak, but in this case there are enough independent sources from the time corroborating that this was how Edward IV and Elizabeth Grey first met.[23]

Thomas More, writing a generation later and having grown up in the household of Archbishop Morton who knew the couple well, claimed that 'when the King beheld and heard her speak, as she was both fair and of a good favour, moderate of stature, well made and very wise, he not only pitied her, but also waxed enamoured of her.'[24] Predictably, he attempted to seduce her. More insists that she 'virtuously denied him' and that her rebuttals were phrased 'so wisely and with so good manner, and words so well set, that she rather kindled his desire than quenched it'.[25] Like Anne Boleyn sixty years later, Elizabeth Grey's refusal to hop into bed with the King struck many people as a manipulative ploy, but that is hindsight writing History. The report written for Angelo Cato, one of Louis XI's advisers, reported at the time that 'the king first fell in love with her beauty of person and charm of manner' but, 'he could not corrupt her virtue by gifts or menaces. The story runs that when Edward placed a dagger at her throat, to make her submit to his passion, she remained unperturbed and determined to die rather than live unchastely with the king'.[26]

Whether she was the puppet-master or, as seems more likely, responding to circumstances as they unfolded, Edward briefly attempted to forget the widow Grey and returned to London, where one contemporary chronicle recorded that 'being a lusty prince' he sought to distract himself from her with a string of lovers, but 'he could not perceive none of such constant womanhood, wisdom and beauty, as was Dame Elizabeth, widow of Sir John Grey of Groby late defunct, he then with a little company came unto the Manor of Grafton, beside Stony Stratford, whereat Sir Richard Wydville, Earl of Rivers, and Dame Jacqueline, Duchess-Dowager of Bedford, were then dwelling; and after resorting to divers times, seeing the constant and stable mind of the said Dame Elizabeth, early in the morning the said King Edward wedded the foresaid Dame Elizabeth there on the first day of May in the beginning of his third year'.[†][27] Immediately after the wedding service, Edward and Elizabeth rushed to bed where they 'tarried upon, two or three hours'.[28] Evidently, neither was disappointed in their new partner and the King returned to Elizabeth's chamber immediately after coming in from hunting the next day.

Warwick's reaction to the King's elopement was one of wounded fury. Elizabeth Grey, or Elizabeth Woodville as she was more commonly known, was the daughter of one Lancastrian and the widow of another. Although her mother belonged to one of the greatest families of the European nobility, her father was regarded as a jumped-up social climber and this allowed her enemies to paint her as a scheming commoner who had used her sexual wiles to entrap the King. Edward's predilections may have been titillated by the fact that the new Queen was about five years older than him, but choosing a woman in her late twenties when heirs still needed to be produced seemed the height of irresponsible folly. It also humiliated Lord Warwick on the international stage, since while Edward was preparing to wed one of his own subjects, Warwick had been discussing the possibility of his marriage to the infant Princess Anne of France. Invigorated by marital life, tired of Warwick's domination and perhaps emboldened by the support he received from his new wife, Edward IV began to undermine his mentor. Within a couple of years, courtiers liked to place bets on whose foreign policy aim would triumph – Warwick's preference for an alliance with France or Edward's for closer ties with Burgundy. In 1468, another royal wedding brought another public embarrassment for Warwick when Edward's younger sister Margaret was married to the Duke of Burgundy. Proud and resentful, the Kingmaker began to plot how to destroy what he had created.

---

† There is some disagreement among modern writers about the best spelling of Elizabeth's maiden name. Some prefer 'Wydeville' or 'Wydvill', I have opted for the more familiar 'Woodville'. Given the fluidity of medieval names, further underlined here by referring to Elizabeth's mother as Jacqueline rather than Jacquetta, the debate boils down to a matter of personal preference.

In the early years of the marriage, Queen Elizabeth Woodville proved her fecundity by giving birth to three daughters, Elizabeth, Mary and Cecily, in quick succession. To her critics' glee, there was no son thus far. The Queen came from a large family and over the course of the reign, four of her sisters were married into the high nobility – the widowed Anne was married to the Earl of Kent, Margaret Woodville to the Earl of Arundel, Mary Woodville to the Earl of Pembroke and the youngest of the Queen's sisters, Katherine, to the Duke of Buckingham. The Queen's father was made an earl in his own right, her brother John was married in 'a diabolical marriage' to the aged Dowager Duchess of Norfolk, a woman about forty years his senior, and another brother became Bishop of Salisbury.[†][29] This influx of Woodvilles and the creation of a network that gave them enough clout to form a political faction unsettled Warwick and his supporters, who were undoubtedly responsible for spreading stories accusing Elizabeth and her mother of involvement in witchcraft.

In 1469, Warwick and the King's younger brother, the Duke of Clarence, rebelled. Their supporters captured the Queen's father and her younger brother, John. Both were executed and their heads displayed on pikes outside the gates of Coventry. Various attempts at reconciliation came to nothing and given what they had done to the Queen's family, Edward IV could never have forgiven them without appearing pathetic. In 1470, Warwick and Clarence fled to France, throwing themselves on the mercy of King Louis XI, a man with such an insatiable appetite for scheming that he was nicknamed 'the Universal Spider'. Blessed with this heaven-sent opportunity to weaken his neighbours and punish Edward for his alliance with Burgundy, Louis encouraged Warwick to reconcile with another celebrated émigré at the French court, Queen Marguerite of Anjou, who had been living there since 1463.

Edward IV's impulsive marriage to Elizabeth Woodville had played right into Marguerite's hands. She had already been joined by the most devout of the Lancastrian stalwarts, like the Earl of Oxford. Now, the man who had put the Yorks on the throne had betrayed them. As much as she may have liked to bury it in his head, Marguerite pragmatically buried the hatchet in a more metaphorical capacity and the two enemies proclaimed a pact of friendship at Angers

† Some of the family's later critics claimed the Dowager Duchess was nearly eighty at the time the twenty-something John Woodville married her, but she was middle-aged. Still quite a gap, but not quite the 'diabolical' six decades implied by the hostile chronicler.

Cathedral on 22 July 1470. Two months later they invaded England. The alliance between Warwick and the Lancastrian Queen terrified Edward who, with the support of his most loyal brother Richard of Gloucester, fled to their sister's court in Burgundy to gather an army of their own. The seven-month pregnant Queen Elizabeth and her three daughters were placed in sanctuary at Westminster Abbey where, on the Feast of All Souls, the great Catholic commemoration of the Dead, she finally gave birth to an heir, named for his father. But what on earth that baby was heir to was suddenly very unclear. Henry VI was back in London, occupying, to his amazement and confusion, the sumptuous apartments that had recently been re-decorated for Elizabeth Woodville. The period known as the Readeption, Henry VI's brief restoration to the throne, had begun. Parliament was treated to a pointed sermon that took as its text the phrase 'Return, O back-sliding children' from the Biblical Book of Jeremiah.[30] As a gesture of royal thanks, one of Warwick's daughters married Henry and Marguerite's son, the Prince of Wales. The restored King, so it was said, was barely capable of speech, but the holy soul was vocal enough to insist upon sending gifts of food, money and clothing to Elizabeth Woodville and her children at Westminster.

When the winter frosts cleared, Edward IV arrived with a fleet and soldiers courtesy of Burgundy. Warwick was defeated and killed; Queen Marguerite was vanquished at the Battle of Tewkesbury a couple of months later. Among the battlefield dead was her only child. She was captured and brought back to London, where both she and her husband were imprisoned at the Tower. As soon as he retook the capital, Edward IV ordered Henry VI's murder. The little oratory where he was praying on the night they killed him can still be seen, beautiful and sad with its patterned tiles and golden crucifix. Nobody believed the government's story that Henry VI actually died of grief.

With no son or husband left to fight for, Marguerite of Anjou was no longer much of a threat. She was ransomed and sent back to France in 1475. One of her touchingly pathetic letters to King Louis XI begs him to remember that her financial situation was totally dependent on 'his good will and pleasure'.[31] She gave up her château at Reculée because she could not afford to maintain it, she dismissed her servants and threw herself on the mercy of a chivalrous seigneur, François de Vignolles, a former vassal of her family who remembered his oaths of loyalty and provided Marguerite with a small château at Dampierre.

There, on 25 August 1482, she died at the age of fifty-two. A modern novel inspired by her life dubs Marguerite 'the Queen of Last Hopes'. It is an appropriate sobriquet. She had taken on an impossible task in marrying a schizophrenic King who was surrounded by a grasping and treacherous nobility, all of whom knew that the King's grandfather had come to power by overthrowing an anointed Sovereign. It was a dangerous precedent that neither she nor the rest of the House of Lancaster could escape. She died a failure and in trying to avoid that fate she made many mistakes. The instability and uncertainty that had ruined her life erupted again a year after funeral. This time to annihilate the House of York.

NO MORE SONS OF THE ROYAL BLOOD

IN HIS final twelve years on the throne, Edward IV worked hard to make the monarchy solvent, avoided accusations of corruption, encouraged foreign trade, patronised the arts, aimed for fairer taxation, committed himself to the suppression of robbery on the kingdom's highways and restored the international prestige of the Crown.[†] As the Renaissance gathered pace across Europe, the court of Edward IV and Elizabeth Woodville was one of such sybaritic splendour that it frequently took foreign visitors' breath away. One account described the court as one that 'fully befits a most mighty kingdom, filled with riches and with people of almost all nations'.[32] The widely-travelled Gabriel Tetzel, a German serving in the household of the Queen of Bohemia's brother, visited England and described Edward's household as 'the most splendid court that could be found in all Christendom.'[33] Tetzel remarked on the court's strict adherence to etiquette and in particular the 'extraordinary reverence' with which the King and Queen were treated by their servants.[34]Given the uncertainty at the start of his reign, etiquette, hierarchy and pageantry were useful tools for Edward IV to exert control over his courtiers. After the birth of her first child, Queen Elizabeth presided over a banquet held to celebrate her position as mother of the King's first legitimate child, regardless of that child's gender. Protocol was turned into political theatre, as Tetzel witnessed:

> The queen sat alone at a table on a costly golden chair. The Queen's mother and the King's sister had to stand some distance away. When the Queen spoke with her mother or the King's sister, they knelt down before her until she had drunk water. Not until the first dish was set before the Queen could the Queen's mother and the King's sister be seated. The ladies and

---

[†] One of the greatest innovations of his reign was the establishment of the first printing press in England, a move supported by the royal household and one that played a large part in the greatest revolutionising of the dissemination of knowledge until the coming of the Internet in the twentieth century. The printing press made it possible to mass produce books that hitherto had all been transcribed by hands, meaning that they were both rare and usually very expensive.

maidens and all who served the Queen at the
table were all of noble birth and had to kneel so
long as the Queen was eating. The meal lasted
for three hours. The food which was served to
the Queen, the Queen's mother, the King's sister
and the others was most costly. Much might be
written of it. Everyone was silent and not a word
was spoken. My lord [the Queen of Bohemia's
brother] and his attendants stood the whole time
the alcove and looked on.

> After the banquet they commenced to
dance. The Queen remained seated in her chair.
Her mother knelt before her, but at time the
Queen bade her rise. The King's sister danced a
stately dance with two dukes, and this, and the
courtly reverence they paid to the Queen, was
such as I have never seen elsewhere, nor have I
ever seen such exceedingly beautiful maidens.
Among them were eight duchesses and thirty
countesses and the others were all daughters
of influential men. After the dance the King's
choristers entered and were ordered to sing. We
were present when the King heard mass in his
chapel. My lord and his company were let in and
I do not think that I have heard finer song in this
world.[35]

This scene has often been cited out of context as proof of
Elizabeth Woodville's arrogance and hauteur, but Tetzel's account
makes it clear that not only was this a special and quasi-religious
occasion, the Queen's readmission to society after successful delivery
of a child, but that Edward IV also demanded similar treatment.
To kneel in front of a king or queen at public functions was not an
humiliation but a privilege that indicated the person's proximity to
the royal body; similar behaviour is recorded at the courts of Joanna
of Navarre, Marguerite of Anjou, Katherine of Aragon and Anne
Boleyn. In this world, who bowed and for how long mattered greatly.

Following her husband's restoration to the throne,
Elizabeth Woodville gave birth six more times. Two of those
children, Margaret and George, died in infancy, but like her own

rambunctiously healthy tribe of siblings, Elizabeth's children were for the most part a vital brood. By the time the last of her children, a daughter called Bridget, was born at Eltham Palace in November 1480, Queen Elizabeth had ten living children, including her two sons from her first marriage. The eldest of those two, Thomas Grey, had benefited from his stepfather's largesse to become Marquess of Dorset, and the eldest of her sons with the King was given his own household at Ludlow as befitting the Prince of Wales. But this image of the King and Queen presiding over a glittering, cosmopolitan court with their 'most sweet and beautiful children' is only one half of the story.

Unquestionably, he loved her and demanded she be treated with the reverence due to a Queen, but Edward IV was nonetheless compulsively unfaithful to Elizabeth Woodville. A string of mistresses continued to distract him and there were bastards. The dynamic among the rest of the royal family was fuelled by cancerous mutual suspicions. When his slippery brother the Duke of Clarence again attempted to betray him, Edward ordered his murder, a decision that carried unfortunate connotations of Cain and Abel. Legend has it that Clarence's chosen method of execution was to be drowned in a barrel of his favourite malmsey wine. Yorkists keen to exculpate Edward from culpability for his brother's death blamed Elizabeth for manipulating him like a modern Herodias. Later, the Tudors would suggest that a third brother, Richard of Gloucester, arranged the murder. There is no evidence that either Richard or Elizabeth were involved. As the murder of Henry VI had shown in 1471, Edward IV could make such decisions on his own.

Back at court, he was drowning in wine at a slower pace than his unfortunate brother, as he indulged his love of food and alcohol with the result that his looks faded and he piled on weight. After stuffing himself to capacity, Edward took emetics to make room for more servings of his favourite gastronomic treats. In 1482, some military responsibilities had to be handed over to his last surviving brother, the Duke of Gloucester, Edward's right hand in the north, because the King was no longer physically capable of carrying them out himself. On 9 April 1483, after a short illness and quite possibly a series of strokes, Edward IV died at Westminster at the age of forty.

The Queen, like most of the country, was stunned but she moved quickly to have the new King, her twelve year old son Edward V, brought back from his establishment at Ludlow to London in the care of his Woodville uncle Anthony. Edward IV's will left Elizabeth with substantial political influence, even if care of the children was co-entrusted to their paternal uncle Richard of Gloucester. Nowadays, both parties have their passionate defenders but the truth seems to be that both Richard and Elizabeth feared the other and chose to act dishonestly rather than seek an understanding. In doing so they set in motion the chain of events that toppled the Yorkist monarchy. Despite having been his brother's most stalwart supporter, Richard showed himself to be very much a man of his time through the alacrity with which he duped and then disinherited the nephews entrusted to his care.

Leaving his home in the north, Richard travelled south to meet his nephew en route to London. Richard later claimed that the Queen Mother was plotting to assassinate him, but if that were the case, it is curious that Anthony Woodville seemed so amenable to a meeting. More truthfully, Richard believed that Elizabeth intended to exclude him from government and subsequently exaggerated his fear of her to justify his actions. He caught up with Edward V, where he made a great pretence of loyalty and friendship before ordering the arrest of the Woodvilles in his entourage. Elizabeth once again fled to Westminster Abbey to seek sanctuary, accompanied by her daughters and youngest surviving son, Richard, Duke of York. On 4 May, supported by Elizabeth's turncoat brother-in-law the Duke of Buckingham, Richard entered London to be proclaimed protector of the realm until the King reached maturity.

But there was a rub impossible to ignore. At twelve, Edward V was seen by many of his contemporaries to be an adult. Twelve, after all, was the canonical age of consent for marriage and the young King was clever, toward and self-possessed. It was not clear that he needed a regent. However, if the boy was left to rule in his own right, he was so devoted to his mother and close to the Woodville side of his family that he would likely side with her against his uncle Richard. Having gone so far, the ugly reality was that Richard's political survival was now contingent on becoming King in his nephew's place. By June, he was issuing orders for his faithful followers to join him from Yorkshire 'to aid and assist us against the Queen, her bloody adherents and affinity'.[36] On 16 June, the King's younger brother was removed from his mother's care under promises of safe conduct. Elizabeth, whose mood can at best be described as catatonic, had made one of the most horrible mistakes of her life. Nine days later, Richard ordered the executions of her brother Anthony and her second son from her first marriage.

As it became clear that Richard was preparing to disinherit his brother's children, some of his allies began to get cold feet. Lord Hastings had no love for the Woodvilles, but he had only supported Richard in the hope of limiting Elizabeth's influence. When he voiced his objections to the usurpation, Richard had him arrested at a council meeting and murdered on the spot. No trial, no execution. Necessity knew no law. A public relations campaign tried to exploit every possible argument that could be found to justify deposing Edward V. Edward IV's impetuous promise to marry Eleanor Talbot if she would sleep with him was cited as a binding promise that rendered the subsequent marriage to Elizabeth Woodville bigamous and her children nothing more than bastards. A story that Edward IV himself was actually the illegitimate son of an archer was circulated, making Richard the senior living descendant of the late Duke of York and Edward V nothing more than the grandson of a commoner and an adulteress.[†]

In 1483, the smear campaign and the climate of fear prevailed. Edward V and his siblings were stripped of their titles and Richard was proclaimed King Richard III. The deposed monarch and his younger brother were seen playing in the Tower of London throughout the summer only to vanish from the records in the autumn of that year. The disappearance of 'the Princes in the Tower' remains a fruitful field for conspiracy theorists and historical fantasists. The suggestion that

† The latter charge, that Edward IV was not the biological son of the Duke of York, is still repeated today and it has gained a currency that it quite simply does not deserve. The story goes that his mother, Cecily Neville, conceived him in Normandy when her husband was at war and that surviving documentary evidence shows that the couple were not together during the summer of 1441 when Edward IV was conceived. However, the Duke only left Rouen in the third week of July and he was back five weeks later. By either date, he could have impregnated Cecily in time for Edward's birth in April 1442. The child would have been born roughly on time if the couple slept together before the Duke went on campaign or slightly premature if he was conceived when his father returned to Rouen. Even during the fighting, the Duke was only a few days' ride from Rouen and so the possibility of him returning briefly cannot be ruled out. The most conclusive evidence of all, aside from Edward's physical resemblance to most of the York menfolk, was the fact that his enormously proud father acknowledged him as his own and that if there had been any possibility of his illegitimacy, Marguerite of Anjou or Warwick would certainly have found that out and used it to their advantage.

they managed to live beyond 1485, only to be conveniently murdered by Henry VII's Machiavellian mother, Lady Margaret Beaufort, is utter nonsense. Richard III's credibility was irreparably damaged by the allegation that he had murdered his nephews and he could have salvaged a significant amount of political kudos in the countdown to his own downfall by displaying the boys, had they still been alive. It is inconceivable that he would have been so stupid as to send either one of them abroad, as is sometimes suggested. The least convincing and most intellectually ludicrous line of defence is the argument that he had no reason to kill them, because he had already made them illegitimate. Giving any credence to such a theory displays a total ignorance of the legislative acrobatics that medieval parliaments were willing to perform in order to suit the throne's incumbent. Had Edward V been liberated by his mother or her supporters, Parliament would have declared him legitimate just as complacently as they had once declared him illegitimate. The only way to ensure that what had been done was not undone was to do what Henry IV had done to Richard II in 1400 and Edward IV had done to Henry VI in 1471 – namely, assassination.

In terms of pointing the finger for one of the most famous murder mysteries in British history, Richard III remains the most likely suspect, despite generations of valiant and often sentimental attempts to exonerate him. Admittedly, it is just about possible that one of Richard's more zealous supporters undertook the deed during the confusion of his coup d'état. But even so, as both King and the boys' former legal guardian, Richard bears the ultimate responsibility for their disinheritance and subsequent disappearance.

Spilled blood does not sleep. Poison spreads. Few royalist causes in history have ever displayed such an unfailing ability to turn on themselves like the Yorkists. Personal animosity, festering resentment, titanic egos and unchecked ambition ensured that their rule was even shorter than the Lancastrians'. The latter's cause began to revive, despite the fact that the closest claimant it had left in terms of blood was Henry VI's nephew, Henry Tudor, a penniless exile living on handouts at the court of the Duke of Brittany. Tudor was the grandson of Catherine de Valois and her enterprising second husband Owen, but he had a faint link to the English throne via his mother's descent from Richard II's uncle, John of Gaunt. Under normal circumstances, Tudor's pretensions to kingship would have seemed laughable, but the disappearance of Edward V split the Yorkists. Some of Richard's own allies, like the Duke of Buckingham, turned on him and although early rebellions against him failed, there were enough high profile desertions to Tudor's court-in-exile to give King Richard cause for concern. The death of his only son in 1484 and then of his Queen, Anne Neville, during a solar eclipse in 1485 elicited almost no sympathy from his subjects, despite the fact that at the death of his son Richard was 'in a state almost bordering on madness, by reason of their sudden grief'.[37] Clouds of humiliation carrying the inescapable odour of panic arrived when Richard was compelled to publicly deny charges that he had poisoned his wife to pave the way for his incestuous seduction of, and marriage to, his stunning niece, Elizabeth of York, sister of the vanished princes.

Even those once loyal to Richard's family were slipping away. The executions, the disappearances, his alleged promotion of loyal northern favourites to positions of influence in the southern shires and his attacks on those who might pose a threat to him meant that by the time Henry Tudor invaded Wales in the summer of 1485 his army was, to quote a modern study of Richard's reign, 'at least as "Yorkist" as Richard's.'[38]

The two forces met at the Battle of Bosworth Field on 22 August 1485. King Richard III fought courageously, even as he was betrayed by some of his servants and suffered multiple injuries that were catalogued after the discovery of his remains in 2013. He was remembered in the centuries to come as a monster, thanks largely to the portraits left of him by Thomas More and William Shakespeare. He was not a monster, but he did monstrous things. The internecine viciousness of the Yorkist court, its pathological paranoia, which made it both untrustworthy and untrusting, its cruelty, its duplicity and its unhinged inability to forget the murky circumstances in which it had first come to power, had bred a generation that was in many ways a collection of people who were mad, bad and dangerous to know. For a century, the English monarchy had been a plaything to men's baser instincts, robbed of the security that made it so successful. Watching the English, the contemporary Philippe de Commynes observed, 'The lords in England killed their enemies, then later the children of their enemies gained revenge when times changed and favoured them and they killed the others.'[39]

Richard III, who prayed devoutly, remained comparatively faithful to his wife and certainly eschewed the promiscuous self-indulgence of his eldest brother, nonetheless was responsible for the disappearance and quite probably the death of two young family members who had been entrusted to his care, acts of tyranny against his nobles and peers, and in alienating the support of those who could have saved him.[40] Today, attempts to rehabilitate Richard have swung so far in the opposite extreme to the Tudors' bile towards him that during the excitement surrounding the discovery of his body in 2013, ordinarily-sombre British television presenters and historians participated in documentaries that cast him as a cross between Sir Galahad and a Disney prince. It was as bizarre as it was misleading. Richard III was born into a treacherous environment and played for high stakes in an unforgiving game. He fell in 1485 not just because of his own actions but also the terrible circumstances of his class and generation.

The House of York had finally destroyed itself.

AS THE LAW
OF CHRIST ALLOWS

THE RULE OF THE TUDORS

'The royal estate of princes, for the excellency
thereof doth far pass and excel all other estates
and degrees of life, which doth represent and
outwardly shadow unto us the glorious and
celestial monarchy which God, the governor of
all things, doth exercise in the firmament.'

Anne Boleyn, Queen of England

ON 19 May 1536, the sword of English medieval monarchy
gleamed one last time when it sliced through the neck of Anne
Boleyn. Anne had spent most of her formative years in France,
where beheading by sword remained more common than England's
farewell with the axe. This biographical detail resulted in the
perfectly understandable conclusion that Anne was allowed to perish
according to the customs of the land she had grown-up in. There
were even suggestions that Henry VIII allowed death by sword as a
final kindness to the wife he had once desired so passionately, raising
the possibility that, in some small way, he was not the uxoricidal

psychopath of popular legend. However, more recently Leanda de Lisle has hypothesised that the choice of a sword to execute the Queen in 1536 had very little to do with easing Anne's final moments and everything to do with the monarchy's, and Henry's, obsession with the legends of King Arthur.[1] Anne, as an adulterous Queen, had corrupted Henry VIII's court in much the same was as Guinevere had Camelot's. Anne's co-accused included her husband's closest friend, Henry Norris, paralleling Guinevere's fornication with noble Lancelot. So perhaps Anne Boleyn died beneath a form of Excalibur, not as a kindly favour to her French upbringing, but to massage her husband's pretensions of being Arthur's heir.

The irony was that in publicly shedding the blood of a crowned Queen, Henry VIII was completing the moral dislocation of the English monarchy which began with the deposition of Edward II in 1327 and gathered pace throughout the fifteenth century, resulting in the cloak-and-dagger assassinations of Richard II, Henry VI and Edward V. Kings had fallen in battle before, that was noble. They had been murdered in secret before, that was ignoble but it still showed a pragmatic deference for the institution of monarchy. Death had come for England's royals in many ways, but never public execution. The tragic drama of Anne Boleyn's final weeks and the illicit passion of her romance with Henry VIII have distracted from the constitutional significance of her death. Henry VIII's unhinged megalomania meant that he saw his wife solely as his creation, his property; he failed to realise that in having her blessed, anointed and crowned before thousands he had elevated her to the kinship of royalty in which her ceremonial importance far outweighed the dynamic of her personal life. Excalibur sliced through not just Anne Boleyn's neck but centuries of monarchist theory.

THE WELSH MOSES

AT THE same time as Henry VI's lifeless body crumpled onto the floor of the Tower of London, the future Henry VII was being bundled into a small boat in the bay of the village of Tenby in southern Wales. The fourteen-year-old, tall, lean, fit, with pale skin, dark hair and watchful eyes, was pitched out into the tail-end of an Atlantic storm that tossed the ship in swells of seasickness-inducing agony until it limped into unexpected safety in the harbours of Brittany. There, Henry VI's nephew and Catherine de Valois' grandson stepped ashore in the company of his uncle Jasper, the dispossessed Earl of Pembroke, to seek sanctuary at the court of François II, ruler of an independent Brittany. Henry Tudor grew up there, fell in love or lust, perhaps fathered a bastard child called Roland, read a lot of Arthurian legends, pined for his brilliant, domineering and devoted mother Margaret, who was working feverishly on his behalf back in England to ingratiate herself with the Yorkist court, and struck up enough of a friendship with the Duke that the latter loyally refused all English attempts to have Henry extradited.

When Richard III seized the throne in 1483, the disappearance of Edward V and his brother revived Henry Tudor's chances. If hitherto he and his mother had only dreamed of persuading Edward IV to restore his father's earldom of Richmond to the boy, the shattering of the Yorkist political class and the trickle, then flood, of political émigrés making their way to Henry's side turned him into a viable contender for the throne itself. His claim was hardly watertight. However, he was all the Lancastrians had left and as Richard III's popularity plummeted, Henry became the rising sun. When Duke François' mental health declined to the point that his treasurer was able to strike a deal to hand Henry over to the English, he was tipped off thanks to one of his mother's spies at Richard's court, faked sickness, donned a disguise and rode hell-for-leather to the Breton border with France where, as the great-grandson of a French monarch, he could expect an offer of sanctuary.

It was from France that he set sail with a medium-sized army, returning to the homeland he had last seen fourteen years earlier, and fell to his knees to recite Psalms and kiss the ground as he landed. The Welsh people still groaned under penalising legislation introduced to punish them for Owen Glendower's rebellion against Henry IV eighty-five years earlier and so the sight of a Welsh-born lord progressing towards the English throne stirred many hopes.[2] A Welsh bard referred to him as 'a Moses who delivered us from our bondage'.[3] Crucially, Henry Tudor was also able to attract significant support in England and his mother used her most recent marriage to the Yorkist Lord Stanley as a convenient cloak under which to intrigue shamelessly with Richard III's disaffected supporters, a policy that paid dividend when he was abandoned by many of them on the battlefield on 22 August 1485.

As Richard's body was carted off for burial, Henry progressed to London to be crowned, proclaimed rightful Sovereign by Parliament and marry Edward IV's eldest daughter, the nineteen-year-old Elizabeth of York. In that order. Henry was very keen to stress that his crown came from military victory and a religious mandate, like the Anglo-Saxons, Normans and early Plantagenets, rather than more recent monarchs' reliance on convoluted ancestral nit-picking and parliamentary quiescence. Those who had supported him in exile were richly rewarded, none more so than his mother and uncle Jasper. A triumphal tour of the northern parts of England amid bumper harvests and beautiful weather culminated in his arrival to joyful scenes in York of all places, where the fountains flowed with wine and the interlocked white and red roses of the York and Lancaster families proclaimed the union of two warring clans through the new King and Queen's marriage, a hope solidified by the Queen's successful delivery of a son nine months after her wedding. The baby was christened Arthur.

New beginnings are more easily proclaimed than realised, however, and the corpse of the Wars of the Roses kept twitching throughout Henry VII's time as King, aggravating the corrosive paranoia he became so famous for. An early uprising led by the rump of Richard III's most devoted adherents ended in ignominious failure when they were deserted by most of their common supporters, thanks to Henry VII's decision to issue promises that if the rebels set down their arms, they could go home unpunished.

Two more serious threats arose against him later, both of which tested Ireland's fluctuations in loyalty, volatile ever since Edward I weakened the monarchy's influence there by becoming too distracted with his wars in Wales, Scotland and France. The Wars of the Roses had resulted in a further dilution of the Crown's authority and the rise of the local nobility at its expense. Welsh Henry's seizure of the throne was not popular in Ireland and the Irish Parliament that met in Dublin two months after the Battle of Bosworth insisted upon opening in King Richard's name, rather than Henry VII's. The country was riddled with internal divisions, particularly on what might tentatively be called ethnic grounds. Its geopolitics were explosively divisive. Tensions festered between the Anglo-Irish, the descendants of the settlers in the twelfth century, and the native Irish, despite the fact that both groups had repeatedly intermarried with each other. Fact did not matter very much and to those who self-identified as native Irish, the Anglo-Irish were contemptuously referred to as the *Gaill* (foreign). In the words of one historian, the Anglo-Irish, 'were bound by the same statutes, and to the same allegiance as the English of England, and spoke English, yet they were also clearly distinct from the English of England, for they were born in Ireland, and most also spoke Irish. The English of Ireland lived in close but uneasy proximity to a culture profoundly different from their own.'[4] It was a set of complex identities that the Tudor government struggled with, just as much as those in Northern Ireland in the twentieth century.

As the fifteenth century wore on, royal control in Ireland had more or less contracted to a region around Dublin that was eventually ringed-in by defensive dykes, walls, fortresses and castles. Within the Pale, English customs like a parliament, a chancellery, a royal council and an English judicial system were maintained and ties to England deepened in reaction to what was seen as the violence of the *Gaedhil* (native Irish).

Dublin had a thriving civic and religious life which saw the city's upper classes invest in hospitals, almshouses for the poor, leper sanctuaries and schools, much like their equivalents in England or on the continent. Dublin's women were particularly keen to participate in the culture of wealthy female benefactresses, endowing establishments like the city's hospital of Saint John the Baptist.[5] Yet even within Dublin, tensions remained. It is a fallacy to assume that everything within the Pale was complacently anglicised and everything outside it implacably hostile.

It was this schizoid sense of identity, running through Irish society, which led Polydore Virgil to conclude, 'these Irishmen excel the others in ferocity, and – being more eager for revolutions – are found readier to support any type of upheaval.'[6] When Henry VII took the throne in 1485, he unintentionally exacerbated Ireland's uncertain sense of identity. He was not popular, not even with the powerful clans of the Anglo-Irish aristocracy, and when a pretender arrived on their shores claiming to be a long-lost prince of the House of York, they knelt before him. Henry's own Lord Lieutenant, the Earl of Kildare, helped organise the adolescent boy's coronation as 'King Edward VI' in Dublin's Christ Church Cathedral, where he was crowned with a make-do crown plucked from a statue of the Virgin Mary.

The boy, who claimed to be the Earl of Warwick, Edward IV and Richard III's nephew who had languished in the Tower ever since Henry VII's seizure of the throne, was in fact an Oxford joiner's son called Lambert Simnel. He bore a passing resemblance to the York family and he was being carefully schooled by priests and former courtiers in his entourage, most of whom knew that the real Warwick was still alive and well, hidden behind the looming walls of the Tower of London. They hired two thousand German mercenaries and sailed the child to Ireland, where they met with local nobles. One Irish priest, Cathal Maguire, archdeacon of the northern diocese of Clogher, applauded the nobility's actions, remarking that the King of 'the Welsh race' was an unacceptable King of England or Lord of Ireland, and that everyone preferred 'Edward VI'.[7]

However, when Simnel's army landed on the Lincolnshire coast, the enthusiasm was more muted, even as they processed through the former Yorkist heartlands in the north. As Francis Bacon observed a century later, 'Their snowball did not gather as it went'.[8] They passed Sherwood Forest and encountered the royal army at the Battle of Stoke, which proved a resounding victory for the Tudors. Most of Simnel's prominent supporters either fell in battle or drowned in the river trying to escape. Touchingly conscious of the fact that the boy had been plucked and groomed for the role based on his appearance, Henry VII pardoned him and threw in a job in the royal kitchens, where Simnel turned the spits in the palace's cavernous fire pits. He proved as conscientious a study as he had when preparing for a throne and he ultimately rose to become master of the King's prized falcons. In the meantime, the real Earl of Warwick was conducted from the Tower to attend Mass at Saint Paul's Cathedral to prove that he was still alive and in the King's custody.

However, while producing the real Earl to disprove the Simnel threat was easily done, when, Anastasia-like, another pretender rose from beyond the grave, it was a lot harder to quash the rumours. The handsome and confident Perkin Warbeck insisted that he was Elizabeth of York's younger brother Richard, who had vanished in the Tower with their brother Edward V in 1483. Elizabeth's estranged aunt Margaret, Dowager Duchess of Burgundy, naturally detested the Tudors and she supported Warbeck's claim. However, given that she had also lent her support to Lambert Simnel, it is difficult to know how accurate this identification was. Exploiting Henry's difficulties as they once had Edward IV's and Richard III's, the governments of France and the Hapsburg Empire endorsed Warbeck's claim. Even more damagingly, given its proximity, was the court of Scotland's support, which was so enthusiastic that it allowed Warbeck to marry their King's kinswoman, Lady Katherine Gordon. Warbeck, styling himself King Richard IV, went to Ireland to finish what Simnel's team had started. He arrived at Cork in 1491 and his subsequent invasion of England helped spark a serious rebellion against the Tudors in Cornwall.

In the end, Warbeck's cause also fell on the battlefield and he was captured and executed, after confessing to fraud, in 1499. The cost to Henry VII's Exchequer had been enormous and the cost to his already fragile sense of trust even greater. For a brave young man with a talent for acting, Perkin Warbeck had come far too close to toppling Henry's throne. Frantic attempts to find the bodies of Edward V and his brother, which could be publicly displayed to refute Warbeck's claim, came to nothing; it was not until the reign of Charles II in the seventeenth century that skeletons allegedly belonging to the two princes were found buried beneath the bottom of a staircase in the Tower.

In the meantime, Queen Elizabeth of York had provided enough children to stabilise the fledgling dynasty. After Prince Arthur's birth, the Queen produced six more children – Margaret in 1489, Henry in 1491, Elizabeth in 1492, Mary in 1496, Edmund in 1499 and Katherine in 1503.[9] Along with her mother-in-law, who penned strict guides on court etiquette, Elizabeth of York added to the pomp of the Tudor court, bringing to it the sophistication and polish she had experienced growing up at her parents'. Both women helped smooth over the roughness of Henry's own manners and the occasional faux-pas which inevitably arose from someone who had spent most of his developmental years in Brittany and France. At times, the King seemed unaware of the full significance of Parliament and his expectation to rule like the French autocrats he had seen as a young man was nowhere more apparent than his desire for money. This he needed badly to financially ground the Crown after years of it haemorrhaging money.

In the first half of his reign, as splendid palaces like Richmond, one of the finest examples of Renaissance architecture in northern Europe, rose along the banks of the Thames and the court sparkled under the watchful eyes of Lady Margaret and Queen Elizabeth, Henry VII's avariciousness was not so blatant. However, a series of bereavements pushed him into a long and dark decline – his eldest son Arthur died during an outbreak of the plague in 1502, only a few months after marrying the Spanish monarchs' youngest daughter, Katherine of Aragon, and a year later Queen Elizabeth died on her thirty-seventh birthday as a result of post-natal complications.[10] Her new-born daughter died a week later and the King locked himself away to mourn. He had been faithful to Elizabeth throughout their marriage which, although born from political necessity in the dying days of the Wars of the Roses, seems to have been a happy one.

The final six years of his reign saw him tightening the screws on anyone and everyone, bleeding them dry and making his councillors hate figures not just for the outraged nobility, who detested Henry VII's preference for the company of hardworking lawyers and civil servants over the blue-bloods of the aristocracy, but also to the vast majority of his subjects. The unpleasantness seeped into his private life. Funds to his widowed daughter-in-law were cut off as he had second thoughts about re-cementing the Spanish alliance as planned by marrying her to his teenage son Henry, now heir-apparent. Princess Katherine worked herself up into a resentful hysteria at her treatment, a mood in keeping with the rest of the country. On-the-rise legal students like Thomas More launched blistering criticisms on the government's rapacity, there were anti-taxation riots in Yorkshire and when Henry VII began to sicken and die from tuberculosis, losing his battle in the spring of 1509, there were few who pitied him and even fewer who mourned. In years to come, Tudor panegyric airbrushed the decline and focused solely on Henry's success in ending the turmoil of the previous generation, restoring England's position as a force to be reckoned with in European politics, and leaving the monarchy rich and solvent for the first time in decades.

BLUFF KING HAL

THE LITERATURE on Henry VIII is vast. His private life so improbable that no novelist would dare dream it up if it had not actually happened. The peaks and troughs of his domestic tribulations are moments of sublime melodrama, crafting the narrative arc for the numerous playwrights, novelists and scriptwriters who have attempted to dramatise his story, from William Shakespeare to the present. Henry and his six unlucky brides almost constitute an industry in their own right. This fame has its pitfalls. The King's romantic mishaps, as well as the brooding charisma projected from the portraits of him by Hans Holbein, have nurtured many myths about the man who ruled England, Wales and Ireland with varying degrees of success from 1509 to 1547. The legend of 'Bluff King Hal', the larger-than-life machismo that made him so popular with the vast majority of his subjects, is the first and by far the most potent of these legends. In fact, the story of Henry's great popularity, still repeated today, was largely a product of the generation after his death when the uncertainties of his children's reigns gave Henry's a retrospective glow. Sources from the time reveal that his subjects' views of Henry were far more ambivalent. Later in his life, conversations overheard between his subjects confirmed that 'if the King knew every man's thought, it would make his heart quake'.[11]

That certainly was not the mood at his coronation in 1509. His was the first undisputed succession since Henry V's nearly a century earlier. When stability and relief were coupled with the King's good looks, Yorkist fair hair and muscular frame, it was not difficult to see why he was swept onto the throne on the crest of a wave of adulation. Even the Venetian ambassador joined in, with letters gushing with faintly erotic excitement at the prettiness of the King's sweat-clad form as it glowed through his expensive shirts while he played tennis.[12] The decadence of his court, with its parties, constant feasts and frequent jousts, was augmented by his petite blonde wife, Katherine of Aragon, who usually knew how to behave and when she did not, learned quickly.

Nonetheless, the seeds of the reign's future malaise were sown in its early days. The Queen was separated from one of her favourite ladies-in-waiting when they dared remonstrate about the King's attempts to seduce one of the Duke of Buckingham's sisters, a scandal that helped isolate the country's premier peer further from a regime that he already seemed to regard as a tacky monstrosity, presided over by a preening child. Hot on the heels of that fracas was the farce of Queen Katherine's first pregnancy, during which she disregarded all medical advice that contradicted her own belief that she was with child. She was not. Her hysterical pregnancy was hushed up, but not before a string of embarrassing letters to and from her father in Spain.[13] The alliance she represented was already beginning to crumble as its usefulness was queried by those close to the King, commencing nearly three decades of diplomatic chop and change. Wars with France were launched in a vain attempt to bring back the glory days of Henry V and Edward III, but the greatest military victory of his reign was ironically carried out under the auspices of Queen Katherine, left behind as regent while her husband played at being a general in France. She had to rally the troops under the command of the aged Earl of Surrey to defeat the invading armies of France's ally, King James IV of Scots. The Scottish King fell in battle and the courtiers had to talk Queen Katherine out of sending his battered corpse to Henry as a prize. She contented herself with his blood-stained doublet.[14]

Within a decade of becoming King, the dominant influence on Henry was a brilliant and industrious Oxford graduate, Father Thomas Wolsey, whose efficiency and eye for detail saw him rise through the court hierarchy to become Henry's favourite adviser, Archbishop of York, a cardinal, Papal legate and Lord Chancellor. The Queen distrusted him and her views were shared by the old guard of the nobility, with whom she enjoyed her closest relationships. Wolsey, the commoner, aggravated their sensibilities, while his attempts to reform the royal household cut off lucrative forms of aristocratic employment, earning him the enmity of prominent families like the Howards, Brandons and Boleyns. By the end of the 1510s, Cardinal Wolsey was the brain behind the Henrician government and, while Henry remained in broad control of the larger picture, he was too bored by hard work and irritated by writing to question the Cardinal's monopolisation of the minutiae.

Henry VIII was not stupid. In fact, he was superbly educated and although he seldom had any idea that was uniquely his own, he busied himself with writing a competent if hyperbolic defence of Papal authority when it was challenged by the advent of the Protestant

Reformation in Germany in 1517. It pleased the Pope, but made little difference elsewhere. The fires of spiritual uncertainty swept the northern half of Europe. Too late did the Vatican realise the extent of the threat or the hunger for ecclesiastical reform. There were those in England, close to the King, who wanted harsh measures to be taken against the spread of the Protestant heresy in England and, at least at first, he agreed with them. For his literary efforts and piety, Pope Leo X awarded him the title 'Fidei Defensor' ('Defender of the Faith'), and Henry dreamed of re-starting the Crusades.

Catholicism's great defender, however, had no son to pick up his mantle if, or rather when, mortality came to demand the price it levies on us all. His son Henry, Duke of Cornwall, had died six weeks after his birth, leaving his mother utterly distraught. Her numerous subsequent pregnancies produced only one surviving child, the precocious Princess Mary, born at Greenwich Palace in February 1516. In the meantime, the King's succession of mistresses culminated with one, Elizabeth Blount, giving birth to his bastard son, Henry FitzRoy, whom he happily acknowledged as his own.[15] Katherine's distress at this illegitimate progeny was exacerbated by her husband's decision to elevate him to the duchy of Richmond, a title which, worryingly from the Queen's perspective, had been enjoyed by Henry's own father before he became King in 1485.[16] The boy's ennoblement took place around the same time as the Queen passed the menopause, forcing her to confront the prospect looming on the horizon of her daughter being displaced in the line of succession by Elizabeth Blount's bastard.[17]

It was not the wisest move Henry ever made. While William the Conqueror had taken the throne in 1066 as a man born out of wedlock, times had changed and one of the main planks of Richard III's quest to disinherit Edward V was his charge that the latter was the offspring of an illegal marriage, making him a bastard unfit to wear the crown. Despite the disaster of the Empress Maud's attempts to take the crown after 1135, there was a lot more to suggest that the people would happily acquiesce to a female Sovereign than an illegitimate one. A healthy and legitimate male heir from a queen of child-bearing age would be the ideal solution to the problem of the succession. To that end, in the middle of the 1520s Wolsey began to put out feelers about the validity of the royal marriage. At the time it was celebrated in 1509, the Archbishop of Canterbury had preached sermons against it, citing texts from the book of Leviticus that condemned the marriage between a former brother- and sister-in-law as incestuous.[18] Back then, no one had paid very much attention, since Pope Julius II's dispensation of Levitical law and the radiant Katherine's insistence that her first marriage to Arthur Tudor had never been consummated meant that no one took the Bible's looming threat of a cursed and childless marriage too seriously.[19] However, with all his sons born dead or dying shortly after their birth, Henry's conscience began one of its convenient flair-ups and Cardinal Wolsey supported him petitioning for an annulment to then marry the King of France's sister-in-law, the sixteen-year-old Renée de Valois, whose mother had fourteen children and whose late sister, Queen Claude, gave birth to seven.

Early talks about a possible royal annulment were held in strictest confidence – who knew what the Queen would do if she got wind of the plan too early? Some of Wolsey's in-palace enemies would no doubt have been delighted to scupper his plans by alerting her, even if most of them seem to have accepted that a second marriage would be in the country's best interests. Aristocratic hatred of the Cardinal had only intensified when he was blamed for arranging the trial and execution of the Duke of Buckingham in 1521. Other aristocrats, compelled to sit in judgement to give him the trial by his peers guaranteed by law, wept as the Duke was sentenced to death for allegedly plotting the deposition of the King. That Buckingham was the King's cousin on his mother's side did absolutely nothing to help him, nor did the decidedly eclectic nature of the evidence against him. The Duke's most recent biographer has suggested that he was certainly guilty of hating Henry's government, but whether those thoughts would have ever have transformed into actions is unknowable.[20]

Cardinal Wolsey's many opponents received a golden opportunity when the King fell in love with Anne Boleyn, the youngest daughter of one of the men Wolsey had managed to aggravate during his impressive career. What began as an unreciprocated infatuation quickly escalated to the point that thoughts of Renée de Valois were banished as the prospect that Anne Boleyn would follow in the footsteps of Elizabeth Woodville became increasingly likely.

THE RISE AND FALL OF ANNE BOLEYN

MORE NONSENSE has been written about Anne Boleyn than almost any other figure in British history.[21] The myriad fictitious and contradictory Annes have produced a cultural afterlife almost as rich and fascinating as the story of the real woman. Since no parish records were kept in England until well into the reign of her daughter, dating Anne's birth is a fraught process – the first of the controversies. Within a century of her death, dates as far flung as 1499 and 1512 had been suggested. Today, the competing works of the late Hugh Paget and Retha Warnicke have distilled the debate down to two none-too-close dates of 1501 and 1507.[22] Although the weight of popular opinion favours the earlier date, for what it is worth, my money has always been on the summer or autumn of 1507.[23] Her place of birth is unknown, although the family originally hailed from Norfolk and her parents spent some of their early married life there, residing at Blickling Hall.

After her grandfather's death in 1505, the family divided most of their time between the court, where Sir Thomas Boleyn's proficiency in languages and skills as a diplomat ensured his career's upward trajectory under Henry VII and Henry VIII, and picturesque Hever Castle in Kent, which survives today as one of the most lovely medieval residences in the British Isles. Her mother, born Elizabeth Howard, was the Duke of Norfolk's daughter and said to be very beautiful. Anne was one of at least five siblings, probably more, with two brothers, Thomas and Henry, dying in infancy. An elder sister, Mary, grew into adulthood, as did their brother George, who was probably born either in 1503 or 1504. Through her mother, Anne was related to most of the great families of the English aristocracy – her maternal aunts included the countesses of Derby, Oxford, Bridgewater and Sussex – and like most of the English nobility by the sixteenth century, she was distantly descended from the numerous offspring of Edward III and Philippa of Hainault.[24] Her father stood to inherit the earldom of his Irish grandfather Thomas Butler, Katherine of Aragon's Lord Chamberlain.[25] Centuries earlier, the Boleyns had made their money in the wool trade and advanced into the nobility by a series of socially advantageous marriages. This allowed some of her opponents to portray Anne as a girl who climbed like ivy, a charge reworked by her latter-day enthusiasts into the story of a plucky young commoner rising to greatness as a self-made woman. Alas, by the time Anne Boleyn was born, the Boleyns were very much one of the club when it came to courtly families and both she and her father benefitted from the Anglo-Irish nobilities' historical tendency to pay as much deference to maternal ancestry as paternal.

She was educated on the continent, first as a ward of the Archduchess Margaret of Austria, the Emperor's daughter who ruled the Netherlands as his regent-cum-governor, and then at the French court, where she acquired a sophisticated cosmopolitan allure, fluency in French, proficiency in Latin, her love of clothes and her talent for music.[26] Whilst there she met and quite possibly befriended the girl who might have been Queen of England in her stead, Renée de Valois, the King's gentle and diminutive sister-in-law. Everywhere she went in the early stages of her career, Anne Boleyn made a favourable impression. Decades later, Renée fell into conversation with Sir Nicholas Throckmorton, the English ambassador, telling him that she had known Anne in childhood and fond memories of her compelled her to think highly of his Queen, Elizabeth I.[27] Renée's brother-in-law, King François I, praised both Anne's charm and her ability to keep admirers at a chaste distance. Long after, when she was England's Queen and relations between the two countries had soured, he changed his tune to claim that Anne had behaved 'little virtuously' during her time in France.[28] However, he also tore into the reputation of Henry VIII's youngest sister Mary, his predecessor's widow, calling her 'a great whore', so it is difficult to take his assessment of either lady at face value, particularly when set against what he said of them when they were actually in his company.[†]

Anne Boleyn returned to the English court in the winter of 1521, where her family connections secured her a position as one of Queen Katherine's maids-of-honour. It is possible that her recently married sister, Lady Mary Carey, was the King's latest paramour, although several historians have cast doubt on whether or not the King's affair

---

† François' comments are usually assumed to refer to Anne Boleyn's elder sister, Mary, who was also briefly in residence at the French court. However, there was no separate phrase for a sister-in-law in the sixteenth century, meaning that Mary Tudor the Elder would have been considered Anne Boleyn's sister once she married into the royal family. Given François' blistering condemnation of her elsewhere, the recent theory that the most famous quote associated with Mary Boleyn was in fact a reference to Mary Tudor, Queen Dowager of France and Duchess of Suffolk, seems convincing.

with the other Boleyn sister ever actually occurred.[29] The veracity of rumours linking the two are hotly contested. If any liaison did take place, it must have been very fleeting and there is little chance that either of Mary Carey's two eldest children were fathered by the King. Given his feverish attempts to prove his fertility and the Queen's barrenness, which was the primary motivating factor behind the elevation of Henry FitzRoy to the top rungs of the peerage, it is improbable that the King would not have recognised Henry Carey if there was a possibility that he was his.

Anne Boleyn made an impact on court life almost immediately. Contemporary estimations of her beauty vary, from courtiers who thought she was very beautiful, right the way through to the famously dismissive assessment of a Venetian diplomat who thought she was 'not one of the handsomest women in the world'.[30] Stories of an extra finger, deformed nail, warts, third nipples and jaundiced skin date from propaganda tracts written long after her death. No deformity is mentioned in any of the eyewitness descriptions of her which, if they existed, is surely incredible.[31] She had long dark hair, a svelte physique that occasionally bordered on the too-thin, and beautiful dark eyes that were described as her best feature. She certainly had charisma, and that in bucketfuls. She was dazzlingly charming with a risqué sense of humour and a needle-sharp brain. Like many highly strung people, she had a tendency towards the neurotic, which produced outbursts of slightly manic bad temper. The world of the court, the palace and the high nobility was all she had ever known and she took to it in England like a duck to water. Court poets wrote sonnets of anguished unreciprocated love to her in which she appeared as the doe beyond every hunter's reach. There was talk of betrothal, first with one of her Irish cousins, the future Earl of Ossory, and later with Lord Henry Percy, the heir to the earldom of Northumberland.

Eventually, the huntsman she could not escape entered the chase. Flirtation was a part of life at a Renaissance court, not so much an exchange of romantic longing as a game of witty one-upmanship, and Henry VIII and Anne Boleyn excelled at it. It is quite possible that Henry was drawn to her under the guise of courtly love that eventually grew into the real thing. Calling it love might admittedly be to mislabel and mislead. From the start, Henry's attitude towards Anne Boleyn was a deeply unhealthy one, which at least one of her biographers has not hesitated to compare to stalking.[32] It was certainly obsessive, possessive and self-loathing. Anne was a prize to be won, not a woman to be understood, and as his pursuit of her increased in ardour she behaved like a doe caught in a clearing. She was clearly flattered by his interest. After all, he was the King, but losing her virginity would make her less desirable on the aristocratic marriage market. The very best she could hope for was a wealthy member of the gentry, since few noble families would want their own exalted bloodline sullied by second-hand goods, even if it was a hand-me-down from the King. Later suggestions that she drew Henry in like a fish on a hook are to accredit her with powers of clairvoyance. Her retreats to her family seat at Hever removed her by miles from Henry's presence and in the days of much slower travel, the chance that he would lose interest entirely was very real. He did not and his letters to her, by turns cloyingly emotional and then agonisingly reproachful, show that even at this early stage he was filled with a desire to control her that sat alongside self-disgust for being so preoccupied with her.

Anne's refusal to become Henry's latest mistress coincided with enquiries about the royal annulment. How much she knew about it at that early stage is hard to say. If she did, her rejection of Henry need not be read as part of a deliberate policy to make herself Queen in Katherine's place. If she had heard whispers on the court grapevine, she may also have heard of the Cardinal's promotion of Renée de Valois as a possible replacement for Queen Katherine. Given her childhood acquaintance with Renée and her fluency in French, it is more than possible that Anne could have become the new Queen's favourite or confidante, a chance that would be lost to her if she became Henry's mistress and Renée's competition. Ambition, fear and uncertainty drove Anne Boleyn's early rejections of Henry VIII. At some point, and the exact chronology is still contested, he became convinced she should be his next wife. Anne hesitated but the fantastic prospect opening up before her sealed her fate, along with the fact that there really was no other viable answer she could give him without destroying herself and her family's careers in the process.

Queen Katherine, in the meantime, had been informed of the King's attempts to divorce her and the reasons for it. She was furious and deeply hurt. She clung to her version of events, that her six-month marriage to Arthur Tudor in 1501 and 1502 had never been consummated, which meant its existence as a marriage at all was in doubt. Her supporters, which at least in the early stages could be counted on one hand when it came to the great and the good of her husband's court, cited a quote from the book of Deuteronomy, which directly contradicted the verse in Leviticus by claiming that if a man died childless then his brother should marry his widow for the sake of family honour.[33] Experts poured over various translations of the holy text to see what precisely they demanded and threatened, and the King entrusted everything into the ever-capable hands of Cardinal Wolsey while the Queen's confessor smuggled panicked letters to her relatives in Europe.

For centuries, stories circulated that Anne Boleyn nurtured a cancerous hatred of Cardinal Wolsey and from the moment the metaphorical engagement ring was placed on her finger, she intrigued ceaselessly in the hope of ruining his career. This is not borne out by the surviving evidence. Initially, her father, her uncle the Duke of Norfolk, and their friends hoped to use her newfound influence with the King to pursue their own long-held grudge against the Cardinal, but Anne had no reason to dislike or distrust Wolsey. At least, not yet. Her instinct for self-preservation and her unfailing ability to show great kindness and support to anyone who helped her, provided that they continue to do exactly what she asked of them, were on full display in 1528 and 1529 as she placed all her confidence in Wolsey, the star of her fiancé's government, in the hope that he would make good on his promises to make her Queen quickly. The two of them exchanged chatty letters peppered with effusive compliments and accompanied by expensive gifts, including gourmet fish for Anne's dinner parties during Lent, when meat was prohibited. Cardinal and queen-to-be were clever enough to know that more could be gained by allying than quarrelling.

However, the Boleyn-Wolsey camaraderie began to unravel in the face of Katherine of Aragon's heroic defence of her queenship. Heroism, while admirable of course, is not always wise and, as Katherine's Hapsburg relatives brought the full force of their superpower status to bear on the indecisive pontiff, the trenches were dug for a six-year battle that would end not only in defeat for the Queen, but the shattering of England's allegiance to the Vatican, the destruction of dozens of careers and the bastardisation of Katherine's only surviving child. As tensions rose over the Queen's refusal to go quietly into a nunnery, life in the palace became a hotbed of espionage, treacherous servants, stolen letters, duplicitous promises and festering feuds barely concealed by the court's inexorable adherence to etiquette. Henry VIII's love letters to Anne were stolen and delivered to Rome by servants in the pay of the Queen, who was anxious to show that her husband was fornicating with another woman while preaching to the Pope about the tenderness of his conscience. Ironically, the letters confirmed that Henry and Anne were abstaining from sex until marriage, but Anne's presence and her conspicuous extravagance helped galvanise public support for Katherine, who played, fairly, the role of the wronged wife to the hilt.

Cardinal Wolsey's promise that he could deliver the divorce from Rome came back to haunt him when the Queen publicly testified that she would accept no verdict but one delivered directly by the Pope himself. Given her family's dominance of the Italian peninsula, she could be assured a favourable hearing in Rome. After this debacle, which he failed either to foresee or contain, Wolsey was dismissed from office and banished to the north, where he died in dejection and disgrace. Anne Boleyn, furious at the delays and what she chose to interpret as Wolsey's game-playing dishonesty, was blamed for orchestrating his demise, even allegedly arranging picnics to keep the King occupied when Wolsey came cap-in-hand to orchestrate a reconciliation, but both Wolsey's most recent biographer and Boleyn's have argued that it was Henry, full of wrath at being thwarted, who was the chief architect of his one-time confidante's destruction.[34] If she did exert any influence in laying waste to Wolsey's career, she did so subtly.

After Wolsey, the next exiling was the Queen's. For the first four years of the divorce, euphemistically referred to as the King's 'Great Matter' by contemporaries, the couple had maintained an excruciatingly polite façade, with the King protesting to a group of no doubt incredulous hangers-on that he hoped desperately that the Pope would declare that his marriage to Katherine of Aragon was valid because, 'if I were to marry again, if the marriage might be good, I would surely choose her above all other women.'[35] His infatuation with Anne Boleyn and her sizable household now financed with a budget that satisfied her every caprice told an altogether different story, but no one was going to point that out as the King waxed loquacious on the purity of his intentions. In 1531, the pretence was abandoned and Katherine of Aragon was moved to one of Cardinal Wolsey's former countryside retreats, the More. She was housed in luxury with a staff of hundreds, but the heartrending humiliation of her demotion caused her to disingenuously claim that the house was a purgatorial ruin.

Queen Katherine loved her daughter, the fourteen-year-old Princess Mary, deeply but Henry decided to separate them as punishment for Katherine's continued refusal to give him his annulment. In a cruel twist, had Katherine of Aragon acquiesced to the annulment in its early stages she could have preserved her child's place in the line of succession, because the Church allowed children to remain legitimate if they were conceived 'in good faith', when two people joined together in an illegal union but had not yet realised it. This had been the option settled on for the children of Louis VII and Eleanor of Aquitaine. Determined not to compromise if she would not, Henry pressed on for the full dissolution of the marriage on the implied grounds that Katherine had lied about the consummation of her first marriage. Her defence of her own title thus helped unintentionally to pave the way for the destruction of her daughter's position and English Catholicism.

Even as it became clear that those at court who were secretly sympathetic to Protestantism were flocking to Anne Boleyn, who was promoting them into positions of influence as she began to flex her political muscles, Katherine of Aragon did not crumble. Indeed, she seemed almost to relish the drama and she embraced the fight with a vigour that appeared ever-more imbalanced. Her letters to her daughter urged her to choose death over compromise, she barricaded herself in her rooms claiming that she feared poison, she refused to acknowledge any servants who would not address her as Queen, and she spoke of martyrdom on the horizon.

That crown was denied her, but it was thrust onto the heads of hundreds of others who shared her religious views. None died to save Katherine's queenship, despite years of romantic pretence that they did. Queens had been shunted aside before on grounds far more dubious than the ones shifting beneath Henry and Katherine. What mattered after 1533 was what Katherine's demotion went hand-in-hand with – the destruction of Rome's spiritual authority in England, Ireland and Wales.

Driven to the point of fury by the Pope's constant dithering over the subject as he hoped to avoid offending either side, Henry's mind proved fertile fields for those who wanted to see the legacy of

Henry IV overturned so that the Bible could once again be published in English or who felt inspired by Martin Luther's blistering denouncements of the corruption and power of the Papacy. Anne Boleyn, who regarded the administering of the death penalty to the Vatican's spiritual opponents as a repulsive horror, received banned books that rubbished the Papal office and distributed them to her servants. She was not, however, a Protestant in the way that we would now understand the word. Indeed, by modern standards, she was a devout Catholic, with a belief in Purgatory, the intercession of the saints, veneration of the Blessèd Virgin Mary, pilgrimage, the efficacy of good deeds in earning one's salvation, and great devotion to the doctrine of Transubstantiation. However, she did believe in the Bible in the vernacular, reform of the clergy and the importance of sermons. It says more for the obdurate anger of the Holy See in the first three decades of the Reformation that these beliefs made her seem like an arch-heretic.

Future generations of Protestants lovingly claimed Anne as one of their own, the 'crop and root' of the English Reformation, who had been chosen by God to fulfil His plan when He had 'given her the mind' to accomplish it.[36] Their respect for her is not difficult to explain, because as impatience mingled with spiritual inquisitiveness, Anne emerged as one of the most powerful figures in the English government and she used that influence to promote the attacks on the Vatican at every turn. Parliament was called to deal with the issue and the echoes of every previous royal quarrel with the Papacy, particularly Henry II's and King John's, rang through Westminster as they reached far back into the national memory to support Henry VIII's claim that the Vatican had no right to intervene in English matters. Even Constantine the Great's presence at the Council of Nicea was invoked to revive the doctrine of caesaropapism, the belief that a monarchy should be heavily involved in its kingdom's faith. The clergy, so it was argued, were trying to serve two masters, the King and the Pope, and that was a recipe for treason. Heavy fines were levied on the clerical caste and laws, piece by piece, were introduced that suffocated the English people's ability to appeal to Rome until the life was choked from it completely.

The exact date of Henry VIII and Anne Boleyn's marriage is debated and it is probable that, as with many medieval royal marriages, they went through two ceremonies: the first either during a visit to the

English colony at Calais or at Dover Castle shortly after their return in November 1532, and the second at Whitehall, Wolsey's former palace now beautified and expanded for Anne, in the third week of January. She was pregnant by the time of her second nuptial Mass, although it is unlikely she could have realised it at that early stage. Not long after there was even discussion of her going on a pilgrimage to the shrine of Our Lady of Walsingham in Norfolk to petition the Virgin Mary for a child if she was not pregnant within a few months.

At Easter, she attended Mass for the first time as Queen and prayers for her were added to services throughout the kingdom. The new Archbishop of Canterbury, Thomas Cranmer, obediently declared that the marriage between Henry VIII and Katherine of Aragon was an incestuous contravention of Biblical law which no earthly authority had the right to dispense, their daughter was demoted from princess to Lady Mary, and at Whitsunday Anne was crowned Queen with Edward the Confessor's crown at Westminster Abbey. A mechanical dragon had been built to belch fire across the river as the delighted Queen and her entourage sailed into the city with the numerous 'banners and pennants of arms [...] of fine gold' reflected in the sunshine.[37] On land, Anne travelled under arches decorated with sculptures of the Muses on Mount Parnassus, statues of her patron saint, mother of the Virgin Mary, choirs of singing children, genuflecting officials and cheering crowds.

The Hapsburgs' ambassador, Eustace Chapuys, described the coronation as 'a cold, poor, and most unpleasing sight to the great regret, annoyance, and disappointment not only of the common people but likewise of all the rest'.[38] However, away from his official epistles to his master, who was Katherine of Aragon's nephew, Chapuys could be seen enjoying a night-time banquet on one of the many barges celebrating on the River Thames in the balmy summer twilight as the mighty cannons of the Tower fired their salvoes to salute the new Queen.[39] An official in the French embassy wrote later that 'the English sought, unceasingly, to honour their new princess' and while he admitted that it was impossible to tell how much that was due to Anne's popularity versus a desire to please Henry, he heard of the court's festivities for the coronation: 'The lords and ladies set to dances, sports of various kinds, hunting expeditions, and pleasures without parallel. Numerous tournaments were held in her honour

[...] as well as magnificent and joyful celebrations, everyone sought to be as attentive and solicitous as possible to serve their new mistress.[40]

The most sincere of the conservative flock, chief amongst them the former Lord Chancellor Thomas More, who had succeeded Wolsey only to resign in unhappiness at the government's pursuit of the Break with Rome, stayed away. Even if, at this stage, they had no grounds to, in More's words, 'murmur or dispute' against 'his Highness being in possession of his marriage and this noble woman really anointed queen'.[41]

However, murmuring soon grew into disputation when Pope Clement VII belatedly tried to put the genie back into the bottle by ruling in Katherine of Aragon's favour. Queen Anne was only a few weeks away from giving birth to her first child, but even as the court tried to cover up its disappointment at the birth of a girl, Princess Elizabeth, on 7 September 1533, they were preparing to strike at those who now sensed very clearly that the Vatican and the Crown were at war with one another in England. The axe and the butcher's cleaver tore into the flesh of dozens of pious souls who perished before large crowds, and royal commissioners were sent to inspect the monasteries and nunneries, suspected bastions of Papist loyalty, with the view to shutting them down.

One of the more blithely ridiculous comments often made about Anne Boleyn, even by her legion of modern-day admirers, is that she was unsuited to the office of queen consort. The sexy, sparky, difficult woman who excelled in the role of royal mistress is supposed to have stumbled and fallen at marriage, because she was too confrontational, too glamorous, too brittle and too outspoken. Such an assessment is surely only possible if the writer in question is wholly ignorant of the kind of women who had previously excelled as queens in England. Did the careers of Matilda of Flanders, Isabelle of Angoulême, Eleanor of Castile, Anne of Bohemia or Elizabeth Woodville end in their ruin or execution? Was the entire roll call of this country's medieval queens consort a bunch of insipid, doe-eyed doormats? Were they not, as Lisa Hilton's beautiful modern study of them suggests, 'an exceptional confederacy: magnificent, courageous, foolish, impetuous – splendid in their royal array'?[42] Katherine of Aragon and Anne Boleyn were the last of the medieval queens consort, the last to be crowned, the last to exert real political influence, and in many ways Anne was more than suited to the role she acquired in 1533. She was clever, sophisticated and elegant, she certainly knew how to dress the part, she was extremely generous to charity, and she was adept at interceding for those less fortunate than herself, particularly if they were women.[43] The allegedly difficult aspects of her personality pale in comparison to comparable flaws in queens like Eleanor of Aquitaine, Eleanor of Provence, Isabella of France or Marguerite of Anjou. What brought about Anne Boleyn's tragic end was not her personality, but her husband's. No King of England before Henry VIII would ever have been so egotistically self-absorbed as to strike against the mystique of monarchy by publicly executing an anointed Queen, but on 19 May 1536 he did just that.[44]

She was arrested shortly after lunch at Greenwich Palace on 2 May 1536, four months after her second miscarriage. Seven men were accused of being her lovers, including her brother George, Lord Rochford, the King's closest gentleman-in-waiting, Henry Norris, the athletic playboy Francis Weston, and a young court-based musician called Mark Smeaton, who was of low enough social rank to be tortured into providing evidence against the others.[45] Two of the accused were released with one, Thomas Wyatt, being told at the time of his arrest not to worry, because he would be set free in due course. Their release cleverly made the government's coup against the Queen seem like a genuine investigation. At her trial, Anne rebutted all the charges at length and held her nerves together, even as she was sentenced to death. The five men were beheaded outside the Tower of London on 17 May and the Queen, her dress defiantly trimmed with ermine, a fur reserved solely for members of the royal family, and protesting her innocence on the Eucharist at her final Mass, was slain two days later. The Archbishop of Canterbury was found weeping hysterically in the grounds of his London palace muttering that Anne would ascend into Heaven and ever since then speculation has run rampant about why Anne Boleyn's life ended with her kneeling before an executioner.

Historians have ranged from those who believe that Anne's flirtatious personality gave credence to vicious court rumours to those who support the more traditional interpretation of her demise, namely that her failure to produce a son left her vulnerable to her husband's tyrannical whims.[46] An attempt in the early 1990s to resurrect the idea that she might actually have been guilty of at least some of the charges foundered on a lack of contemporary evidence, not just in

Anne's defence of herself but also in the prosecution's clumsy and error-littered case against her. The man who organised the arrests and trials was Thomas Cromwell, the son of a blacksmith from Putney. He had replaced Cardinal Wolsey, his former mentor, as the man Henry VIII could not do without. After the Break with Rome, he had helped co-ordinate the dissolution of the monasteries and ensured that their confiscated wealth was poured into the King's treasury rather than into socially-improving programmes like new schools and hospitals, which caused Queen Anne to compare him to the Old Testament villain, Haman.

Due to this dispute, Cromwell is often accused of framing the Queen before she had him dismissed and selecting her lovers from the list of men who were likely to side with her politically. This is by far the most popular interpretation of what happened to Anne Boleyn in 1536 and there is too much evidence in its support to dismiss it entirely. However, there is much to be said for the suggestions made by two of Henry VIII's modern biographers, J. J. Scarisbrick and Derek Wilson, who argue that Cromwell would never have dared move against Anne in such a scandalous and dangerous way had he not been told to, however tacitly, by the King. The pornographic charges against her (the alleged incestuous seduction of her brother was recounted in particularly excruciating detail), the inconsistencies in the prosecution's case and the nature of her death show far more of Henry's influence than Cromwell who was, first and foremost, the King's servant. Henry's unhinged obsession with his glamorous second wife had reached its tragic finale or, in Professor Scarisbrick's words, 'devastating infatuation had turned into bloodthirsty loathing'.[37] Henry, with an ego that was enormous but fragile, destroyed a woman who, with many of the other kings of England, might have made a very successful Queen consort.

After Anne Boleyn's death, Henry VIII's final decade on the throne witnessed a serious uprising against him, known as the Pilgrimage of Grace, which spread across most of the north. As its name suggests, its main motivation was religious in nature. It railed against the destruction of the monasteries and the ransacking of centuries of tradition. It was only defeated when the King's deceitful promises of pardon managed to disperse the rebels long enough for the Crown to swoop in, brutalise the region and order mass executions. One of its leaders, Robert Aske, was strung up by chains to die of exposure outside the gates of York. Festering religious tensions, exacerbated by the King's swing back towards conservatism in middle-age, plagued the nation. Thomas Cromwell was executed for treason and heresy in 1540 as the country jittered with fear at the prospect of a retaliatory Catholic crusade led by the Hapsburg Empire and France. The King resorted to debasing the coinage to maintain both the splendour of his court, his resurgently aggressive foreign policy, and the building of defences against the feared invaders. Inflation ran amok, people grumbled and the court turned into a backbiting maze of shifting alliances. The King died on 28 January 1547 at the age of fifty-five. In his final years, his lack of exercise and enormous appetite caught up with him to ruin his health, condemning him to a decline full of pain. He left a country racked by economic, cultural and sectarian problems.

Henry, of course, is far more famous today for his private life than for his politics and it is this that explains his posthumous fame. After Anne Boleyn's execution, he married four more times. In contrast to the twenty-two years he spent with Katherine and the ten with Anne, his relationships with his four final brides lasted for a combined total of eleven years. None of these later queens exerted significant political influence and none of them was ever crowned, marking a dilution of the Queen's office from its heyday in the Middle Ages. They did, however, help enshrine Henry VIII in popular legend and their stories give us some idea of how tumultuous life was in his court.

His third wife, Jane Seymour, whom he married eleven days after Anne Boleyn's execution, has been dismissed by historians as 'a woman of no family, no beauty, no talent' and 'one of the least remarkable women ever to play a part in history.'[48] She was certainly no beauty and, unlike every Queen of England before her, her father was not a royal, an aristocrat or even in line to inherit an aristocratic title. In many ways, Jane Seymour represented the ultimate example of the Tudors' penchant for creating new money. New men had been a staple of Henry VII's government as he attempted to free the monarchy from dependence on the great families of the nobility, who he blamed for the longevity of the Wars of the Roses, and his successors continued that policy. Jane Seymour and her family were not connected to any of the great aristocratic clans in 1536 and as such she and they were entirely dependent on Henry VIII's goodwill. They had been made by him, they could thus be destroyed by him.

From the little surviving evidence that we have, it seems that Jane Seymour's political views were predominantly conservative, but Henry prevented her from expressing them too often. Her husband's religious policy actually became more radical during Jane's reign, not less. She was a strict disciplinarian with her servants, an effective administrator of her estates and entirely obedient to her husband. She was pregnant within about seven or eight months of her wedding and she gave birth to the long-awaited son at Hampton Court Palace on 12 October 1537. The child was christened Edward amidst scenes of widespread rejoicing. The Bishop of Worcester got rather carried away when he compared the baby's birth to that of Saint John the Baptist. In the immediate aftermath of the gruelling three-day labour, Queen Jane seemed to be in good health and she was well enough to attend a christening party for four hundred guests on the 15th. The next day, she suffered from diarrhoea and took to her bed. Tragically, post-natal complications had set in. As the Bishop of Carlisle was summoned to administer the Last Rites, Henry was still debating whether to cancel his return trip to his lodge at Esher where he had been hunting during the final stages of his wife's pregnancy.[49] The Queen died twelve days after her son's birth. She was given a state funeral at Windsor Castle and almost before she was cold, the hunt was on to find Henry a replacement bride.

By 1537, there were sound diplomatic reasons for his advisers pressuring Henry to accept an international bride rather than promoting one of his own subjects again. The Break with Rome had made England a pariah state and the Pope was still working on his plan to unite the great Catholic powers of France and the Hapsburg Empire in a war against Henry. The obvious solution was to select a bride from either one of the two and thus pre-emptively divide them. The problem with that plan was that both Henry VIII's religion and his private life made him an unattractive candidate from the Europeans' point of view. The Emperor's gorgeous niece, Christina of Denmark, reportedly quipped that she would only marry Henry if she had the necessary safeguard of two heads. The French brides were equally dismissive. Marie de Guise allegedly quoted Anne Boleyn's last jest about having a little neck, before adding insult to injury by accepting the proposal of Henry's estranged nephew, King James V of Scotland. (Together, they became the parents of Mary, Queen of Scots.) When Henry suggested that he would like to bring all the prospective royal and aristocratic French candidates to Calais so he could personally inspect them, the French ambassador acidly responded that the women of France were not accustomed to being lined up and appraised like horses at market.

With the much-feared alliance between the Empire and France finally materialising, Cromwell persuaded the King to propose marriage to the twenty-four-year-old Anne of Cleves, the younger sister of Wilhelm, Duke of Cleves. Wilhelm was the head of the Schmalkaldic League, a federation of Lutheran or Lutheran-sympathising German princes, who Cromwell hoped could provide valuable assistance by distracting the Hapsburgs if they attempted to invade England. After some delays due to winter storms, Anne made it to England to be married at Greenwich Palace on 6 January 1540. Henry claimed to find her physically repulsive, odorous and told his doctors that he could not sustain an erection in her presence. She was richly rewarded for her co-operation in the divorce, which was finalised six months later.

Before the month was out, Henry married Catherine Howard, the orphaned niece of the Duke of Norfolk. The young Queen was pretty and vivacious, but a year into the marriage a former family servant made allegations concerning Catherine's youthful romances with two men called Henry Manox and Francis Dereham. Subsequent enquiries also uncovered a love letter from the Queen to a very good-looking gentleman of the court called Thomas Culpepper, written after Catherine's marriage into the royal family. It could now be argued that the Queen had been guilty of adultery and she was executed at the Tower of London on 13 February 1542. Her alleged lover, her childhood fiancé and her favourite lady-in-waiting, Lady Rochford, met a similar fate. Henry remained single for over a year.

The King's sixth and final wife was another Katherine – born Katherine Parr and widow of Lord Latimer when Henry proposed marriage to her in the spring of 1543. She does not seem to have been overly enthusiastic about his offer, but a refusal, however polite, was never really an option. Attractive and intelligent, Katherine Parr was a committed Protestant but wisely learned to trim her spiritual sails to suit her husband's. Her theatrical subservience to him was what saved her when one of her book suppliers, Anne Askew, was savagely tortured and burned at the stake in 1546 for distributing radical Protestant literature. After Henry VIII's death in 1547, the formerly decorous Katherine caused quite the scandal by eloping with Jane Seymour's roguish brother, Thomas. Her stepdaughter, Mary Tudor, was appalled at this affront to propriety and even the youngest, fifteen-year-old Elizabeth, seemed uneasy.[50] Eighteen months later, Katherine died in childbirth at the age of thirty-six. Her baby daughter did not long survive her and her fourth husband was executed for treason in 1549. Henry was buried next to his third wife, Jane Seymour, a dynastic statement as their son succeeded to the throne as King Edward VI.

DEBORAH AND JOSIAH

THERE WERE three men who wielded great influence in England during Edward VI's reign, none of whom was the King. It was not that the young man lacked the brains to rule, indeed a case could be made for Edward VI being our most intellectually gifted Sovereign. His proficiency in foreign languages (as a child he was taught Greek by the regius professor at Cambridge) was matched by his athletic prowess and his grasp of history, mathematics, the arts and theology. He lacked only maturity. He came to the throne shortly after his ninth birthday and died before his sixteenth. Initially, power was held by his maternal uncle Edward Seymour, who elbowed the competition out of the way in the weeks after Henry VIII's death to make himself Lord Protector and Duke of Somerset. Factional politics were not buried with the behemoth-like Henry VIII and Edward Seymour's career ended in his death on trumped-up charges of treason. He was replaced by John Dudley, who followed his slaughtered colleague into the dukedoms by making himself Duke of Northumberland.[51] Like the departed Edward Seymour, he struggled unsuccessfully against Henry VIII's legacy of a diplomatically isolated kingdom with rising inflation and an ambitious foreign policy that it could no longer afford to maintain.

The third figure at the heart of the Edwardian monarchy was Thomas Cranmer, the quiet and gentle-mannered Cambridge don who had been appointed Archbishop of Canterbury thanks in part to the Boleyn family's faith in him. Since then he had served Henry VIII diligently, towing the line as the government shifted religion in a more conservative direction, helping with the dissolution of Henry's marriages to Anne of Cleves and Catherine Howard, and soothing Henry VIII's conscience on his deathbed. However, as soon as he was free of Henry, Cranmer showed where his true religious allegiances lay and he helped co-author the Protestant settlement of Edward's reign. It was a much more theologically aggressive policy than Henry VIII's, though less bloody in its application. Beautiful art, from holy statues to stained glass windows, was smashed, desecrated and whitewashed. Purgatory and prayers for the dead were declared nonsense, Latin was removed entirely from religious services, a new Book of Common

Prayer was made mandatory and a thousand years of art, faith and history were swept away.

Even rebellions, brought on by mounting economic hardship and people's alienation at the new religion being forced upon them by the court, did not knock the government off course. The King, young though he was, was a zealous Protestant who regarded the next-in-line, his elder half-sister Mary Tudor, with condescension and then concern for her continued devotion to the theology of her ancestors. Early in the reign there had been talk of arranging a marriage for Edward with his second cousin Lady Jane Grey, the eldest daughter of the Duke and Duchess of Suffolk and a granddaughter of Henry VII on her mother's side.[52] She was only a few months older than Edward, equally well-read and she shared his devotion to Protestantism.[53] (She once referred to Catholicism as 'the stinking and filthy kennel of Satan'.)[54] The marriage plans had come to nothing, but Jane once again dominated the King's thoughts when, in the spring of 1553, he realised that he was dying.

A variety of theories have been put forward to explain why this apparently healthy young man died before his sixteenth birthday. Renal failure, tuberculosis and measles, which left him fatally weak to secondary infections, have all been suggested.[55] In increasing pain, he worked tirelessly with Northumberland to write a will that cancelled out his father's, disinheriting Catholic Mary in favour of Protestant Jane. The thought of seeing the country return to the old religion was too much for Edward to bear and when some of his advisers protested at the thought of abandoning the heiress-apparent, he rebuked them sharply. Cutting out Mary on the grounds that she was a bastard and therefore unfit to reign also meant condemning Edward's other half-sister, nineteen-year-old Elizabeth, who was a Protestant but who had likewise been declared the product of an illegal union by an obedient Act of Parliament. Edward viewed Elizabeth's disinheritance as collateral damage and when he passed away on 6 July 1553, cradled in the arms of a childhood playmate, the council obeyed his last wishes and proclaimed Jane Grey, or rather Jane Dudley as she had become ever since her politically-motivated marriage to Northumberland's son Guildford, the first Queen regnant of England and Ireland.[56]

Famously she lasted nine days, the shortest reign in British history.[57] As Anne of Cleves and Princess Elizabeth, the other senior members of the royal family, waited quietly in the countryside to see which way the wind would blow, Mary Tudor rallied her supporters to be carried south by the combined momentum of Northumberland's unpopularity and her own charisma.[58] She entered London to scenes of adulation and displayed her mettle a year later when she gave rousing speeches to her troops in the face of an uprising against her in Kent. It had ostensibly been a protest against the Queen's forthcoming marriage to her second cousin Prince Philip of Spain, but Mary suspected it had aimed at her deposition, to replace her either with Princess Elizabeth or a restored Queen Jane.

The heavy presence of Protestantism in the rebel camp gave the Queen a target for her ire. The teenage Jane was offered her life if she converted. When she refused, she was beheaded at the Tower on 12 February 1554. Eyewitnesses in the crowd recorded that they were stunned by the amount of blood that gushed forth from such a tiny body.[59] Elizabeth was incarcerated in the fortress, despite her protestations of innocence. With absolutely no evidence against her, Mary eventually had to let her go and the princess's imprisonment played badly with the city of London, where she was very popular. For the rest of the reign, Elizabeth was denied any signs of royal favour and for much of it she was kept under a form of house arrest in the Oxfordshire countryside.

In Oxford itself, Elizabeth's godfather, Thomas Cranmer, met his end amid the flames after Mary restored Papal supremacy and the heresy laws. Nearly three hundred Protestants went to their deaths because of it and their bravery garnered a great deal of sympathy for their cause. The Queen's marriage to Philip, who became King of Spain upon his father's abdication in 1556, was not popular and the alliance it represented even less so after a joint war against France resulted in the French conquest of Calais, the last fragment of the Plantagenets' continental empire. The Queen was humiliated by it as much as she was by her two phantom pregnancies, echoes of her mother's four decades earlier, and when she died in November 1558, most likely as a result of ovarian cancer initially mistaken for a pregnancy, her ladies-in-waiting expressed the hope that she would be united with children in Heaven, having been denied them on Earth.[60]

The pathetic tragedy of Mary's final few months contrasts strongly with the black legend of her as 'Bloody Mary', the tyrannical demon of Protestant myth and popular legend. It also detracts both from her failures as a Queen, particularly in foreign relations, and her successes. Mary I had proved her father wrong. A woman could rule England in her own right. She had done so no more unsuccessfully than any of the men who had come before her and, despite their damaged relationship, when Elizabeth I took the throne in 1558, she praised her sister's memory at her first council meeting before authorising a magnificent and respectful funeral for her, the cost of which ran to £7,763 (just over £2 million or $3.4 million today).[61] A few weeks later, the coronation of the new Queen took place with lessons learned, but also inspiration derived, from the old.

THE QUEEN OF SCOTLAND
RISES ON THE WORLD

ELIZABETH TUDOR AND Mary Stewart carried with them the deaths of the English and Scottish monarchies and the birth of the British. Elizabeth was the elder of the two, by nearly a decade, and whereas her early childhood had been characterised by privilege and the affection of a doting mother, Mary lost her father when she was six days old and had to be smuggled out of the country when the English armies invaded on the orders of Henry VIII to capture her and bring her south to London as a bride for the future Edward VI. Ships bore Mary to her mother's relatives in France, the Guise family, arguably the greatest aristocratic clan in Europe at the time.[62] There, they used their influence at the French court to have her betrothed to the Dauphin François and Mary, a tall and elegant beauty like her mother, grew up surrounded by luxury and adoration. The court poet, Pierre de Ronsard, wrote:

> Just as we see, half rosy and half white,
> Dawn and the Morning Star dispel the night
> In beauty thus beyond compare impearled
> The Queen of Scotland rises on the world [63]

In contrast, Elizabeth Tudor endured uncertainty and demotion as her father's chop-and-change attitude to brides left her at the mercy of the fluctuations of fortune. When she became Queen in 1558, the French saw the perfect opportunity to annoy her by proclaiming Mary of Scotland to be Mary Tudor's rightful successor. Elizabeth was a bastard and a Protestant, whereas Mary was the legitimate granddaughter of Henry VII's eldest daughter, Margaret.[64] What was probably intended as no more than a spirited riposte to the English Crown's continued reverence for Edward III's claims to the French throne was viewed by Elizabeth as a serious threat and her government began to finance the hard-line of the Protestant Reformation in Scotland, which was making many difficulties for Mary's mother and regent, Marie de Guise.

Matters did not improve when Mary's husband, King François II, died shortly before Christmas in 1560, quite possibly from meningitis, leaving her a childless widow at the age of seventeen. She initially wanted to remain in France, but her mother-in-law, Catherine de Medici, disliked the Guise family and did not want Mary to marry her other son, the new King Charles IX. Mary returned to rule a kingdom she had last seen as a girl and she was horrified by what she found, although too polite and far, far too charming to let it show in all but her most unguarded moments. Her education in France, which had aimed at equipping her to execute the role of Queen consort, had left her hopelessly unprepared for ruling in her own right, especially in a country where she was regarded as a Papist foreigner. The governing body of the new Scottish strand of Protestantism, the Presbyterian Kirk, commanded by the fearsome John Knox, wielded great influence and its aristocratic supporters, the Lords of the Congregation, received under-the-table funding from the English.

Elizabeth veered between feeling sympathy for Mary's plight, augmented by a sense of the solidarity of female rule, and nightmare-inducing suspicion. The latter eclipsed the former permanently when Mary married their mutual cousin Henry, Lord Darnley, an English aristocrat with descent from both the Scottish and English royal houses. Elizabeth saw the wedding as an act of aggression by newlyweds planning to produce a child who the whole world would regard as the rightful heir. Mary had chosen poorly in more ways than one. Darnley's bisexuality was no great obstacle to the marriage, but his hedonism, alcoholism, narcissism, dishonesty, adultery and treachery were. He helped destabilise her already-fragile government, allied with the Presbyterian nobles to murder her Italian-Catholic secretary David Rizzio in front of her at a supper party, and when he was found half-naked and strangled near the smoking ruins of an Edinburgh townhouse in February 1567, there was no shortage of suspects. Mary subsequently married one of the accused, the volatile James Hepburn, 3rd Earl of Bothwell, and the ensuing scandal wove together with her other problems to sweep her off her throne. She refugeed south to England, appealing to Elizabeth for protection.

Unfortunately, Elizabeth lost all sense of perspective when it came to Mary, Queen of Scots. She cross-questioned anyone who had met Mary about her beauty, acumen and accomplishments. In terms of beauty, Mary trounced Elizabeth and every other princess in Europe, but Elizabeth was thrilled to discover that she was considered slightly too tall. Intellectually, Elizabeth emerged triumphant. She spoke more languages, had such a sophisticated grasp of Latin that she could comfortably enter into conversations and debates in it with Oxford dons, played better as a musician and inspired a more stable kind of loyalty. Nonetheless, Mary haunted Elizabeth and the greatest fear was the impact of Mary's charisma. John Guy, one of Mary's modern biographers, captured the essence of her allure when he wrote, '"charmante" and "la plus parfaite" were the adjectives most commonly applied to her singular blend of celebrity. Not just physically mesmerizing with her well-proportioned face, neck, arms, and waist, she had an unusual warmth of character with the ability to strike up an instant rapport. Always high-spirited and vivacious [...] Gregarious as well as glamorous, she could be genial to the point of informality as long as her 'grandeur' was respected. Many contemporaries remarked on her almost magical ability to create the impression that the person she was talking to was the only one whose opinion really mattered to her.'65

Mary's arrival in the still predominantly Catholic north of England created a headache for Elizabeth, who abandoned her normal parsimony and hurled money at the problem to provide Mary with a lavish household in the hope of distracting attention from the fact that she had placed her in a cage, albeit a gilded one. As much as her instinctive, visceral monarchism had been outraged by the Kirk's actions, her talent for survival left her relieved that Mary no longer commanded the kingdom on her northern doorstep. Mary and Darnley's son, James VI, was a baby left in the reassuringly Protestant care of the lords who had snatched him from his terrified mother during the drama of her deposition. Regardless of its noxious ideological implications, Elizabeth had no immediate pragmatic motive for helping destroy the new government in Scotland.

And so for nineteen years, Mary Stewart languished in the English countryside, denied a chance to meet Elizabeth and driven to despair as her youth ebbed away from her. A revolt by the most powerful families of the northern nobility, which sought to turn the clock back to the previous century when their influence had not been so thoroughly checked by the monarchy, was followed by a plot that aimed to restore the Catholic faith and marry Mary to the country's premier Catholic nobleman, Elizabeth's kinsman, the Duke of Norfolk. The rebellion was crushed with maximum severity and the Duke was beheaded, but Elizabeth refused to punish Mary. From her own imprisonment in her sister's reign, Elizabeth had learned that a royal's name could be used in an enterprise that they had not approved of. 'I have had good experience and trial of this world. I know what it is to be a subject, what to be a sovereign,' she told a group of MPs, 'what to have good neighbours and sometimes meet evil-willers. I have found trust in treason, and seen great benefits little regarded'.[66] No matter how many plots against her arose, nearly all of them with the ultimate goal of assassinating her for Mary's sake, Elizabeth would not appease either her advisers or Parliament by attacking Mary in any meaningful way. Her father and her sister had executed queens, Elizabeth did not want to spill royal blood in the same way.

She did not have the same laudable qualms about persecuting Catholics. The arrests, the fines, the imprisonments, the grotesque executions that plagued the English and Welsh Catholic community with increasing severity over the final three decades of Elizabeth I's long reign were not born from any fiery sense of religious totalitarianism, but from a mixture of paranoia and *realpolitik*. On 25 February 1570, Pope Pius V tried, too late, to help the rebels against her by issuing the bull Regnans in Excelsis, which excommunicated Elizabeth, referred to her as 'the servant of crime', a usurper who no Catholic should obey.

At a stroke, the Vatican had condemned thousands of English and Welsh Catholics to living as outcasts in their own country. The Protestant majority in the south concurred with the increasing vitriolic speeches in Parliament that called for harsh measures to be taken against the enemy within, while Elizabeth, who had come to the throne trivialising the internecine viciousness of the Protestant-Catholic dispute, eventually and reluctantly concurred with her closest advisers, the strongly Protestant William Cecil, Lord Burghley, and her spymaster, Francis Walsingham, who wanted the full penalty of the law exacted for every single case of recusancy. Even Elizabeth's beloved Robert Dudley, Earl of Leicester, sided with the anti-Catholic faction, egging her on to greater acts of repression against a beleaguered minority.

Elizabeth, a sincere but not a fundamentalist Protestant, often found their zeal irritating and she once stormed out of church when a chaplain began preaching against her sympathy for liberal, we might call it 'high', Anglicanism. When she first came to the throne the Acts of Uniformity and Settlement had restored the independence of the

Church of England, making her its Supreme Governor and enacting a theologically liberal character, which she sincerely hoped would, in time, win over as many Catholics as possible. Once Pope Pius V threw down the gauntlet and with the presence of an alternative Catholic monarch living within the kingdom, Elizabeth could not back down on the religious question. When petitioned to grant them toleration, she answered, 'If I grant this liberty to Catholics, by this very fact I lay at their feet my honour, my crown and my life'.[67] In 1584, Prince William the Silent, the leader of the Protestant Dutch rebellion against the Spanish Crown that still ruled over them, was assassinated by a Catholic spy. In England, a Bond of Association was drawn up in which the signees vowed to kill a Catholic heir if Queen Elizabeth met the same end. The following year, Parliament passed the Act for the Surety of the Queen's Person, which made it possible to pursue a legal prosecution against an heir to the throne if they conspired against the current monarch. Mary had been surrounded by her enemies.

Matters came to a head in the summer of 1586 when Francis Walsingham presented Elizabeth with seemingly irrefutable evidence that Mary had consented to a plot organised by a Catholic gentleman called Sir Anthony Babington, whereby he agreed to free her from captivity, murder Elizabeth and place Mary on the throne. When the case was presented to the ex-Queen of Scots, she denied all complicity and accused Walsingham of forgery. How far she was involved is unknowable, but it does seem highly improbable that she was totally innocent. A more likely explanation is that Walsingham, who watched her every move, allowed her to become so deeply involved until he had enough to persuade Elizabeth to order execution. At least one of Elizabeth's modern biographers has suspected that she knew the game Walsingham was playing and waited to see how Mary would behave. We have no way of knowing for certain, since Elizabeth's feelings seem to have been as confused as they were confusing.

Mary was beheaded at Fotheringhay Castle in Northamptonshire on 8 February 1587, her legendary beauty vanished after years of disappointment, loneliness and lethargy. She died heroically in an immaculately choreographed performance in which, rosary and crucifix in hand, she sought to separate her death from the grubbiness of politics to instead bathe herself with the aura of martyrdom. This she did with great success and there were anti-English riots in

Paris when the news broke. Queen Elizabeth's reaction was scarcely more restrained. She had been pressured into signing the death warrant by public opinion, Walsingham's evidence, her own fear and parliamentary hysteria. Before the execution, she agonised to a delegation from Parliament, 'What will my enemies not say, that for the safety of her life a maiden queen could be content to spill the blood even of her own kinswoman?'[68] Once the deed was done, she suffered some kind of nervous breakdown. They had never met, but the long and agonised relationship between the two cousins had defined one another's lives in a way that no husband, lover, friend, foe or servant ever could.[69]

THAT GOOD OLD PRINCESS

A YEAR after Mary, Queen of Scots died, Elizabeth's former brother-in-law, King Philip II of Spain, launched the Armada against her. The greatest Catholic power hurled itself against its Protestant counterpart and lost. Its defeat was by no means a foregone conclusion, despite the fact that even some in command of the great fleet had tried in vain to warn King Philip that it was not ready. Until English naval skill and a strong gale, depicted as a blast of God's nostrils in triumphal Protestant woodcuts, dispersed it, the prospect of the Armada landing on the southern coast was a terrifying possibility.

In those weeks, Elizabeth I achieved not just her own apotheosis but her monarchy's as well. Not until George VI and his Queen, Elizabeth Bowes-Lyon, took to the streets of a Blitz-devastated London was there a monarch who stood among their people in a time of crisis and fear to define to perfection the great bond between throne and populace. Elizabeth I, fifty-three years old, unmarried and past the point where people expected it, defied her advisers' pleas that she keep away from immediate danger to instead join the troops camping at Tilbury. She went to talk to them in the inimitable and wonderful way she always spoke to her people. She walked among them, she charmed them, she wept and laughed with them; she adored them and she made that adoration plain. Her godson noted years later, 'Her speech did win all affections'.[70] At Tilbury, that popular touch became a caress when she began by telling the soldiers of her contempt for Philip II and his deputy Alessandro, Duke of Farnese, before going on to articulate the philosophy of her queenship and the bonds she believed united her with her people.

> My loving people
>
> We have been persuaded by some that are careful of our safety, to take heed how we commit our selves to armed multitudes, for fear of treachery; but I assure you I do not desire to live to distrust my faithful and loving people. Let tyrants fear. I have always so behaved myself that, under God, I have placed my chiefest strength and safeguard in the loyal hearts and good-will

of my subjects; and therefore I am come amongst you, as you see, at this time, not for my recreation and disport, but being resolved, in the midst and heat of the battle, to live and die amongst you all; to lay down for my God, and for my kingdom, and my people, my honour and my blood, even in the dust.

I know I have the body of a weak, feeble woman; but I have the heart and stomach of a king, and of a king of England too, and think foul scorn that Parma or Spain, or any prince of Europe, should dare to invade the borders of my realm; to which rather than any dishonour shall grow by me, I myself will take up arms, I myself will be your general, judge, and rewarder of every one of your virtues in the field.

I know already, for your forwardness you have deserved rewards and crowns; and We do assure you on a word of a prince, they shall be duly paid. In the mean time, my lieutenant general shall be in my stead, than whom never prince commanded a more noble or worthy subject; not doubting but by your obedience to my general, by your concord in the camp, and your valour in the field, we shall shortly have a famous victory over these enemies of my God, of my kingdom, and of my people.[71]

In the middle of the victory celebrations, Elizabeth's childhood friend-turned-adult-love, the Earl of Leicester, passed away. She was heartbroken. It has long been surmised that Elizabeth would have married Leicester had he not already been married and his first wife, Amy Dudley (née Robsart), had not then been found dead in circumstances that looked suspiciously like murder. However, during a bout of serious illness when she thought she was about to die, Elizabeth made a point of denying that she had ever taken Leicester into her bed, no matter how much she loved him. Despite mountains of speculation, there is in fact no firm evidence at all to suggest that Elizabeth I was not a virgin as she claimed. The risk of pregnancy, the loss of her reputation, death in childbed or yielding her authority to a man made celibacy by far her safest choice. We will never know, of course, what happened every day and night of her life, but it is worth pointing out that it should not be taken as axiomatic, as it too often is, that Elizabeth Tudor lied about her life-long virginity.

The death of a man she might have married if she could marked the beginning of Elizabeth's decline. One by one, the constants of her life fell away from her. She nursed Lord Burghley herself on his deathbed, Francis Walsingham passed, her childhood governess Blanche Perry, who had become the chief lady of Elizabeth's privy chamber, died at the age of eighty-three in 1590, and a cousin on the Boleyn side, Katherine, Countess of Nottingham, died, producing a grief so severe it hastened Elizabeth's own end in 1603.

Her contemporaries were replaced at court by new bloods, chief of whom was Lord Burghley's son, the Machiavellian Robert Cecil, and Leicester's warrior stepson Robert Devereux, Earl of Essex. Despite their fawning praise of her, they were privately contemptuous of Elizabeth's settled conservatism, her aversion to war and her refusal to name an heir. Remembering how people had flocked to her while her sister lay dying in 1558, Elizabeth refused to name an heir directly, 'saying,' as her godson recalled, 'she would not have her winding sheet set up before her face'.[72] So innate was the Queen's faith in the institution she led that she believed it was nonsense to suggest that primogeniture would not do the work for her. Whoever had the best ancestral claim to the throne when she died would become the next King or Queen. To her it was simple, to her courtiers it was maddening. For their own peace of mind, everyone wanted to know who, in the words of the loyalist spy Thomas Wilson, would succeed 'that good old princess, the now queen.'[73] The Queen caked herself in white make-up and wore gowns designed to dazzle and intimidate, rather than to flatter. In a deeply misogynist world it was better for her to appear frighteningly bizarre and other-worldly than betray even the faintest sign of aging weakness.

A sense of hopeless frustration, political ennui, was nurtured by atrocious weather and correspondingly poor harvests. Corruption was endemic in the late Elizabethan state and feeling against it ran high. Rebellion, led by Hugh O'Neill, Earl of Tyrone, convulsed Ireland. Elizabeth had continued her grandfather and sister's policies of trying to stabilise and expand the monarchy's presence on the island. O'Neill's quests for political power of his own were helped by tensions between Crown loyalists, who were given areas of land to settle outside the Dublin Pale, and the Irish-speaking majority. Religion added a new spice to the animosity, with most of Ireland remaining Catholic and the majority of settlers practicing Protestantism. Violence spread. In a particularly horrific sequence of events, O'Neill's supporters attacked a Crown-sponsored settlement in Munster, Ireland's most southerly province, and murdered all the men living there, before slaughtering the children in front of their mothers, who were then gang-raped, facially mutilated and driven naked into the nearby hills to die of exposure.[74] When pressed to offer O'Neill a pardon in the hope of buying peace, Elizabeth erupted at the thought of clemency for 'the author of so much misery to our loving subjects'.[75] When Lord Essex, who was sent to Ireland to crush O'Neill, ended up offering him terms in despair at what he felt was an unwinnable war, Elizabeth was apoplectic. She cut the proud Earl off from her largesse and he rebelled against her, possibly with the intention of speeding up the day when she was succeeded by her young Scottish cousin, King James VI. The city of London did not heed his cry, however, and the Queen ordered his execution with great reluctance. She had cared for him once as the stepson of her cherished Leicester and she admired his spirited bravado. But he was a traitor who had put himself above the national good. For Elizabeth, that was a crime that must be punished.

When her father snatched spiritual authority from the Pope, his title as head of the new Church had initially been completed by the pious caveat, 'as far as the law of Christ allowed'.[76] When Elizabeth became Queen, she chose to be Supreme Governor of the Church, rather than Supreme Head, to avoid criticism that the monarchy was usurping the prerogatives of Christ. This was how she saw herself, God's deputy on Earth, a Sovereign lieutenant entrusted with safeguarding her people from the ravages of civil war, invasion, lawlessness and instability. In the pursuit of this, she committed many terrible acts, especially through her treatment of her Catholic subjects. It has been argued here that the choice was essentially forced upon her by a stupidly belligerent pontiff, but that does not serve to make it any more appealing or less tragic. In her defence, she ultimately succeeded in holding the kingdoms together through nearly half a century of peace. Ten years into her reign, she made this prayer that captures, I think, the core of her attitude towards her country:

Dear Lord most mighty, stretch forth your right hand over me to protect and defend me from my enemies so that they never overcome me. Give me, O Lord, the assistance of the Holy Spirit and the comfort of your grace. Let me know you and love you and trust you with all my heart. I acknowledge that I receive the government of this Church and kingdom from you, so grant me the ability to govern a peaceful and quiet country which is well ordered. Let me rule over a perfectly reformed Church which will reflect your glory. Grant my subjects, dear Lord, faithful and obedient hearts so that they will follow and obey your word and commandments according to the Bible. As a nation we will give thanks and praise for all the benefits we have received from you.

May we rejoice and praise your Holy name.

Grant this, O merciful Father, for Jesus Christ's sake, our only Mediator to you, dear Lord.

Amen.

EPILOGUE

THE WORD 'MUST'

ELIZABETH I DIED on 24 March 1603 at Richmond Palace, a few months before her seventieth birthday. It was a strange coincidence that the woman immortalised in English memory as the Virgin Queen was born and died on the eve of two holy days associated with the Virgin Mary.[1] In an age before Protestantism, when queens were still seen in England as earthly handmaidens of Christ's Mother, great significance would doubtless have been attached to this. As it was, Elizabeth I, the last English Queen, died on a day associated with a *fin-de-siècle*: new year's eve. In 1603, her people still marked new year on the Feast of the Annunciation, 25 March. She had kept going, right to the end, despite the fact that her body seemed worn out and her spirits exhausted. During the opening of Parliament, the fragile old lady had nearly lost her balance thanks to the weight of her robes. When one of her advisers told her that she must go to bed, she disdainfully told him, 'Little man, the word 'must' is not used to princes'.[2] According to her godson, Sir John Harington, Elizabeth I slipped away quietly, shortly after 'hugging' the hand of the Archbishop of Canterbury as he spoke gently to her of the reality of Heaven. Harington reported that 'she took great delight in hearing prayers and would often at the name of Jesus lift up her hands and eyes to heaven.'[3]

At the eleventh hour, Parliament tried to bully Elizabeth into naming her successor by holding out the threat that a previous monarch could not be buried until a new one was formally installed. She outmanoeuvred them, as she always had done, by stipulating in her will that she did not want her body to be autopsied, which meant no embalming and so her funeral went ahead on schedule, before putrefaction set in.

An era had ended and another contemporary wrote that with Elizabeth's death many of her subjects felt as if 'the most resplendent sun [had] setteth at last in a western cloud'.[4] All the frantic behind-the-scenes intrigues paid dividend in the peaceful accession of her third cousin, King James VI of Scots, who became James I of England and Ireland. Elizabeth I's faith in monarchical primogeniture was justified and the House of Stewart, or Stuart as the English, Welsh and Irish called them, ruled until 1714. Although James I's dreams of formally uniting the two former enemies beneath one government were not technically realised until the reign of his great-granddaughter with the Act of Union in 1707, the personal union that he and his heirs symbolised birthed Great Britain, its expanding empire and a British, rather than an English, monarchy.

In the centuries to come, the royal institution was to pride itself on uniting the nation during the horrors of war, while ordinarily extolling the virtues of peace, prosperity, unity, patriotism and good government. Just under four hundred years after Elizabeth I's death, the Golden Jubilee celebrations of Elizabeth II demonstrated just how successful that policy had been. When the prospect of Scottish secession from the United Kingdom reared its head in 2014, there were subtle but clear signs from the Palace that Her Majesty did not want to be Queen of a separate Scotland and that she, along with the majority of her subjects, believed that the country was, to quote the 'No' campaign, better together.[5]

Elizabeth I served as the perfect bridge between the English monarchy that died with her and the British Crown, which took its first steps at her funeral. She, and indeed the entire medieval monarchy's celebration of martial valour and Arthur's gleaming sword, had a moment comparable to Agincourt at Tilbury with the defeat of the Spanish Armada with scenes, however subsequently eulogised, of a monarch at one with her troops and apparent displays of Divine providence in the gales that scattered England's enemies. Yet, the Queen at the centre of the tableau found war abhorrent and expensive, and spent most of her reign trying to avoid it. It was only when necessity thrust it upon her that she rose to take on the role that patriotic histories loved her in best of all: Gloriana, warrior-Queen. Elizabeth I was far more popular with subsequent generations for her aversion to war than she was with many of her courtiers, who found the Queen's habitual pacifism embarrassing and dishonourable.

Despite her magnificent riposte to Robert Cecil in 1603, most of England and Britain's monarchs had been governed by the word 'must'. That, in its most reductive form, is the answer to the question of the institution's longevity. Where other monarchies, like those in France, Austria-Hungary and Russia, fought against change and only attempted to implement it when it had clearly been forced upon them, Britain's moved and moves subtly, implementing a dozen tiny changes with each new generation that maintain the appearance of continuity while avoiding ossification.[6]

This policy has its roots in the medieval legacy of England's kings. William II embraced his Anglo-Saxon subjects when he realised that their support was more valuable than his Norman lords', Henry I, Edward IV and Henry VII utilised the best and brightest in their kingdoms to take advantage of new forms of learning to produce more efficient and sophisticated government, and even in kings who were backed into a corner, like King John and his son Henry III, there had been an awareness that they must do what reality demanded of them. With the exception of Richard II, who was deposed, the English monarchy had no Ludwig II, no castles of imagination at the expense of political necessity.

The greatest kings to the Middle Ages were men like William the Conqueror, Henry II, Richard the Lionheart, Edward I and Edward III – monarchs who had won their spurs on the battlefield and maintained, or expanded, their glory in the same arena. This may seem distasteful to us and it is undoubtedly a positive thing that the British monarchy came to reflect changed attitudes towards war as a necessary sacrifice rather than a hoped-for glory, but the legend that flowed from Camelot helped explain not just the country's applause for victories and contempt for defeat, but also the expectation for a lavish chivalric court to surround the royal family and the development of good government alongside that, in which the people could participate in the running of the realm.

Mary, Queen of Scots' final motto was the haunting phrase 'In the End is My Beginning'. By the time it died to be born anew in 1603, the English monarchy had already crafted an extraordinary story, one of History's greatest, full of horror and majesty, hope and despair, aspiration and brutality. The tombs, the ruined castles, the time-worn portraits, the jewels and the country itself stand as its warnings and its tributes.

ACKNOWLEDGEMENTS

Over the course of writing this book, I have incurred many debts of gratitude. First and foremost, I must thank Tim Ridgway, who was so supportive of this work and tolerated so many delays as I finished a book on another set of royals with a far less successful political record. Writing the story of the English monarchy has been a rich and rewarding experience, for which it is not possible to thank Tim sufficiently for his enthusiasm and encouragement.

I would like to thank the staff at the Linen Hall Library in Belfast, who do such a wonderful job in maintaining a space so conducive to the study of books and the writing of new ones.

Those friends and colleagues who shared their time and expertise, both invaluable, have my deepest gratitude – Sara Cockerill; Dr James Davis of Queen's University, Belfast; Leanda de Lisle; Dr Steven Gunn of Merton College, Oxford; Hugo Hanna; Rafe Heydel-Mankoo; Susan Higginbotham; Janice Hyndman; Laura McCosker; Ciarán Noade; Jim de Piante; Claire Ridgway; Mary-Eileen Russell; Dr Dion Smythe of Queen's University, Belfast, and Kathryn Warner, who took time off from her own biography of Edward II to very kindly offer her thoughts of chapter five. Scott De Buitléir spent hours going over my notes and theories on Henry II's intervention in Ireland and he was painstakingly patient in lending me the benefit of his superb grasp of the Irish language, both ancient and modern, to explain the pitfalls of translation. Any errors or discrepancies are entirely my own.

Finally, it would not be possible to complete a project like this without the support of good friends and family. My parents were, as ever, invaluable. My thanks to Claire Handley, who hosted a lovely weekend away to the windswept beauty of Portballintrae on the north coast of Northern Ireland, one of my favourite places, when I finished the first draft of this manuscript. Eric Spies and Tom Woodward were early cheerleaders of this project, and it was with Eric and his sister Lauren that I first visited the Plantagenet tombs at Fontevraud. Lucy Williams, who has an ear for poetry and language, helped me decide upon the working subtitle of this book, and although in the end it became the title for the prologue rather than the frontispiece, it helped define its focus. She was very kind to discuss my thoughts with me and she, like everyone who helped, has my deepest thanks.

Gareth Russell
Belfast,
Michaelmas, 2014

BIBLIOGRAPHY

PRINTED PRIMARY SOURCES

Arnold, T. (ed.), Henry of Huntingdon: Historia Anglorum
  (London, 1879)
Bede, Ecclesiastical History of the English People,
  trans. A. M. Sellar (London, 1907)
Blakman, John, Henry the Sixth, M. R. James (ed.) (London, 1919)
Eadmer of Canterbury, Eadmer's History of Recent Events,
  trans. Geoffrey Bosanquet (London, 1964)
Brewer, J. S., James Gairdner and R. H. Brodie (eds), Letters and
  Papers, Foreign and Domestic of Henry VIII
  (London, 1862 – 1932)
Brown, R., G. Cavendish-Bentinck, H. F. Brown, and A. B. Hinds
  (eds), Calendar of State Papers and Manuscripts Relating to
  English Affairs, Existing in the Archives and Collections of
  Venice and in Other Libraries of Northern Italy
  (London, 1864 – 1947)
Butler, H. E. and W. J. Millor (eds and trans.), C. N .L. Brooke
  (rev.), The Letters of John of Salisbury (Oxford, 1979 – 1986)
Childs, Wendy R. (ed. and trans.), Vita Edwardi Secundi
  (Clarendon, 2005)
Crawford, Anne (ed.), Letters of the Queens of England
  (Stroud, 2002)

Delaborde, M. F. (ed.), Œuvres de Rigord et de Guillaume le
    Breton, historiens de Philippe-Auguste (Paris, 1882 – 1885)

Denholm-Young, N. (ed.), Vita Edwardi Secundi: Monarchi
    Cuiusdam Malmesberiensis (London, 1957)

Douglas, D. C., and G. W. Greenway (eds), English Historical
    Documents (London, 1953)

Ellis, Henry (ed.), The new chronicles of England and France, in two
    parts: by Robert Fabyan. Named by himself: The concordance
    of histories. Reprinted from Pynson's edition of 1516. The
    first part collected with the editions of 1533, 1542, and 1559
    (London, 1811)

Ellis, Henry, Three Books of Polydore Vergil's English History
    (London, 1844)

Forester, Thomas (ed. and trans.), The Chronicle of Henry of
    Huntingdon, comprising of the History of England from
    the invasion of Julius Caesar to the Accession of Henry II
    (London, 1853)

Gerald of Wales, The History and Topography of Ireland, (rev. ed.),
    J. J. O'Meara (London, 1982)

Gildas, De Excidio et Conquestu Britanniæ,
    trans. Michael Winterbottom (Chichester, 1978)

Giles, J. A. (ed.), Petri Blesensis Archidiaconi Opera Omnia
    (Oxford, 1847)

Giles, J. A., Galrifi la Baker de Swinbroke chronicon Angliæ
    temporibus Edwardi II et Edwardi III (London, 1847)

James, M. R. (ed.), De Nugis Curialium (London, 1914)

Keynes, Simon and Michael Lapidge (eds), Alfred the Great:
    Asser's Life of King Alfred and Other Contemporary Sources
    (London, 1983)

King, Edmund (ed.), William of Malmesbury: The Historia Novella,
    trans. K. R. Potter (London, 1999)

Letts, Malcolm (ed.), The Travels of Leo of Rozmital through
    Germany, Flanders, England, France, Spain, Portugal and Italy
    1465-1467 (Cambridge University Press, 1957)

Madden, Frederick (ed.), Matthaei Parisiensis, Monachi Sancti
    Albani, Historia Anglorum, sive, ut Vulgo Dictur,
    Historia Minor. Item Ejusdem Abbreviatio Chronicorum
    Angliae (London, 1866-69)

Mancini, Dominic, The Usurpation of Richard the Third, trans C.
    A. J. Armstrong (Second edition, Oxford, 1969)

Map, Walter, Courtiers' Trifles (Oxford, 1983)

Maxwell, Herbert (ed.), Scalaronica: The Reigns of Edward I,
    Edward II and Edward III as Recorded by Sir Thomas Gray of
    Heton, knight (Glasgow, 1907)

More, Thomas, The History of Richard III, Richard S. Sylvester (ed.)
    (Yale University Press, 1963)

Orderic Vitalis, The Ecclesiastical History of England and
    Normandy, trans. Thomas Forester (London, 1853)

Potter, K. R., and Davis, R. H. C. (eds and trans.), Gesta Stephani
    (Oxford, 1976)

Pryce, Huw (ed.), The Acts of Welsh Rulers, 1120 – 1283
    (University of Wales Press, 2005)

Stevenson, Joseph (ed.), Calendar of State Papers, Foreign, Elizabeth,
    1560 – 61 (London, 1865)

Stevenson, Joseph (ed.), Chronica de Mailros, e Codice Unico
    (Edinburgh, 1835)

Stubbs, William (ed.), Chronica magistri Rogeri de Hovedere
    (London, 1868 – 1871)

Stubbs, William (ed.), Chronicles of the Reigns of Edward I and
    Edward II (London, 1883)

Stubbs, William (ed.), De gestis regnum anglorum libri quinque:
    Historiae novellae libri tres
    (Cambridge University Press, 2012)

Stubbs, William (ed.), Gesta regis Henrici secundi Benedicti abbatis:
    the chronicle of the reigns of Henry II and Richard I,
    AD 1169 – 1192 (London, 1867)

Stubbs, William (ed.), The Historical Works of Ralph Diceto
    (London, 1876)

Stubbs, William (ed.), Willelmi Malmesbiriensi monachi de gestis
    regum Anglorum (London, 1887-1889)

Swanton, Michael (ed. and trans.), The Anglo-Saxon Chronicles
    (London, 2000)

Tacitus, The Annals, trans. Alfred John Church and William
    Jackson Brodribb (London, 1909)

UNPUBLISHED DISSERTATIONS

Noade, Ciarán, 'The Anglo-Norman Invasion and the Episcopacy of Armagh'
(MA thesis submitted to Queen's University, Belfast, 2011)
McCosker, Laura, 'Health and Social Welfare in Medieval Dublin'
(MA thesis submitted to Queen's University, Belfast, 2012)

SECONDARY SOURCES

Adair, Jamie, 'Purple Wedding: Joffrey and the Death of Eustace of Boulogne', History Behind Game of Thrones (2014)
Allmand, Christopher, Henry V (London, 1992)
Amt, Emile, 'William FitzEmpress', Oxford Dictionary of National Biography (Oxford University Press, 2004)
Arkin, M., 'When the Jewish goose stopped laying the golden eggs', Jewish Affairs (1955)
Ashley, Maurice, The Life and Times of King John (London, 1972)
Atkinson, E. G., The Jews in English History (London, 1912)
Barker, Juliet, Agincourt: The King, the Campaign, the Battle (London, 2005)
Bartlett, Robert, England under the Norman and Angevin Kings (Oxford University Press, 2000)
Barlow, Frank, The English Church, 1066 – 1154 (London, 1979)
Barlow, Frank, Edward the Confessor (Second edition, Yale University Press, 1997)
Barlow, Frank, 'William II', Oxford Dictionary of National Biography (Oxford University Press, 2004)
Barraclough, Geoffrey, The Medieval Papacy (Norwich, 1979)
Bernard, G. W., 'The Fall of Anne Boleyn: A rejoinder', English Historical Review (1992)
Bernard, G. W., The King's Reformation: Henry VIII and the Remaking of the English Church (Yale University Press, 1997)
Bernard, G. W., Anne Boleyn: Fatal Attractions (Yale University Press, 2010)

Bernard, G. W., The Late Medieval Church: Vitality and
    Vulnerability Before the Break with Rome
    (Yale University Press, 2013)
Bevan, Bryan, Edward III: Monarch of Chivalry (London, 1992)
Bordo, Susan, The Creation of Anne Boleyn: A new look at
    England's most notorious queen (New York, 2013)
Boswell, John, Christianity, Social Tolerance and Homosexuality:
    Gay People in Western Europe from the beginning of the
    Christian era to the fourteenth century
    (University of Chicago Press, 1980)
Bowsky, William (ed.), The Black Death (New York, 1971)
Bredero, Adriaan H., Bernard of Clairvaux: Between Cult and
    History (Edinburgh, 1996)
Brigden, Susan, New Worlds, Lost Worlds: The Rule of the Tudors,
    1485 – 1603 (London, 2000)
Brooks, Nicholas, The Early History of the Church of Canterbury:
    Christ Church from 597 to 1066
    (Leicester University Press, 1984)
Bruce, F. F., The Spreading Flame: The Rise and Progress of
    Christianity from its First Beginnings to the Conversion of the
    English (London, 1995)
Bruce, Marie Louise, Anne Boleyn (London, 1972)
Callahan, Thomas, 'The making of a monster: the historical image
    of William Rufus', Journal of Medieval History (1981)
Carmi Parsons, John, Eleanor of Castile: Queen and Society in
    thirteenth century England (New York, 1995)
Carroll, Stuart, Martyrs and Murderers: The Guise Family and the
    Making of Europe (Oxford University Press, 2011)
Cartledge, Paul, Alexander the Great: The Hunt for a New Past
    (London, 2004)
Chadwick, H. M., Studies on Anglo-Saxon Institutions
    (Cambridge, 1905)
Chadwick, Henry, The Early Church (London, 1990)
Chambers, James, The Norman Kings (London, 1981)
Chaplais, Pierre, Piers Gaveston: Edward II's adoptive brother
    (London, 1994)
Chazan, Robert, The Jews of Medieval Western Christendom, 1000
    – 1500 (Cambridge University Press, 2006)

Cheetham, Anthony, The Life and Times of Richard III
(London, 1972)

Cheney, C. R. (ed.) and Michael Jones (rev.), A Handbook of Dates
(Cambridge University Press, 2004)

Chibnall, Marjorie, The Empress Matilda: Queen Consort, Queen
Mother and Lady of the English (Oxford, 1993)

Cockerill, Sara, Eleanor of Castile: The Shadow Queen
(Stroud, 2014)

Davies, R. R., ' Mortimer, Roger (V), first earl of March (1287–
1330)', Oxford Dictionary of National Biography
(Oxford University Press, 2004)

Dodd, Gwilym and Anthony Musson (eds), The Reign of Edward II:
New Perspectives (Woodbridge, 2006)

Douglas, David C., The Normans (Bury St Edmunds, 2002)

Duffy, Eamon, The Stripping of the Altars: Traditional Religion in
England, c. 1400 – c. 1580
(Second edition, Yale University Press, 2005)

Duffy, Eamon, Saints, Sacrilege and Sedition: Religion and Conflict
in the Tudor Reformations (London, 2012)

Dunn, Jane, Elizabeth and Mary: Cousins, Rivals, Queens
(London, 2004)

Elman, P., 'The economic causes of the expulsion of the Jews in
1290', Economic History Review (1937)

Erlanger, Philip, Margaret of Anjou: Queen of England
(London, 1970)

Flanagan, Marie Thérèse, Irish Society, Anglo-Norman Settlers,
Angevin Kingship: Interactions in Ireland in the late twelfth
century (Oxford University Press, 1989)

Fletcher, Christopher, Richard II: Manhood, Youth and Politics,
1377-99 (Oxford University Press, 2008)

Fletcher, Richard, The Conversion of Europe: From Paganism to
Christianity, 371 – 1386 AD (London, 1997)

Foster, Joseph, The Royal Lineage of Our Noble and Gentle Families
together with Their Paternal Ancestry (London, 1886)

Fraser, Antonia, Mary Queen of Scots (London, 1976)

Fraser, Antonia, The Six Wives of Henry VIII (London, 1998)

Fraser, Antonia, Marie Antoinette: The Journey (London, 2002)

Fraser, Antonia, The Warrior Queens: Boadicea's Chariot
(London, 2002)

French, W. H. C., The Early Church: From the beginnings to 461
    (London, 1992)
Frieda, Leonie, Catherine de Medici (London, 2005)
Gambero, Luigi, 'Patristic Intuitions of Mary's Role as Mediatrix
    and Advocate: The Invocation of the Faithful for her Help',
    Marian Studies (2001)
Gillingham, John, Richard I (London, 1999)
Goldsworthy, Adrian, Caesar (London, 2007)
Green, Chris, 'Scottish independence: The Queen breaks silence on
    referendum debate – as think tank warns of £14bn black hole
    if Scotland votes Yes', The Independent (2014)
Gunn, Steven, 'Henry VII's "New Men"', Total Politics (2012)
Guy, John, My Heart is My Own: The Life of Mary Queen of Scots
    (London, 2004)
Gwyn, Peter, The King's Cardinal: The Rise and Fall of Thomas
    Wolsey (London, 1992)
Hamilton, J. S., Piers Gaveston, Earl of Cornwall, 1307 – 1322:
    Politics and Patronage in the reign of Edward II
    (London, 1988)
Hamilton, J. S., 'Menage á Roi: Edward II and Piers Gaveston',
    History Today (1999)
Harris Nicolas, Nicholas, The Literary Remains of Lady Jane Grey:
    with a memoir of her life (London, 1825)
Harris, Barbara J., Edward Stafford, Third Duke of Buckingham,
    1478 – 1521 (Stanford University Press, 1986)
Harvey, John, The Plantagenets, 1154 – 1485 (London, 1948)
Henderson, Philip, Richard Cœur de Lion: A Biography
    (London, 1958)
Herman, Eleanor, Sex with the Queen: 900 years of vile kings, virile
    lovers, and passionate politics (New York, 2006)
Hicks, Michael, Anne Neville: Queen to Richard III (Stroud, 2006)
Higginbotham, Susan, The Woodvilles: The Wars of the Roses and
    England's Most Infamous Family (Stroud, 2013)
Hillaby, Joe, 'London: the 13th-century Jewry revisited', Jewish
    Historical Studies (1990-1992)
Hilton, Lisa, Queens Consort: England's Medieval Queens
    (London, 2008)
Hodgkin, Thomas, The History of England from the Earliest Times
    to the Norman Conquest (New York, 1906)

Hollister, C. Warren, Monarchy, Magnates and Constitutions in the
     Anglo-Norman world (London, 1986)
Hollister, C. Warren, 'Henry I', Oxford Dictionary of National
     Biography (Oxford University Press, 2004)
Holmes, Frederick, Grace Holmes and Julia McMorrough, 'The
     Death of Young King Edward VI', New England Journal of
     Medicine (2001)
Honeycutt, Lois L., Matilda of Scotland: A Study in Medieval
     Queenship (Woodbridge, 2003)
Hooton, Christopher, 'Game of Thrones' "Purple Wedding": George
     R. R. Martin explains thinking behind Joffrey's demise', The
     Independent (2014)
Horrox, Rosemary, Richard III: A study in service (Cambridge
     University Press, 1989)
Howard, Ian, Harthacnut: The Last Danish King of England
     (London, 2008)
Howell, Margaret, Eleanor of Provence: Queenship in thirteenth
     century England (Oxford University Press, 1998)
Humble, Richard, The Saxon Kings (London, 1980)
Hume, David, History of England (London, 1871)
Hutchinson, Harold F., The Hollow Crown: The Life of Richard II
     (London, 1961)
Hyams, P. R., 'The Jewish Minority in Medieval England, 1066 –
     1290', Journal of Jewish Studies (1974)
Hyde, Harford Montgomery, The Love That Dare not Speak its
     Name: A candid history of homosexuality in Britain
     (London, 1970)
Ives, Eric, 'The Fall of Anne Boleyn Reconsidered', English
     Historical Review (1992)
Ives, Eric, The Life and Death of Anne Boleyn: The Most Happy
     (Oxford, 2004)
Ives, Eric, Lady Jane Grey: A Tudor Mystery (Oxford, 2009)
Jenkins, Elizabeth, Elizabeth the Great (London, 1958)
Johnson, Paul, Elizabeth: A study in power and intellect
     (London, 1974)
Jones, Dan, Summer of Blood: The Peasants' Revolt of 1381
     (London, 2010)
Jones, Michael K., Agincourt 1415 (Barnsley, 2005)

Jones, Michael K., and Malcolm G. Underwood, The King's
    Mother: Lady Margaret Beaufort, Countess of Richmond and
    Derby (Cambridge University Press, 1992)
Jones-Pierce, T., 'The Growth of Commutation in Gwynedd in the
    Thirteenth Century', Bulletin of the Board of Celtic Studies
    (1941)
Jordan, W. C., The French Monarchy and the Jews (London, 1989)
Keefe, Thomas K., and C. Warren Hollister, 'The making of the
    Angevin empire', Journal of British Studies (1972-1973)
King, Edmund (ed.), The Anarchy of King Stephen's Reign
    (Oxford University Press, 1994)
Knowles, David and R. Neville Hadcock, Medieval Religious
    Houses England and Wales (London, 1971)
Lambert, Royston, Beloved and God: The Story of Hadrian and
    Antinous (London, 1984)
Lane Fox, Robin, Alexander the Great (London, 1973)
Laynesmith, J. L., The Last Medieval Queens
    (Oxford University Press, 2006)
Lee, Christopher, The Sceptred Isle: The Dynasties (London, 2002)
Leyser, Henrietta, Medieval Women: A Social History of Women in
    England, 450 – 1500 (London, 1995)
Licence, Amy, The Six Wives and Many Mistresses of Henry VIII
    (Stroud, 2014)
Liebermann, Felix, The National Assembly in the Anglo-Saxon
    Period (Halle, 1913)
Lindsey, Karen, Divorced, Beheaded, Survived: A Feminist
    Reinterpretation of the Wives of Henry VIII (Boston, 1996)
Lipscomb, Suzannah, 1536: The Year That Changed Henry VIII
    (London, 2006)
Lisle, Leanda de, After Elizabeth: How James King of Scots Won
    the Crown of England in 1603 (London, 2004)
Lisle, Leanda de, The Sisters Who Would Be Queen: The Tragedy of
    Mary, Katherine and Lady Jane Grey (London, 2008)
Lisle, Leanda de, Tudor: The Family Story (London, 2013)
Lisle, Leanda de, 'Anne Boleyn's last secret', The Spectator (2013)
Loach, Jennifer, Edward VI (Yale University Press, 2002)
Longford, Elizabeth Pakenham, Countess of (ed.), The Oxford Book
    of Royal Anecdotes (Oxford University Press, 1989)

Loyn, H. R., Anglo-Saxon England and the Norman Conquest
(Second edition, London, 1991)

MacNalty, Arthur, Henry VIII: A Difficult Patient (London, 1952)

Maddicott, John R., The Origins of the English Parliament
(Oxford University Press, 2010)

Mann, Stephanie A., Supremacy and Survival: How Catholics
Endured the English Reformation (New Rochelle, 2009)

Marr, Andrew, The Diamond Queen: Elizabeth II and Her People
(London, 2012)

Mason, Emma, The House of Godwine: The History of a Dynasty
(London, 2004)

Matthews, Gervase, The Court of Richard II (London, 1968)

Maunder, Chris (ed.), Origins of the Cult of the Virgin Mary
(London, 2008)

McLynn, Frank, Lionheart and Lackland: King Richard, King John
and the Wars of Conquest (London, 2007)

Morgan, D. A. L., 'The political after-life of Edward III: the
apotheosis of a warmonger', English Historical Review (1997)

Morris, Marc, A Great and Terrible King: Edward I and the Forging
of Britain (London, 2009)

Mortimer, Ian, 'The Death of Edward II in Berkeley Castle', English
Historical Review (2005)

Mortimer, Ian, The Fears of Henry IV: The Life of England's Self-
Made King (London, 2008)

Mortimer, Ian, The Perfect King: The Life of Edward III, Father of
the English Nation (London, 2008)

Moynahan, Brian, The Faith: A History of Christianity
(London, 2003)

Mundill, Robin R., The King's Jews: Money, Massacre and Exodus
in Medieval England (London, 2010)

Neale, John E., 'Sayings of Queen Elizabeth', History (1925)

Neale, John E., Queen Elizabeth (London, 1934)

Ní Mhaonaigh, Máire, 'Diarmait Mac Murchada', Dictionary of
Irish Biography (Cambridge University Press, 2009)

Ó Cróinín, Dáibhí, Early Medieval Ireland, 400 – 1200
(London, 1995)

Okerlund, Arlene, Elizabeth: England's Slandered Queen
(Stroud, 2006)

Omrod, W. Mark, Edward III (Yale University Press, 2011)

Owen, D. D. R., Eleanor of Aquitaine: Queen and Legend
    (Oxford, 1996)
Owst, G. R., Literature and Pulpit in Mediaeval England
    (Cambridge University Press, 1933)
Paget, Hugh, 'The Youth of Anne Boleyn', British Institute of
    Historical Research (1981)
Paine, Lauran, Saladin: A Man for All Ages (London, 1974)
Payne, Richard, The Dream and the Tomb: A History of the
    Crusades (London, 1984)
Penn, Thomas, Winter King: The Dawn of Tudor England
    (London, 2011)
Philips, Seymour, Edward II (Yale University Press, 2010)
Poole, A. L., Henry the Lion (Oxford University Press, 1912)
Porter, Linda, Crown of Thistles: The Fatal Inheritance of Mary
    Queen of Scots (London, 2013)
Porter, Linda, Mary Tudor: The First Queen (London, 2009)
Potter, Jeremy, Pretenders (London, 1986)
Prestwich, Michael, Edward I (London, 1990)
Prestwich, Michael, Plantagenet England: 1225 – 1360
    (Second edition, Oxford University Press, 2007)
Price, Munro, The Fall of the French Monarchy: Louis XVI, Marie
    Antoinette and the baron de Breteuil (London, 2003)
Ramsay, James, The Angevin Empire (London, 1903)
Ridgway, Claire, The Fall of Anne Boleyn: A Countdown
    (Lúcar, 2012)
Ridley, Jasper, The Life and Times of Mary Tudor (London, 1973)
Ridley, Jasper, Henry VIII (London, 1984)
Ross, Charles Derek, Edward IV
    (University of California Press, 1974)
Roth, Cecil, A History of the Jews in England (Oxford, 1978)
Rubin, Miri, The Hollow Crown: A History of Britain in the Late
    Middle Ages (London, 2006)
Runciman, Steven, A History of the Crusades
    (Cambridge University Press, 1954)
Russell, Gareth, The Emperors: How Europe's Rulers were
    Destroyed by the First World War (Stroud, 2014)
Saul, Nigel, Honour and Fame: Chivalry in England, 1066 – 1500
    (London, 2011)

Scarisbrick, J. J., Henry VIII
(Second edition, Yale University Press, 1997)

Schiff, Stacy, Cleopatra: A Life (London, 2011)

Schriber, C., Arnulf of Lisieux: the dilemmas of a twelfth-century Norman bishop (London, 1990)

Seward, Desmond, The Last White Rose: The Secret Wars of the Tudors (London, 2011)

Sharpe, Richard, Adomnán of Iona, Life of St Columba (Harmondsworth, 1995)

Skidmore, Chris, Death and the Virgin: Elizabeth, Dudley and the Mysterious Fate of Amy Robsart (London, 2011)

Slocombe, George, William the Conqueror (London, 1959)

Smith, Lacey Baldwin, Fools, Martyrs and Traitors: A History of Martyrdom in the Western World (New York, 2012)

Southern, R. W., Saint Anselm and his biographer: a study of monastic life and thought, 1059 – c. 1130 (London, 1963)

Southern, R. W., Medieval Humanism and other studies (London, 1970)

Southern, R. W., Saint Anselm: a portrait in a landscape (London, 1990)

Speed, John, The Historie of Great Britain (London, 1611)

Starkey, David, Six Wives: The Queens of Henry VIII (London, 2004)

Starkey, David, Crown and Country: The Kings and Queens of England: A History (London, 2010)

Stokes, H. P., 'The relationship between the Jews and the royal family of England in the thirteenth century', Transactions of the Jewish Historical Society (1918)

Strickland, Agnes, Lives of the Queens of England (London, 1840 – 1848)

Sturdy, David, Alfred the Great (London, 1995)

Sullivan Jr., Garrett A., Patrick Cheney and Andrew Hadfield (eds), Early Modern English Drama: A Critical Companion (Oxford University Press, 2006)

Trachtenburg, Joshua, The Devil and the Jews (London, 1943)

Thomas, Charles, Tintagel: Arthur and Archaeology (London, 1993)

Tremlett, Giles, Catherine of Aragon: Henry's Spanish Queen (London, 2010)

Turner, Ralph V., King John (London, 1994)

Walker, Curtis H., 'Eleanor of Aquitaine and the Disaster at
    Cadmos Mountain on the Second Crusade', American
    Historical Review (1950)

Walker, Greg, 'Rethinking the fall of Anne Boleyn', Historical
    Journal (2002)

Warner, Kathryn, 'The Adherents of Edmund of Woodstock, Earl of
    Kent, in March 1330', English Historical Review (2011)

Warner, Kathryn, 'Edward II's Death and Afterlife Revisited (2)'
    (Online, 2013)

Warner, Kathryn, Edward II: The Unconventional King
    (Stroud, 2014)

Warner, Marina, Alone of All Her Sex: The myth and the cult of the
    Virgin Mary (Second edition, London, 1990)

Warnicke, Retha M., 'Anne Boleyn's Childhood and Adolescence',
    The Historical Journal (1985)

Warnicke, Retha M., 'Sexual Heresy at the Court of Henry VIII',
    The Historical Journal (1987)

Warnicke, Retha M., The Rise and Fall of Anne Boleyn: Family
    politics at the court of Henry VIII
    (Cambridge University Press, 1989)

Watt, Nicholas, Patrick Wintour and Severin Carrell, 'Scottish
    independence: Queen was asked to intervene amid yes vote
    fears', The Guardian (2014)

Weir, Alison, Britain's Royal Families: A Complete Genealogy
    (London, 2002)

Weir, Alison, The Lady in the Tower: The Fall of Anne Boleyn
    (London, 2009)

Weir, Alison, Mary Boleyn: 'The Great and Infamous Whore'
    (London, 2011)

Weir, Alison, Isabella: She-Wolf of France, Queen of England
    (London, 2012)

Wertheimer, Laura, 'Adeliza of Louvain and Anglo-Norman
    queenship', Haskins Society Journal (1997)

Wilkinson, Toby, The Rise and Fall of Ancient Egypt: The History
    of a Civilisation from 3000 BC to Cleopatra (London, 2011)

Williams, Neville, The Life and Times of Henry VII (London, 1973)

Wilson, A. N., The Elizabethans (London, 2011)

Wilson, Derek, A Brief History of Henry VIII: Reformer and Tyrant
    (London, 2009)

Winston, Richard, Thomas Becket (London, 1967)

Wise, Terence, The Wars of the Crusades, 1096 – 1291 (London, 1978)

Woodruff, Douglas, The Life and Times of Alfred the Great (London, 1974)

Wormald, Patrick, The Making of English Law: King Alfred to the Twelfth Century (Oxford, 1999)

ENDNOTES

AUTHOR'S NOTE

1 Muircheartach, sometimes spelled Muirchertach, roughly translates as Murtagh, but this name does not enjoy a close enough link to justify a translation. My sincere apologies to anyone who might disagree; it was done solely for clarity's sake.

PROLOGUE

1 Marc Morris, A Great and Terrible King: Edward I and the Forging of Britain (London, 2009), p. 165.
2 There are over two hundred surviving copies of Monmouth's History, a very high number for the period.
3 Charles Thomas, Tintagel: Arthur and Archaeology (London, 1993), p. 23.
4 Sara Cockerill, Eleanor of Castile: The Shadow Queen (Stroud, 2014), p. 225. The tomb was destroyed in the seventeenth century.

CONQUEST

1 The identity of the first pharaoh is still a subject of debate. In ancient sources he is sometimes referred to by the Greek version of his name, Menes. He has been identified with two early pharaohs, Narmer and Hor-Aha, with the weight of academic opinion favouring the former as the king who unified Egypt in about 2950 BC. See Toby Wilkinson, The Rise and Fall of Ancient Egypt: The History of a Civilisation from 3000 BC to Cleopatra (London, 2011), pp. 17-19, 25-27.

2 Stacy Schiff, Cleopatra (London, 2011), p. 101.

3 For a discussion of Cleopatra's appearance, see Schiff, p. 38-9, and Adrian Goldsworthy, Caesar (London, 2007), pp. 533-4.

4 Antonia Fraser, The Warrior Queens: Boadicea's Chariot (London, 2002), p. 64.

5 The Roman historian Tacitus believed that Boadicea committed suicide by drinking poison; Dio Cassius suggested she died of illness after grief at losing the battle of Watling Street. Tacitus's version of events seems to be the more likely of the two.

6 Fraser, Warrior Queens, p. 110-111.

7 Another suggestion, that her body lies beneath what is now Platform 8 of King's Cross Station, helped make that the most famous part of the train station until the creation of the fictitious Platform 9 ¾ by J.K. Rowling. Both are, alas, unlikely to be there.

8 The Gospel according to Saint Luke, 23:1-12.

9 Royston Lambert, Beloved and God: The Story of Hadrian and Antinous (London, 1984), pp. 90-4.

10 Robin Lane Fox, Alexander the Great (London, 2004), p. 113; Paul Cartledge, Alexander the Great: The Hunt for a New Past (London, 2005) p. 10.

11 Tacitus, The Annals, trans. Alfred John Church and William Jackson Brodribb (London, 1909), xv. 44.

12 Constantine did not formally convert by rite of baptism until shortly before his death in 337, but after the Edict of Milan his tolerance for, interest in, and patronage of, Christian issues suggest where his loyalties lay. For a persuasive argument on Constantine's spiritual evolution see Henry Chadwick, The Early Church (London, 1990), pp. 125-7.

13 Brian Moynahan, The Faith: A History of Christianity (London, 2003), p. 104.

14 Moynahan, p. 105.

15 As of the nineteenth century, there have been many Christians who venerate the "Garden Tomb" as the site of the Resurrection. The

Basilica of the Holy Sepulchre is said to cover both the site of the Crucifixion and the original site of Christ's tomb, as well as four or five of the Stations of The Cross.

16 Constantine's opening speech to the council urged the bishops to find unity of direction for the sake of peace in the empire. He also weighed-in on various theological debates by indicating support for bishops like Eusebius of Cæsarea.

17 See chapter 7, As the Law of Christ Allows.

18 See Richard M. Price, 'Theotokos and the Council of Ephesus' in Chris Maunder (ed.), Origins of the Cult of the Virgin Mary (London, 2008), pp. 89-103, for the argument that the debate at Ephesus over the title was essentially Christological in nature, but that the title had entered regular usage by Christians invoking the Virgin at least a century before and its popular development was a product of emerging Marianism, rather than Christological debates. For theories placing its use even earlier and the implicit arguments that the great ecclesiastical councils only confirmed the accepted spiritual practices of the Christian majority by the time of Nicea, see Luigi Gambero, 'Patristic Intuitions of Mary's Role as Mediatrix and Advocate: The Invocation of the Faithful for her Help' in Marian Studies (2001).

19 The creed adopted after the Council of Constantinople (381).

20 Richard Fletcher, The Conversion of Europe: From Paganism to Christianity, 371 – 1386 AD (London, 1997), p. 25.

21 Moynahan, p. 109.

22 Gildas, De Excidio et Conquestu Britanniæ, trans. Michael Winterbottom (Chichester, 1978), section XXIII.

23 It has less plausibly been suggested that Bertha and Liudhard received the church of Saint Pancras, but excavations in Saint Martin's in the nineteenth century unearthed artefacts belonging to Liudhard that seemingly corroborate the story that the Queen's chapel was located there in the sixth century.

24 Fletcher, Conversion of Europe, p. 117; Nicholas Brooks, The Early History of the Church of Canterbury: Christ Church from 597 to 1066 (Leicester University Press, 1984) p. 8.

25 Fletcher, Conversion of Europe, p. 117.

26 For a discussion of Saint Aidan's partnership with the Northumbrian royal household and nobility see Fletcher, Conversion of Europe, pp. 165-8.

27 Fletcher, Conversion of Europe, p. 119.

28 Bede, Ecclesiastical History of the English People, trans. A. M. Sellar (London, 1907), iii. chapter v.

29 Fletcher, Conversion of Europe, p. 93.

30 Simon Keynes and Michael Lapidge (eds), Alfred the Great: Asser's
    Life of King Alfred and Other Contemporary Sources (London, 1983),
    p. 68.
31 Douglas Woodruff, The Life and Times of Alfred the Great
    (London, 1974), p. 210.
32 Lois Honeycutt, Matilda of Scotland: A Study in Medieval Queenship
    (Woodbridge, 2003), p. 35.
33 Woodruff, p. 210.
34 See in particular the chroniclers' treatment of William II and King
    John in chapters 2 and 5, respectively.
35 Anglo-Saxon Chronicle
36 Ibid.
37 For the story of Zadok the Priest, Nathan the Prophet and King
    Solomon, see the first book of Kings, 1:34-40.
38 Some of the original crown jewels were destroyed after the abolition
    of the monarchy in 1649, but any replacements made after the
    Restoration generally honoured the original symbolism.
39 The body of Harold I was allegedly hurled into a 'fen', a kind of
    wetland best described as a swamp or bog.
40 See the original frontispiece of Emma's self-commissioned biography
    Encomium Emmæ Reginæ.
41 An earlier monastery dedicated to the patronage of Saint Peter had
    allegedly been built near the site in the seventh century. However, it
    was Edward the Confessor who began the construction of the abbey as
    a royal burial ground.
42 The first epistle to the Corinthians, 7:1.
43 Marina Warner, Alone of All Her Sex: The myth and the cult of the
    Virgin Mary (London, 1990), p. 73.
44 Frank Barlow, Edward the Confessor (Second edition, Yale University
    Press, 1997) , p. 82.
45 Barlow, Edward the Confessor, pp. 106-9.
46 Lisa Hilton, Queens Consort: England's Medieval Queens
    (London, 2008), p. 21.

GOD, LIFE AND VICTORY

1   Hilton, Queens Consort, p. 21.
2   There is some debate over whether or not King Harold did sustain
    his famous wound to the eye at Hastings. The account of the battle
    by the Bishop of Amiens, written shortly after the event, reports that
    Harold was eventually hacked apart by Norman knights. The Bayeux

Tapestry shows two figures near the label Harold Rex Interfectus Est, ('Harold the King is Killed'). One figure has an arrow apparently piercing his eye and another lies prone, as he is trampled underfoot. It seems unlikely that these are two separate figures, but rather part of a sequence that confirms the story that Harold sustained a terrible injury but kept fighting until he eventually fell at enemy hands.

3 Anglo-Saxon Chronicle
4 Elizabeth, Countess of Longford, The Oxford Book of Royal Anecdotes (Oxford University Press, 1989), p. 48.
5 Emma Mason, The House of Godwine: The History of a Dynasty (London, 2004), p. 178.
6 Orderic Vitalis, The Ecclesiastical History of England and Normandy, trans. Thomas Forester (London, 1853)
7 Hilton, p. 33.
8 Longford, p. 50.
9 Robin R. Mundill, The King's Jews: Money, Massacre and Exodus in Medieval England (London, 2010), p. 9.
10 Orderic Vitalis.
11 Ibid.
12 Frank Barlow, The English Church, 1066 – 1154 (London, 1979), p. 2.
13 Vita B. Simonis, Patrologia Latina (London, 1853)
14 Hilton, p. 38.
15 The Gospel according to Saint Matthew, 25:52.
16 Anglo-Saxon Chronicle.
17 George Slocombe, William the Conqueror (London, 1959), p. 255.
18 Anglo-Saxon Chronicle.
19 William of Malmesbury, De gestis regnum anglorum libri quinque: Historiae novellae libri tres, William Stubbs (ed.) (Cambridge University Press, 2012), i. 313.
20 Eadmer's History of Recent Events, trans. Geoffrey Bosanquet (London, 1964), p. 53.
21 Longford, p. 51.
22 Frank Barlow, 'William II' in Oxford Dictionary of National Biography (Oxford University Press, 2004)
23 Longford, p. 61.
24 Longford, p. 58.
25 Hilton, p. 45.
26 Anne Crawford (ed.), Letters of the Queens of England (Stroud, 2002), p. 20.
27 The story of the prophet Samuel's commitment to the temple is found in the Old Testament (1 Samuel, 1:21-8). The Virgin Mary's childhood experiences, which enjoyed widespread belief in the Middle Ages, are recounted in the early second-century text The Protevangelium of

James, the first two-thirds of which cover the Virgin's life prior to the Annunciation recorded in the canonical New Testament.

28 Hilton, p. 43.

29 Hilton, p. 45.

30 Hilton, p. 49.

31 Orderic Vitalis.

32 C. Warren Hollister, 'Henry I' in Oxford Dictionary of National Biography (Oxford University Press, 2004)

33 Longford, p. 60.

34 Edmund King (ed.), William of Malmesbury: Historia Novella, trans. K. R. Potter (Oxford University Press, 1999), p. 3.

35 Robert Bartlett, England under the Norman and Angevin Kings (Oxford, 2000), p. 41.

36 Historia Novella, p. 14.

37 Edmund King (ed.), The Anarchy of Stephen's Reign (Oxford University Press, 1994), p. 301-2.

38 Orderic Vitalis.

39 Maud's father Henry I and Stephen's mother Adela were both children of William I; Matilda of Boulogne and Maud were granddaughters of Malcolm III of Scotland through his daughters, Mary, Countess of Boulogne and Queen Matilda of England.

40 Thomas Forester (ed. and trans.), The Chronicle of Henry of Huntingdon, comprising of the History of England from the invasion of Julius Caesar to the Accession of Henry II (London, 1853), p. 712-13.

41 Historia Novella, p. 18; The Anglo-Saxon Chronicle.

42 Longford, p. 63.

43 Ibid.

44 Orderic Vitalis.

45 K. R. Potter and R. H. C. Davis (ed. and trans.), Gesta Stephani Regis Anglorum (London, 1975), p. 153.

46 Chronicle of Henry of Huntingdon, p. 78.

47 Anglo-Saxon Chronicle.

48 Historia Novella, p. 22.

49 Anglo-Saxon Chronicle.

50 Gesta Stephani, p. 96-7.

51 Christopher Hooton, 'Game of Thrones' "Purple Wedding": George R. R. Martin explains thinking behind Joffrey's demise' in The Independent (15 April 2014); Jamie Adair, 'Purple Wedding: Joffrey and the Death of Eustace of Boulogne' in History Behind Game of Thrones (17 April 2014).

FROM SCOTLAND TO SPAIN

1   Marie Thérèse Flanagan, Irish Society, Anglo-Norman Settlers,
    Angevin Kingship: Interactions in Ireland in the late twelfth century
    (Oxford University Press, 1989), p. 174.
2   Frank McLynn, Lionheart and Lackland: King Richard, King John
    and the Wars of Conquest (London, 2007), p. 16.
3   Hilton, p. 118.
4   See Curtis H. Walker, 'Eleanor of Aquitaine and the Disaster at
    Cadmos Mountain on the Second Crusade' in American Historical
    Review (1950) for the best discussion of Eleanor's alleged involvement
    in the Cadmos incident.
5   William of Tyre.
6   Hilton, p. 104.
7   William of Tyre.
8   Hilton, p. 118, quoting a poet attached to Eleanor's court.
9   M. R. James (ed.), De Nugis Curialium (London, 1914), pp. 237-242.
10 Patrologia Latina.
11 Peter of Blois to the Archbishop of Palermo, c. 1177, in Patrologia
    Latina.
12 Ibid.
13 McLynn, p. 5.
14 William Stubbs (ed.), The Historical Works of Ralph Diceto
    (London, 1876), i. 351.
15 J. A. Giles (ed.), Petri Blesensis Archidiaconi Opera Omnia
    (Oxford, 1847), i. 193.
16 The site of King Richard and King John's birth in Oxford, Beaumont
    Palace, no longer exists but its name is recorded in Beaumont Street,
    which runs from Worcester College at one end to the Ashmolean
    Museum and the Randolph Hotel at the other. A plaque at the
    Worcester end of the street marks Richard's birth there.
17 Gerald of Wales, The History and Topography of Ireland, (rev. ed.) J. J.
    O'Meara (London, 1982), viii. 292-3.
18 Walter Map, Courtiers' Trifles (Oxford, 1983), p. 450-1.
19 D. C. Douglas and G. M. Greenway (eds), English Historical
    Documents (London, 1953), ii. 410.
20 W. J. Millor and H. E. Butler (eds and trans.), The Letters of John of
    Salisbury (Oxford University Press, 1979–86), ii. 581.
21 The Annals of Clonmacnoise.
22 Máire Ní Mhaonaigh, 'Diarmait Mac Murchada' in Dictionary of Irish
    National Biography (Cambridge University Press, 2009)
23 Ibid.

24 Ibid.
25 Ibid.
26 I am grateful to Ciarán Noade for his discussion with me of the Laudabiliter of Pope Adrian IV.
27 That was the explanation put forth in one contemporary chronicle written by Gervase of Canterbury.
28 Henry was subsequently known as 'the Young King' in imitation of the French monarchy, which tended to crown the next-in-line as a sort of junior King in his father's lifetime in the hopes of guaranteeing a more peaceful and undisputed succession when the time came.
29 Emile Amt, 'William FitzEmpress' in Oxford Dictionary of National Biography (Oxford University Press, 2004)
30 Lacey Baldwin Smith, Fools, Martyrs and Traitors: A History of Martyrdom in the Western World (New York, 2012), p. 240.
31 A. L. Poole, Henry the Lion (Oxford University Press, 1912), p. 220.
32 Before Becket's death, Henry made only two known visits to Canterbury, but after the defeat of the rebellion in 1174 he made nearly a dozen.
33 McLynn, p. 74.
34 The Gospel according to Saint Matthew, 28:6
35 John Speed, The Historie of Great Britain (London, 1611), p. 481.
36 David Hume, History of England (London, 1871), i. 279.
37 See in particular Ridley Scott's Robin Hood (2010).
38 I am grateful to Kathryn Warner for pointing out that 'sodomy' in medieval German applied solely to bestiality, confirming the variables possible when analysing what it meant in medieval political discourse. Elsewhere it was taken to specify blasphemous acts or a lack of hospitality.
39 John Gillingham, 'Richard I' in Oxford Dictionary of National Biography (Oxford University Press, 2004).
40 Ibid.
41 McLynn, p. 246.
42 William Stubbs (ed.), Chronica magistri Rogeri de Hovedere (London, 1868 – 1871), iii. 216-7.

DILUTED MAGNIFICENCE

1 Maurice Ashley, The Life and Times of King John (London, 1972), p. 19.
2 Isobel's name is sometimes given as Isabella, Isabella, Hawisa and even Joan.

3   John descended from Henry's legitimate children via his daughter, the Empress Maud/Matilda, while Isobel descended through Henry's bastard offspring via his son Robert, Earl of Gloucester, a loyal supporter of the Empress during her quarrel with King Stephen.

4   Isabelle's mother, Alice de Courtenay, a granddaughter of King Louis VI of France, had previously been married to Guillaume, Count of Joigny. Their marriage ended in annulment between 1184 and 1186. It was only sometime after, and we have no idea of knowing exactly how long after, that Alice married Isabelle's father, Aymer, Count of Angoulême. A document dating from 1191, when Aymer made a gift to the abbey of St.-Armand-de-Boixe, is the first recorded proof we have of Alice being referred to as his wife. This puts the date of Isabelle's parents' marriage between 1185 (at the very earliest) and 1191.

5   Hilton, p. 146.

6   Longford, p. 87. This would put the date of Arthur of Brittany's death to 3 April 1203.

7   Hilton, p. 148.

8   Hilton, p. 151.

9   Longford, p. 102.

10 Ashley, p. 200.

11 Sir Frederick Madden (ed.), Matthaei Parisiensis, Monachi Sancti Albani, Historia Anglorum, sive, ut Vulgo Dictur, Historia Minor. Item Ejusdem Abbreviatio Chronicorum Angliae (London, 1866-69). Subsequently referred to as Historia Anglorum.

12 Ibid.

13 As with so many proposed royal engagements in the Middle Ages, nothing came of either match. Yolanda of Brittany ultimately married Henry III's half-brother, Hugh XI, Count of Lusignan, and Marjorie of Scotland married the former English regent's son, Gilbert Marshal, 4th Earl of Pembroke.

14 Historia Anglorum.

15 Hilton, p. 175.

16 Historia Anglorum.

17 Chronicle of Melrose Abbey.

18 Antonia Fraser, Marie Antoinette: The Journey (London, 2002), p. 366.

19 The First Barons' War was the rebellion against King John, which ended with William Marshal's victory shortly after John's death.

20 After the restoration of royal authority, Eleanor of Provence appealed to Rome for help in restoring the finances of the Queen's household. Pope Clement IV sanctioned a triennial levy of one-tenth of clerical incomes in England, from which it is estimated that Eleanor personally

obtained approximately £15,000 to pay off some of the debts she had
incurred during the war.

21 Morris, p. 22.

22 Eleanor's exact date of birth is unknown, but given that forty-nine
candle-bearers were included in her funeral it seems that she was forty-
nine at the time of her death in November 1290, indicating 1241. Sara
Cockerill places her birth to late in that year, perhaps 23 November,
see Cockerill, pp. 38-40.

23 This was the conclusion I reached in the course of my research for
Gareth Russell, 'Jews, Money and the Queen's Household: Eleanor
of Provence and Eleanor of Castile', submitted to Queen's University,
Belfast. I am grateful to Dr Dion Smythe for his supervision and
encouragement during that process. This is not to imply that
Queen Eleanor was in favour of Jewish rights vis-á-vis Christians or
sympathetic to Judaism in the way we would now understand it.

24 Cockerill, p. 101.

25 My thanks to Sara Cockerill for our discussions on Edward I and
Eleanor of Castile's marriage and his fidelity to his wife.

26 Morris, p. 194.

27 See Sara Cockerill's biography of Eleanor, pp. 247-54, for a balanced
assessment of Eleanor's attitude to her children. She seems to have
been an encouraging parent, who took a great interest in her offspring's
upbringing, but 'her relations with them were less intense and more
distant than the modern idiom expects.'

28 Morris, p. 115.

29 Morris, p. 136.

30 T. Jones-Piece, 'The Growth of Commutation in Gwynedd in the
Thirteenth Century' in The Bulletin Board of Celtic Studies (1941).

31 Morris, p. 151.

32 Morris, p. 176.

33 Huw Pryce (ed.), The Act of Welsh Rulers, 1120 – 1283 (University of
Wales Press, 2005), pp. 626-8.

34 The Gospel according to Saint Luke, 1:26-38.

35 For a fuller discussion of the role of the Feast of the Annunciation in
medieval calendars see C. R. Cheney (ed.) and Michael Jones (rev.), A
Handbook of Dates (Cambridge University Press, 2004), p. 12-13.

36 Morris, p. 186.

37 Robert Chazan, The Jews of Medieval Western Christendom, 1000 –
1500 (Cambridge University Press, 2006), p. 159.

38 Mundill, p. 14.

39 Mundill, p. 146.

40 Mundill, p. 17.

41 Joe Hillaby, 'London: the 13th-century revisited' in Jewish Historical
    Studies (1990-1992), p. 150.
42 Morris, p. 228.
43 Ibid.
44 Mundill, p. 158.
45 E. G. Atkinson, The Jews in English History (London, 1912), p. 8.
46 Mundill, p. 166.
47 Morris, p. 231.
48 Agnes Strickland, Lives of the Queens of England (London, 1840-48),
    i. 80.
49 Joshua Trachtenburg, The Devil and the Jews (London, 1943), p. 12.
50 Morris, p. 252.
51 Morris, p. 240.
52 Morris, p. 289.
53 As of 2014, the plan remains for the stone to be brought back to
    Westminster for future coronations to complete the anointing of a
    British, rather than English, sovereign.
54 Morris, p. 290.
55 Morris, p. 311.
56 Hilton, p. 206.
57 Morris, p. 354.
58 Morris, p. 359.
59 Morris, p. 326.
60 Morris, p. 221.

ENEMIES FOREIGN AND DOMESTIC

1 Leanda de Lisle, Tudor: The Family Story (London, 2013), p. 1.
2 My thanks to Kathryn Warner for bringing this touching anecdote to
   my attention.
3 Eleanor Herman, Sex with the Queen: 900 years of vile kings, virile
   lovers, and passionate politics (New York, 2006), p. 59.
4 Alison Weir, Isabella: She-Wolf of France, Queen of England
   (London, 2012), p. 148.
5 Vita Edwardi Secundi; The Scalacronica.
6 Gesta Edwardi de Carnarvon.
7 Ranulphi Castrensis, cognomine Higden, Polychronicon (sive
   Historia Polycratica) ab initio mundi usque ad mortem regis Edwardi
   III in septem libros dispositum. Subsequently referred to as the
   Polychronicon.

8 Morris, p. 349.
9 W.M. Omrod, 'The Sexualities of Edward II' in Gwilym Dodd and Anthony Musson (eds), The Reign of Edward II: New Perspectives (Woodridge, 2006), p. 22.
10 Kathryn Warner, Edward II: The Unconventional King (Stroud, 2014), pp. 27-30.
11 In 1304, Gaveston was granted the wardship of an orphan, Roger Mortimer, meaning that he must have been at least twenty-one by that stage. He is usually referred to as Edward II's contemporary and put together this indicates he was born between 1281 and the summer of 1283.
12 Chronicon Galfridi le Baker.
13 Vita Edwardi Secundi
14 Warner, Edward II, p. 42.
15 Morris, p. 359.
16 Bryan Bevan, Edward III: Monarch of Chivalry (London, 1992), p. 5.
17 Vita Edwardi Secundi.
18 Vita Edwardi Secundi. I am grateful to Kathryn Warner for our conversations on Edward II's allocation of the earldom and the arguments, pro- and contra-, for it playing a role in alienating Marguerite of France.
19 Hilton, p. 213-14.
20 Alan Stewart, 'Edward II and male same-sex desire' in Garrett A Sullivan Jr., Patrick Cheney and Andrew Hadfield (eds), Early Modern English Drama: A Critical Companion (Oxford University Press, 2006), p. 82.
21 John Boswell, Christianity, Social Tolerance and Homosexuality: Gay People in Western Europe from the Beginning of the Christian Era to the Fourteenth Century (University of Chicago Press, 1980), pp. 295-300.
22 J.S. Hamilton, Piers Gaveston, Earl of Cornwall, 1307 – 1312: Politics and Patronage in the Reign of Edward II (London, 1988), believes that Edward II and Gaveston were lovers, but argues that it was politics and concerns over the monopolisation of patronage which led to the assassination.
23 See Leonie Frieda, Catherine de Medici (London, 2005), p. 283-4, for the theory that Philibert Le Vayer, sieur de Lignerolles, was assassinated either on the Queen Mother's orders or with her connivance.
24 Vita Edwardi Secundi.
25 David Starkey, Crown and Country: The King and Queens of England: A History (London, 2010), p. 224.
26 A contemporary cited in Warner, Edward II, p. 88
27 Weir, Isabella, p. 142.

28 Vita Edwardi Secundi.
29 The Wigmore Chronicle.
30 Ian Mortimer, The Perfect King: The Life of Edward III, Father of the English Nation (London, 2008), p. 25.
31 Bevan, p. 4.
32 Bevan, p. 10-11.
33 Mortimer, Perfect King, p. 64.
34 Murimuth dated the King's murder to 22 September 1327 in Chronicon and Continuatio chronicarum.
35 Warner, Edward II, p. 244.
36 The Baker Chronicle.
37 Mortimer, Perfect King, p. 200-201 and Appendix 2, pp. 405-410.
38 Ian Mortimer, Perfect King, Appendix 3, pp. 411-418.
39 R. R. Davies, 'Mortimer, Roger (V), first earl of March (1287 – 1330)' in Oxford Dictionary of National Biography (Oxford University Press, 2004).
40 Mortimer, Perfect King, p. 1
41 Mortimer, Perfect King, p. 333.
42 Mortimer, Perfect King, p. 278.
43 Candidates for the mysterious lady include Catherine Montagu (née Grandison), Countess of Salisbury, or Edward III's future daughter-in-law Joan, Countess of Kent and Baroness Wake of Liddell.
44 William Bowsky (ed.), The Black Death (New York, 1971), p. 14.
45 The Gospel according to Saint Luke, 2:34-5. An actual feast day to Our Lady of Sorrows was not assigned to the whole Catholic Church until the nineteenth century, nonetheless it had been celebrated in many parts of Christian Europe from the fifteenth century and evidence for devotion to the Virgin Mary in that guise dates from the early thirteenth century, with the cult exploding in popularity after the traumatic impact of the Black Death.
46 Dan Jones, Summer of Blood: The Peasants' Revolt of 1381 (London, 2010), p. 14.
47 Jones, Summer of Blood, p. 16.
48 Hilton, p. 270.
49 Mortimer, p. 390-1.
50 D. A. L. Morgan, 'The political after-life of Edward III: the apotheosis of a warmonger' in English Historical Review (1997), p. 861.
51 The description comes from Queen Anne's tomb at Westminster Abbey.
52 Jones, Summer of Blood, p. 33.
53 Parliament Rolls.
54 G. R. Owst, Literature and Pulpit in Mediaeval England (Cambridge University Press, 1933), p. 5.

55 Jones, Summer of Blood, p. 7-8.
56 St. Albans Chronicle.
57 Jones, Summer of Blood, p. 147.
58 Jones, Summer of Blood, p. 159.
59 Westminster Chronicle.
60 St. Albans Chronicle.
61 Historia Vitae et Regni Ricardi II.

SPILLED BLOOD DOES NOT SLEEP

1 Ian Mortimer, The Fears of Henry IV: The Life of England's Self-Made King (London, 2008), p. 1.
2 There is some debate over 1366 or 1367 as the year of Henry's birth, but the majority of his biographers favour the latter.
3 Mortimer, Henry IV, p. 121.
4 Her name is sometimes given as Joan, Joanne or Johanna.
5 The Earl of Oxford in question was Richard de Vere, 11ᵗʰ Earl of Oxford, a cousin of Richard II's favourite who died in exile. The 11ᵗʰ Earl had maintained the family's loyalty to Richard II, but went on to serve Henry V loyally in his wars against France.
6 Christopher Allmand, Henry V (London, 1992), p. 420-1.
7 For the Church's view on the Virgin as Queen of Heaven, see the Book of Revelation, 12:1.
8 Juliet Barker, Agincourt: The King, the Campaign, the Battle (London, 2005), p. 320.
9 Allmand, p. 132.
10 Allmand, p. 178.
11 The record for the youngest accession in British history to date goes to Mary, Queen of Scots who succeeded to the throne of Scotland when she was six days old in December 1542.
12 French coronations usually took place at Rheims, but since his rival uncle Charles was crowned there, Henry VI was crowned in Paris.
13 De Lisle, Tudor, p. 8.
14 Henry Ellis (ed.) Three Books of Polydore Vergil's English History (London, 1844), xxix. 62.
15 De Lisle, Tudor, pp. 9 and 25 argues convincingly that this version of how Catherine and Owen met was corroborated by Owen's last words on the scaffold – although one supposes the swimming story favoured in other accounts may also have taken place at some point in the early stages of their romance.

16 It is sometimes suggested that Owen Tudor and Catherine de Valois never actually married. However, given that no aspersions were cast on the legitimacy of their eldest son Edmund until long after he was dead, all impartial evidence points to the fact that the couple were married privately at some indeterminate point between Owen first joining Catherine's household in 1427 and the birth of their first child in 1430.

17 De Lisle, Tudor, p. 9.

18 John Blakman, Henry the Sixth, M.R. James (ed.) (London, 1919), p. 8-9.

19 Edward III was Henry VI's great-great-grandfather and the Duke of York's great-great-great-grandfather.

20 De Lisle, Tudor, p. 25.

21 De Lisle, Tudor, pp. 25 and 436 suggests that the lady was Owen's former lover and the mother of his illegitimate child.

22 Susan Higginbotham, The Woodvilles: The Wars of the Roses and England's Most Infamous Family (Stroud, 2013), p. 13.

23 One of Elizabeth's modern biographers suggests that the couple met before, at Henry VI's court. See Arlene Okerlund, Elizabeth: England's Slandered Queen (Stroud, 2006), p. 25. However, I am not convinced that Elizabeth was a regular presence at Henry VI's court and even if she was, there is insufficient evidence to support the theory that their meeting beneath the oak tree renewed a long-standing acquaintance.

24 Thomas More, The History of Richard III, Richard S. Sylvester (ed.) (Yale University Press, 1963), ii. 61-2.

25 More, Richard III, ii. 62.

26 Dominic Mancini, The Usurpation of Richard the Third, trans C.A.J. Armstrong (Second edition, Oxford, 1969), p. 61.

27 'Hearne's Fragment of an Old Chronicle, from 1460 – 1470' in The Chronicles of the White Rose of York (London, 1845), p. 15-16. It was common to date a medieval monarch's chronology by their years on the throne.

28 Henry Ellis (ed.), The new chronicles of England and France, in two parts: by Robert Fabyan. Named by himself: The concordance of histories. Reprinted from Pynson's edition of 1516. The first part collected with the editions of 1533, 1542, and 1559 (London, 1811), p. 654; Okerlund, p. 32.

29 Charles Derek Ross, Edward IV (University of California Press, 1974), p. 93.

30 The Book of Jeremiah, 3:22.

31 Philip Erlanger, Margaret of Anjou: Queen of England (London, 1970), p. 243.

32 Okerlund, p. 200.

33 Malcolm Letts (ed.), The Travels of Leo of Rozmital through Germany, Flanders, England, France, Spain, Portugal and Italy 1465-1467 (Cambridge University Press, 1957), p. 45.

34 Ibid.

35 Travels of Leo Rozmital, p. 47-8.

36 Anthony Cheetham, The Life and Times of Richard III (London, 1972), p. 96.

37 The Croyland Chronicle; NASA estimates that the solar eclipse on 16 March 1485, the date of Queen Anne's death, lasted for just under five minutes, with a central duration of four minutes and fifty-three seconds.

38 Rosemary Horrox, Richard III: A study in service (Cambridge University Press, 1989), p. 325.

39 Nigel Saul, Honour and Fame: Chivalry in England, 1066 – 1500 (London, 2011), p. 354.

40 It is sometimes stated that Richard had no affairs during his marriage to Anne Neville, but the date of birth of his illegitimate son is contested, which makes this assertion problematic, though by no means impossible.

AS THE LAW OF CHRIST ALLOWS

1 I am grateful to Leanda de Lisle for sending me her article 'Anne Boleyn's last secret' in The Spectator (17 August 2013).

2 These were justified given Henry VII's removal of the anti-Welsh laws.

3 Neville Williams, The Life and Times of Henry VII (London, 1973), p. 63.

4 Susan Brigden, New Worlds, Lost Worlds: The Rule of the Tudors, 1485 – 1603 (London, 2000), p. 17.

5 Laura McCosker, 'Health and Social Welfare in Medieval Dublin' (Unpublished MA thesis submitted to Queen's University, Belfast, 2012)

6 Polydore Vergil.

7 Brigden, p. 26.

8 Williams, p. 60.

9 There is debate over Princess Mary's birth, with both 1495 and 1496 being suggested. I have opted for 1496 here. The divisive piece of evidence is an entry in the prayer book of her paternal grandmother Margaret, Countess of Richmond and Derby, who recorded her granddaughter's birth by writing, 'Hodie nata Maria tertia filia Henricis VII, 1495'. However, Mary was born on 18 March and in

1495/1496 the English still marked the start of a new calendar year on the Feast of the Annunciation, which fell one week later on 25 March. Based on this change, Mary Tudor would have been born in 1495 by her own reckoning but 1496 to most of the rest of Europe and in our own calendar. I am grateful to Dr Steven Gunn and Dr James Davis, with whom I discussed this theory. Another note on the children of Henry VII is that some sources list a seventh child, Edward, who died in infancy. Alison Weir, Britain's Royal Families: A Complete Genealogy (London, 2002), p. 152, lists him.

10 Prince Arthur's death is sometimes given as tuberculosis, but it occurred during an outbreak of the sweating sickness and there is little evidence to clinch a diagnosis of consumption. Cancer has also been suggested.

11 J. S. Brewer, James Gairdner and R. H. Brodie (eds), Letters and Papers, Foreign and Domestic of the Reign of Henry VIII (London, 1862 – 1932), xiv. 1239. Subsequently referred to as LP.

12 J. J. Scarisbrick, Henry VIII (Second edition, Yale University Press, 1997), p. 13-14.

13 For a discussion of the 1510 pregnancy see David Starkey, Six Wives: The Queens of Henry VIII (London, 2004), pp. 114-18. It is possible that there had been a miscarriage at a very early stage, but even this is open to debate. The Queen's confessor and the Spanish ambassador were dubious about her insistence to be pregnant, but Katherine seems to have been naïve rather than dishonest.

14 In a letter to Henry, Katherine confirms that she wanted to send him James IV's body but had to desist because 'Englishmen's hearts would not suffer it'. See Linda Porter, Crown of Thistles: The Fatal Inheritance of Mary Queen of Scots (London, 2012), p. 191-2.

15 It is not true that Henry VIII only enjoyed two mistresses in his lifetime. For a modern investigation of his love life see Amy Licence, The Six Wives and Many Mistresses of Henry VIII (Stroud, 2014).

16 Henry VI made Edmund Tudor Earl of Richmond, but Henry VIII elevated the title to a dukedom for his son.

17 Eric Ives, The Life and Death of Anne Boleyn: The Most Happy (Oxford, 2004), p. 90, plausibly suggests the cessation of sexual relations between Henry and Katherine in 1524/1525.

18 Leviticus, 20:21.

19 The debate over whether or not the marriage between Arthur Tudor and Katherine of Aragon was consummated is a fraught one – see Starkey, Six Wives, Antonia Fraser, The Six Wives of Henry VIII (London, 1998), Giles Tremlett, Catherine of Aragon: Henry's Spanish Queen (London, 2010) and Licence, Six Wives, for differing interpretations.

20 Barbara J. Harris, Edward Stafford, Third Duke of Buckingham,
    1478 – 1521 (Stanford University Press, 1986), p. 202-3.

21 For a well-researched and effervescent appraisal of Boleyn's place in
    popular culture see Susan Bordo, The Creation of Anne Boleyn: A new
    look at England's most notorious queen (New York, 2013).

22 Hugh Paget, 'The youth of Anne Boleyn' in British Institute of
    Historical Research (1981) and R. M. Warnicke, 'Anne Boleyn's
    Childhood and Adolescence' in Historical Journal (1985).

23 Gareth Russell, 'The Age of Anne Boleyn' (Online, 2010)

24 The number of people who are often surprised and delighted to find
    that they have royal ancestry dating back to the Boleyns, the Middle
    Ages or the Conquest is explained by Edward III's children. The
    growth in the British population between Edward's time and our
    own means that the majority of people in the British Isles or of British
    ancestry are likely to be, in some small way, very distantly descended
    from that king. See Mortimer, Perfect King, p. 412.

25 Retha M. Warnicke, The Rise and Fall of Anne Boleyn: Family politics
    at the court of Henry VIII (Cambridge University Press, 1989), p. 8.
    The Earl's bequests of various family heirlooms to Thomas Boleyn,
    coupled with his specific linking of them to when 'mine ancestors
    at first time … were called to honour, and hath since continually
    remained in the same blood; for which cause my father commanded
    upon me his blessing' suggests to me that Thomas Boleyn was the
    grandson Thomas Butler hoped would succeed him. However, given
    the situation in Ireland and Boleyn's contesting cousins, the family
    would have to wait for royal approval. The stability of the earldom was
    a sensitive matter given its importance to the monarchy in Ireland; the
    family's estates near Kilkenny were administered in such a way that
    they were sometimes viewed as a 'second Pale'.

26 Anne Boleyn complained of her weakness in Latin, but that does not
    mean she could not speak it. At worst, it meant she had some grasp
    at it and at best, she was behaving as her daughter would by modestly
    denying a language she was in fact accomplished in.

27 Joseph Stevenson (ed.), Calendar of State Papers, Foreign, Elizabeth,
    1560 – 61 (London, 1865), ii. 489-90.

28 LP, viii. 985.

29 In the nineteenth century and early twentieth century, J. A. Froude
    and Sir Arthur MacNalty, author of a medical history of Henry VIII,
    all doubted that Henry was ever romantically involved with Mary. This
    was contested by the gentlemen's near-contemporary, A. F. Pollard, the
    King's biographer, and more recently in Alison Weir, Mary Boleyn:
    'The Great and Infamous Whore' (London, 2011), pp. 106-111.

30 Calendar of State Papers and Manuscripts Relating to English Affairs,
    Existing in the Archives and Collections of Venice and in Other
    Libraries of Northern Italy, R. Brown, G. Cavendish-Bentinck, H.
    F. Brown, and A. B. Hinds (eds) (London, 1864 – 1947), iv. 105
    (subsequently referred to as Cal. SP. Ven.); LP, v. 1114; Cal. SP. Ven, iv.
    824.

31 For a full discussion of the myths surrounding Anne Boleyn's
    appearance see Warnicke, Rise and Fall, Appendix A, pp. 243-7.

32 Karen Lindsey, Divorced, Beheaded, Survived: A Feminist
    Reinterpretation of the Wives of Henry VIII (Boston, 1996),
    pp. 56-60.

33 Deuteronomy, 25:5.

34 Peter Gwyn, The King's Cardinal: The Rise and Fall of Thomas Wolsey
    (London, 1992), pp. 549-98, and G. W. Bernard, Anne Boleyn: Fatal
    Attractions (Yale University Press, 2010), pp. 49-54.

35 Ives, Anne Boleyn, p. 97.

36 John Aylmer, An harborowe for faithfull and trewe subiectes
    (Strasbourg, 1559).

37 LP, vi. 563.

38 Lauren Mackey, Inside the Tudor Court: Henry VIII and his Six Wives
    through the writings of the Spanish Ambassador, Eustace Chapuys
    (Stroud, 2014), p. 100.

39 Mackey, p. 101.

40 Ives, Anne Boleyn, p. 182.

41 Ives, Anne Boleyn, p. 47.

42 Hilton, p. 10.

43 For a good discussion of Anne Boleyn's performance as Queen see Ives,
    Anne Boleyn, pp. 205-17, 246-59.

44 The debate on Anne Boleyn's downfall has produced many works
    of competing scholarship. For the different arguments see, amongst
    others, Retha M. Warnicke, 'Sexual Heresy at the Court of
    Henry VIII' in The Historical Journal (1987), G. W. Bernard, 'The Fall
    of Anne Boleyn: A rejoinder' in English Historical Review (1992), E.
    W. Ives, 'The Fall of Anne Boleyn Reconsidered' in English Historical
    Review (1992), Greg Walker, 'Rethinking the fall of Anne Boleyn' in
    The Historical Journal (2002) and Suzannah Lipscomb, 1536: The Year
    That Changed Henry VIII (London, 2006).

45 There are two well-received narrative accounts of Anne Boleyn's
    downfall currently in print: Alison Weir, The Lady in the Tower: The
    Fall of Anne Boleyn (London, 2009) and Claire Ridgway, The Fall of
    Anne Boleyn: A Countdown (Lúcar, 2012).

46 She miscarried in 1534 and 1536; there is also a possibility of a natural
    abortion, very early on, in 1535.

47 Scarisbrick, p. xii.

48 Starkey, Six Wives, p. 585; Marie Louise Bruce, Anne Boleyn (London, 1972), p. 274.

49 Derek Wilson, A Brief History of Henry VIII: Reformer and Tyrant (London, 2009), p. 275.

50 Linda Porter, Mary Tudor: The First Queen (London, 2009), p. 153; Leanda de Lisle, The Sisters who would be Queen: The Tragedy of Mary, Katherine and Lady Jane Grey (London, 2008), p. 34-5.

51 The Percy line, the traditional earls of Northumberland, had been temporarily separated from the title after the death of Anne Boleyn's one-time suitor, the 6th Earl, in 1537 and the execution of his brother for treason. The earldom was restored to the Percy family following John Dudley's downfall under Mary I.

52 Jane was the daughter of the Frances Grey (née Brandon), the daughter of Henry VII's youngest surviving daughter, Mary Tudor, Queen Dowager of France, and her second husband, Charles Brandon, Duke of Suffolk.

53 Both of Jane's modern biographers agree that she was born slightly earlier than October 1537, the traditional date. See de Lisle, Sisters, p. 319-20, and Eric Ives, Lady Jane Grey: A Tudor Mystery (Oxford, 2009), p. 36. October 1537 is not a credible date because her mother's itinerary reveals that she was being entertained at a friend's country house in Essex and then attended the royal court throughout October.

54 De Lisle, Sisters, p. 139.

55 Jennifer Loach, Edward VI (Yale University Press, 2002), pp. 160-2, suggests renal failure; Frederick Holmes, Grace Holmes and Julia McMorrough, 'The Death of Young King Edward VI' in New England Journal of Medicine (2001), argue for tuberculosis; Porter, Mary Tudor, pp. 184-6, suggests a bacterial pulmonary infection which left Edward defenceless against secondary infections.

56 She was the first to be proclaimed, unlike the Empress Maud in the twelfth century, who was styled Domina Anglorum until her coronation, which never took place.

57 It is sometimes stated that Jane was technically Queen for thirteen days, rather than the more-famous nine. This number, which was used by Eric Ives in his 2009 study of Jane's career, is made by dating her accession from the moment of Edward VI's death on 6 July 1553 until Mary I's forces took the Tower of London on 19 July. However, Jane was officially proclaimed sovereign on 9 July, banqueted under a canopy of state for the first time that evening, took possession of the Tower on the following day and then relinquished the symbols of her

authority on the 19th, which supports her most popular nickname of 'the Nine Day Queen'.

58 There is some difficulty in deciding on the proper way to title both Mary and Elizabeth Tudor after their father's death in 1547. Both sisters had been styled as princess from the time of their birth until the dissolution of their mothers' marriages, after which they were addressed by the honorific of Lady, even after both were rehabilitated into the Succession. Throughout their brother's reign, they were interchangeably referred to by both titles, due to their positions as first and second in line to the throne, and Elizabeth was often referred to as Princess Elizabeth during Mary's time as Queen. For consistency's sake, I have decided to err on the side of charity in giving both women the higher title.

59 Sir Nicholas Harris Nicolas, The Literary Remains of Lady Jane Grey: with a memoir of her life (London, 1825), p. 58-9.

60 Porter, Mary Tudor, pp. 402-4, argues that the Queen may have been killed by an outbreak of the sweat, rather than succumbing to cancer.

61 Porter, Mary Tudor, p. 407.

62 There is only one full English-language study of this remarkable family currently in print, despite how central they are to understanding not just the trajectory of Mary Stewart's career but also of the Reformation in England, Scotland and France – Stuart Carroll, Martyrs and Murderers: The Guise Family and the Making of Europe (Oxford University Press, 2011).

63 Antonia Fraser, Mary Queen of Scots (London, 1976), p. 89.

64 Margaret Tudor (1489 – 1541) was the eldest daughter of Henry VII and wife of James IV, King of Scots. She was the mother of King James V, the father of Mary, Queen of Scots.

65 John Guy, My Heart is My Own: The Life of Mary Queen of Scots (London, 2004), p. 2.

66 Paul Johnson, Elizabeth: A study in power and intellect (London, 1974), p. 290.

67 Leanda de Lisle, After Elizabeth: How James King of Scots Won the Crown of England in 1603 (London, 2004), p. 174.

68 Johnson, p. 291.

69 The relationship is certainly fascinating. For a beautiful exploration of it, and one which is unusually slightly more sympathetic to Elizabeth than Mary, see Jane Dunn, Elizabeth and Mary: Cousins, Rivals, Queens (London, 2004).

70 De Lisle, After Elizabeth, p. 154.

71 The historical accuracy of this famous speech has been questioned, but the evidence against it seems unconvincing. For its authenticity see

Sir John Neale, 'Sayings of Queen Elizabeth', History (1925), which, despite its age, remains compelling.

72 De Lisle, After Elizabeth, p. 5.

73 The Camden Miscellany (London, 1936), xvi. 5.

74 De Lisle, After Elizabeth, p. 105.

75 Ibid.

76 Scarisbrick, p. 276.

EPILOGUE

1 She was born on 7 September 1533, the eve of the Feast of the Nativity of the Blessèd Virgin Mary, and she died on 24 March 1603, the eve of the Annunciation.

2 Elizabeth Jenkins, Elizabeth the Great (London, 1958), p. 323

3 Johnson, p. 437.

4 Sir John Neale, Queen Elizabeth (London, 1934), p. 390.

5 Chris Green, 'Scottish independence: The Queen breaks silence on referendum debate – as think tank warns of £14bn black hole if Scotland votes Yes' in The Independent (15 September 2014); Nicholas Watt, Patrick Wintour and Severin Carrell, 'Scottish independence: Queen was asked to intervene amid yes vote fears' in The Guardian (16 December 2014).

6 Munro Price, The Fall of the French Monarchy: Louis XVI, Marie Antoinette and the baron de Breteuil (London, 2003), Gareth Russell, The Emperors: How Europe's Rulers were Destroyed by the First World War (Stroud, 2014) and Andrew Marr, The Diamond Queen: Elizabeth II and Her People (London, 2012).

ABOUT THE AUTHOR

Gareth Russell read History at Saint Peter's College at the University of Oxford and he then gained his honours in medieval history with a postgraduate at Queen's University, Belfast. His first novel, Popular, set in Belfast, was published in 2011. Since then he has written another novel, which was adapted for the stage, as well as two works of non-fiction and several plays. He is currently working on a full-length biography of Queen Catherine Howard. He is a columnist for Eile magazine, Tudor Life, and author of the blog Confessions of a Ci-Devant.

ILLUSTRATED
Kings and Queens of England

CLAIRE RIDGWAY, TIMOTHY RIDGWAY, VERITY RIDGWAY

LOVE THE HISTORY?
WHY NOT MAKE THIS YOUR
NEXT READ ...

ILLUSTRATED
KINGS AND QUEENS OF ENGLAND

With stunning colour illustrations of the 59 English kings and queens from Alfred the Great to Elizabeth II, **Illustrated Kings and Queens of England** is packed with interesting facts about the wonderful English monarchy.

This coffee-table book shows the fascinating progression of English history. Every monarch has a biography plus details of their birth and death dates, the dates they ruled and details of their offspring.

Each monarch is accompanied by a vintage Victorian etching, lovingly restored to perfect condition and vividly colourized. These images bring each monarch to life. Anyone with a love of British history will adore this keepsake book.

See English history as you've never seen it before.

MadeGlobal Publishing

Non-Fiction History

- Jasper Tudor - **Debra Bayani**
- Illustrated Kings and Queens of England - **Claire Ridgway**
- A History of the English Monarchy - **Gareth Russell**
- The Fall of Anne Boleyn - **Claire Ridgway**
- George Boleyn: Tudor Poet, Courtier & Diplomat - **Claire Ridgway**
- The Anne Boleyn Collection - **Claire Ridgway**
- The Anne Boleyn Collection II - **Claire Ridgway**
- Sweating Sickness in an Nutshell - **Claire Ridgway**
- Mary Boleyn in a Nutshell - **Sarah Bryson**
- On This Day in Tudor History - **Claire Ridgway**
- Two Gentleman Poets at the Court of Henry VIII - **Edmond Bapst**
- A Mountain Road - **Douglas Weddell Thompson**

Historical Fiction

- Cor Rotto - **Adrienne Dillard**
- The Claimant - **Simon Anderson**
- The Truth of the Line - **Melanie V. Taylor**
- The Merry Wives of Henry VIII - **Ann Nonny**

Other Books

- Easy Alternate Day Fasting - **Beth Christian**
- 100 Under 500 Calorie Meals - **Beth Christian**
- 100 Under 200 Calorie Desserts - **Beth Christian**
- 100 Under 500 Calorie Vegetarian Meals - **Beth Christian**
- Interviews with Indie Authors - **Claire Ridgway**
- Popular - **Gareth Russell**
- The Immaculate Deception - **Gareth Russell**
- The Walls of Truth - **Melanie V. Taylor**
- Talia's Adventures - **Verity Ridgway**
- Las Aventuras de Talia (Spanish) - **Verity Ridgway**

Please Leave a Review

If you enjoyed this book, *please* leave a review at the book seller where you purchased it. There is no better way to thank the author and it really does make a huge difference! *Thank you in advance.*

23647464R00204

Made in the USA
Middletown, DE
30 August 2015